W9-AGC-459

Lyrics of the
Troubadours and
Trouvères

FREDERICK GOLDIN is a member of the Department of English at the City College, and of the Doctoral Program in Comparative Literature at the Graduate School, of the City University of New York. He has written previously on the medieval lyric in *The Mirror of Narcissus* and in several articles.

Lyrics of the Troubadours and Trouvères

An Anthology and a History

TRANSLATIONS AND INTRODUCTIONS BY

Frederick Goldin

ANCHOR BOOKS
ANCHOR PRESS/DOUBLEDAY
GARDEN CITY, NEW YORK

The Anchor Books edition is the first publication of
Lyrics of the Troubadours and Trouvères
Anchor Books edition: 1973

ISBN: 0-385-00877-5
Library of Congress Catalog Card Number 72-96275
Copyright © 1973 by Frederick Goldin
PRINTED IN THE UNITED STATES OF AMERICA
ALL RIGHTS RESERVED
First Edition

To my *father* and to the memory of my *mother*

Acknowledgments

I am grateful to friends and colleagues who listened to many of these translations and introductions and whose useful and encouraging suggestions helped me: Joan M. Ferrante, George D. Economou, Renata Karlin, Saul N. Brody, Esther Casier Quinn.

I owe a special debt to Professor Harry Bober, of the Institute of Fine Arts, New York University, who put into my hands the illustration on the cover of this book.

I am grateful for the help I received from David Goldberg and Milton J. Schubin.

I want to thank the three editors at Doubleday who worked with me on this book: Susan Burchardt Watt took it in, Judith Dollenmayer encouraged it along, William Whitehead brought it out. I cannot imagine how any author could have been more fortunate—and three times in a row. And I am grateful to William Strachan for his patience and precision.

I want to thank my daughters, Cheryl and Lisa, who helped me in many ways, not the least by reading many passages aloud, both from the originals and the translations, and thus through their voices revealing things to me I had not seen before. And in this atmosphere of familiar voices and continual wonder, my son, Paul, helped me too.

My wife, Dione, helped me in ways too numerous to recount, but most of all by just being there.

Foreword

The troubadours were poets and composers who wrote their songs for courtly audiences throughout the southern part of France, beginning in the eleventh century. These lyrics, though they benefited much from literary tradition, had no real antecedents, for they were composed for an audience that had never existed before, a courtly society with the leisure to place a great value on refinement, and eager to pay for the depiction of its own image. Among the troubadours were some of the finest lyric poets who ever wrote, and their songs, though they inspired the poets of every nation of Europe, are like none other.

The romance language in which they wrote is generally called Provençal today, a term that nobody is satisfied with, since this language and literature extended far beyond the area called Provence. Soon after these songs appeared, courtly poets writing in other languages adopted their basic themes and techniques and vocabulary. In northern France, writing in French, these poets were the trouvères.

The lyrics of the troubadours and trouvères, whether they are read or not, have never stopped affecting Western literature. If we read a modern work of any genre in which a beloved one is somehow glorified by a lover's longing; or in which the lover looks to the beloved not simply as a partner but as someone who gives his life meaning and protects him from failure; or in which the lover grieves and rages over the unworthiness, or worst of all the ordinariness, of the beloved, then, whether we think about it or not, we are reading a work that owes to these early courtly poets the preparation for its existence. Though the love songs were the most important, many other kinds of song were written that have nothing to do with love—they were political, moral, and religious songs—and here too the conventions thus established have kept their original force.

In these selections I have tried to give a good representation of each poet's work and of the development of lyric poetry from

the earliest known troubadour down to the year 1250 or there-
abouts. The introductions trace the history of the lyric. The
reader who wants to know something of a poet's life will find the
essential facts in the first paragraph or two. The selections are
limited to the early period, which ended around 1250. After that,
the troubadour lyric declined. This has meant leaving out some
important French poets of the thirteenth and fourteenth centuries, but their work is better known and more available than
that of the earlier, founding poets included here.

F. G.

Contents

PART I

Lyrics of the Troubadours

Guide to the Pronunciation
of Old Provençal

As a rule of thumb, pronounce the consonants as in English, with the following exceptions:

C before a front vowel (*e* or *i*) is pronounced *ts* in the earlier lyrics. In the thirteenth century this sound was reduced to a simple *s*.

Ch is pronounced the way we pronounce it (*tch*, as in "catch"). Note that when this sound is final it is often represented by an *h* or a *g*. Thus *fah* or *fag* is pronounced *fatch*.

Palatal *l* (like Spanish *llamar*, or Italian *egli*), which is approximated by the sound in "million," is represented by various spellings: ll, lh, il, ill, li, lli. Example: *fuelha*. Note that the letter *i* is there only to indicate palatalization and should not be pronounced as a letter: Borneil and Bornelh are pronounced exactly the same.

Palatal *n* (like Spanish *señor*, Italian *signore*), approximated by the sound in "onion," is usually represented by *gn* or *nh*: *senher*.

Q is pronounced like a *k*, whether or not it is followed by *u*.

R is rolled as in modern Italian or Spanish.

Z as a final letter is pronounced *ts: dolenz* pronounced *dolents*.

As to the vowels, pronounce *i* and *u* as in modern French.

When it comes to *a*, *e* and *o*, our simple guide breaks down. For Old Provençal distinguished between an open and close quality in these vowels, the different sounds resulting from their Latin derivations, and no nonphilological rule will hold. We can only choose the least misleading way out.

The close *a* was pronounced like the vowel sound in modern French *pâte, âge, sable* approximately as in father."; The open *a* as in *patte, chat, là, femme*; approximately as in "what."

The close *e* was pronounced like French *é*, as in *thé, été*; English "gate." The open *e* like French *è*, as in *père, terre*; English "there."

2

The close *o* was originally pronounced like the sound in German *Sohn,* or French *chaud,* or English "so." (Late in the thirteenth century it changed to the sound represented by modern French *ou,* as in *amour;* this did not yet occur in the time of the earlier poets.) The open *o* was pronounced as in French *port,* English "cloth."

In the twelfth century, pretonic *o*—that is, an unstressed *o* occurring immediately before a stressed syllable—was pronounced like a short *u.* Thus *movér* should be pronounced *muvér.*

In a simple guide we can only say this: *e* is always close before *m* or *n.* Let us also say that it is close before any other consonant, with these exceptions: it is usually open in all the perfect endings except the first person plural (*cantèi, cantèst, cantèt, cantém, cantètz, cantèron*) ; and it is open in the second person plural of the present tense (*partètz*). If you follow these rules you will probably be right more than half the time, as far as *e* is concerned. For the other vowels we can only say: think Spanish when you come to them.

In the diphthongs each letter retains its value. In diphthongs ending with *u* for example, the second element is pronounced like the vowel in modern French *fou,* English "too." Thus the diphthong *au* is pronounced áoo; *eu,* eóo; *ou,* óhoo. The diphthongs *ai, ei, oi,* are pronounced: áee, éhee, óee, all in one breath. The same rules hold for triphthongs, which always stress the middle letter: *iéu.*

Sometimes an unstressed word became attached to a previous word and lost its vowel. Thus *e lo vins* ("and the wine") became *e·l vins.* The raised dot is used by most editors to indicate this occurrence. It has no effect on pronunciation: *e·l* is pronounced *él.*

GUILLAUME IX

(*1071–1127*)

Guillaume, the seventh Count of Poitiers and the ninth Duke of
Aquitaine, was the lord of an immense realm. He succeeded his
father in 1086, and from that moment to the end of his life his
rule involved him in interminable conflicts with his own vassals,
the lords of other domains, the King of France, and the Church.
In 1101 he led a disastrous crusade into the Holy Land. In 1120
he aided the King of Aragón in a victorious battle against the
Moors. Guillaume is depicted by contemporary chroniclers as
witty, boisterous, riotous, salacious, "as though he believed all
things were moved by chance, and not ruled by Providence"; and
he was excommunicated many times for various reasons: many
disputes with the Church regarding rights, and a liaison with the
Vicomtesse de Châtellerault that he refused to terminate. He told
the papal legate, who was bald: "The comb will curl the hair
on your head before I put aside the Vicomtesse."

Guillaume is the first troubadour whose songs are extant, and
he is sometimes regarded as the originator of the courtly love
lyric. In any case, whether he is really the first troubadour or
rather the first whose work survives, this boisterous misruler of
his realm was a first-rate poet. In eleven little lyrics, which are
all that we have today, he shows his mastery of the basic metrical
forms and the essential themes that would hardly vary in the
troubadour lyric in the following generations; and, most important of all, he perfects the technique of composing a song for
performance before an audience. For versification and theme are
of the essence of all poetry; but the special distinction of the
troubadour lyric is that it depends for its coherence and effect on
a live relation between the poet, or the singer, and an attending
audience.

The troubadour technique of composing for an audience required the singer to strike many different attitudes in the course of the song. He had to step out of one rôle and into another constantly, and smoothly, in a sequence that would be full of surprises and yet coherent: it all had to make sense. When it comes to this technique, Guillaume is a virtuoso. He can do big-bellied bawdiness and the timid-lover bit to perfection. What a stud he plays in the story of Agnes and Ermessen, and how he trembles in the rôle of the obedient servant! One scholar (Pio Rajna) called him a "trovatore bifronte," a poet with two faces; but one can count more faces than that, and as many voices. He has this extensive repertory, not because he is a two-faced hypocrite, but simply because he is a performer.

To trace the development of this technique of performance in Guillaume's poetry takes a few pages; but it is worth all our trouble, because there is no better way to see what the troubadours were doing, and therefore no better way to approach the other poets who set out on the path that the troubadours opened, the Minnesänger, the stilnovisti, the trouvères. And since the meaning of "courtly love" is much disputed, it is best for us to begin with the songs that Guillaume composed on an altogether different theme, the ones in which he plays a bawdy man.

These songs are funny in different ways, and in different meters, but they all have a common theme:

> *dirai vos de con, cals es sa leis,*
> (I shall tell you about cunt,)

the singer says to his male companions, "I shall tell you what its law is." The *leis de con,* running its course with a blind necessity, is the force that causes all of the singer's predicaments in these songs. It is blind because it regards nothing but itself, and irresistible because nothing has any permanence where it holds sway. The human beings who are driven by it, like Agnes and Ermessen and their "pilgrim," go walking through the world in one disguise or another, each taking the other for something else and being taken, for they will become whatever they have to be-

come to get what they want. All their certainties are nullified
in a single instant's surprise, in a throw of the dice. Nor do the
objects of this law have any reliable identity. Their effective
reality lasts only as long as someone's lust is focused on them;
they exist, therefore, only as appearances, as handsome bodies,
and they are appraised like horses.

Under the rule of the *leis de con* all actions have the status of
accidents, for this "law" allows no motive but instinctual appetite
in the individual, and no other rule but chance in the world.
Everyone wanders around till he or she bumps into someone
else, and then lust astounds them both with its possibilities. In
the world in which they wander, there is no personal dignity and
no moral coherence. That is what makes it a world of fun—who
wants to trudge beneath the weight of his dignity all the time?
The festival spirit breathes where it will, seeking encounters
without consequences. That is why these songs are merry. However, prolonged incoherent experience is terrifying; and, in fact,
every encounter in these songs has its consequence, and it is
always unpleasant, an embarrassment or a great vexation. The
wonder of these merry songs is that they are merry about sad
and frightening things.

In the boasting song, the singer introduces himself as a "master," a man of skill who can be counted on in all the most important things: he can put good "colors" on a song, he knows
all the rules of courtly life, he makes the best love in the world.
So generous is the singer's self-esteem, it even embraces the man
who brought him up, whom he blesses for making him a *maestre
certa,* a self-confident and dependable master. Then comes the
first throw of the dice and everything vanishes, all that skill and
training, all that pride in past accomplishments. There is no
further basis for certainty and pride, that wise man whose counsel everyone sought is flabbergasted, that whole famous identity
is dismantled.

It is true that fortune favors him the second time he throws
the dice; but, coming second, his success is as chancy as his failure,
it cannot be counted on. No one can tell in one instant what the
next instant will bring. The singer may claim to be a distinguished man among his neighbors, but chance is a greater leveler

even than death; for the way a man dies may be the last confirmation of his personal style and his moral stance, but an accident comes from a mindless causality and can take no heed of character or merit. The poet chooses the image of the dice throw to represent the master's skill in action; and in this, if we distinguish between the poet and the boastful man he impersonates, we can see a deliberate moral intelligence at work; for when dice are thrown, all distinctions are obliterated, all men are truly equal. The world of this master may seem to be full of fun, a festival world where no one has to have any identity, so that everyone can share the joys of irresponsibility; but it takes no chilly moralist to see that this fun is the accident of a vast uncertainty, and that this world is utterly without continuity, a world of unique instances. This song, with its initial pride in rules and techniques and its final concession to the sovereign power of chance, imitates in its very form a game of dice.

This sense of the unreliability of instances goes all through Guillaume's poetry. In the wonderful song made "of nothing" (no. 3), in the fifth strophe, the speaker tells us that he has a friend but does not know who she is because he has never seen her; in the sixth, that he does not miss her because he has another friend who is better, and the whole thing doesn't matter anyhow. And it really doesn't, it can't, because the one he loves cannot have any identity, everything that might realize her—location, worth, the lover's esteem—is denied as soon as it is affirmed. The things a man sees and wants, and the man himself, have no abiding quality, they dissolve into one another, become their opposites. They have no defined existence, and so they cannot be esteemed, and their world cannot be continuous and significant, but only a realm of accidents. "Guillaume IX was not unaware that animal instinct or appetite contradicts itself. That which the appetite ardently desires soon reveals itself as empty of meaning: a nothing" (Mario Casella). Thus the *leis de con*, the transforming power of lust, turns the whole world into a dream: nothing is real except the closest thing, and even then only the appearance is real, and only for a time. The only permanent facts are the force of desire—*am*, I love—and the embarrassment or discontent in which it ends.

Guillaume can sound more notes than one, however, and he writes other songs about a love that is altogether different from the one he describes for the companions. These are songs of "courtly love," far more refined than the songs of *con* and obviously intended for a wider courtly audience. The lady in these songs is no soldier's mount: she commands respect, she is imperious, celebrated for her virtuous qualities; although, in the remoteness of her perfection, she is still hardly realized as an individual. The difference in the rôles the singer plays is even more striking: before, he had to make noises like a mute, *babariol, babariol, babarian;* now he has to be eloquent.

The reason for all these differences is the setting in which the lover's experience unfolds. The songs of *con* may be full of place names, but whatever happens happens in no particular place: it is "somewhere in Auvergne," or at a "gaming table" in a chamber, not otherwise located. There is no necessary relation between the setting and the action, and that is as it should be, for the pursuit of lust can take place anywhere. But in at least three of Guillaume's songs the lover's experience with the lady unfolds in a very definite setting: in the court.

Now this setting, unlike the others, cannot be ignored or transformed by the *leis de con:* just the opposite is true, the lover's lust must suffer certain restraints if it is to get what it wants. The objective setting has laws of its own, a reality that precedes each person's appetites. The law of lust cannot be fulfilled unless it is itself obedient to the rules of courtliness. Some of these rules are spelled out in the fifth and sixth strophes of *Pus vezem de novelh florir* (no. 6) : in order to get the woman now, the lover has to be obedient; he has to be pleasant and courteous to neighbors and strangers alike, and obliging to everyone in the lady's realm; he has to know how to do charming and graceful things; and he has to keep from speaking vulgarly in court. As we have seen, the absence of a setting in the other songs is an eloquent proof of the self regard and irresistibility of the law of *con:* the lover and the lady (or ladies) he is interested in at the moment go their ways on no particular ground, and whatever social forms appear—contracts of vassalage, formulas of greeting, rituals of hospitality—are adopted in an instant as vehicles for lust. But here, in this song, the lover is surrounded by various personages of the court, and in order for him to get the lady into bed, he has to have the good opinion of these other people, he has to convince them of his good manners, his personal grace, his eloquence: his courtliness.

Ovid, in *The Art of Love*, gives advice that at first hearing sounds a lot like what we have here and indeed has been proposed as one of the sources of Guillaume's song (for example, by Dimitri Scheludko). Ovid bases every hope and strategy on the *leis de con* ("All women can be caught," I, 269–274); and on that basis advises the lover to win the favor of whoever is close to the lady (specifically, her handmaid: I, 351ff), to avoid speaking roughly (II, 167), and to be obedient to the lady's caprices (II, 197–232; 529–534). That sort of thing: recommended for every man on the make. But the behavior that Guillaume describes is more than a strategy for some lone lover, it is the established and definitive behavior of a social class, the behavior that distinguishes it as a class: it is the defining visible form of courtly life. The lover has to love like a courtly man, and the setting is now so essential to his love, as the only means of its expression, that his unsuccess in love necessarily implies his failure as a courtly man. Love has become the enactment of courtliness: the way a man loves is the surest sign of his identity as a courtly man.

We can again sense these new social and aesthetic obligations imposed on lust if we recall Guillaume's Ovidian boasts in the song of the gaming table, where his savoir-faire in court is but one aspect of his universal aptitude. He is good in court and good in bed because he is just plain good. He is a worthy man to begin with, in this morality of skill, and his boast about knowing the ropes at court was never meant as a proof that he deserves love. But here, in this new song, the lover has to win a certain approval before he can get anything else. And that is no arbitrary requirement. He has to prove his standing in life, his authenticity as a courtly man, his human reality. The "setting" now is hardly distinguishable from the experience. The movement of lust has been detoured from the straight path to its object; it has to travel along the lines of a different energy, namely, the force with which a man holds on to his place in a community.

The longing for love now is more than a sexual instinct: it is the courtly expression of the longing to be a recognized identity, to be part of a society in which one has some significance. "The inner conformity to the law of love leads to the willing participation in a society" (Theophil Spoerri). And the lack of love is not to be explained now on the basis of poor strategy or the neglect of Ovidian rules. The lover has to look for the causes of his failure in himself, and he must know the bitterness of guilt and despair. The echoes of Ecclesiastes in the third and fourth strophes of *Pus vezem de novelh florir* could never have been sounded in the other songs. For there the only abiding reality was lust and every objective setting, the whole world, was *de dreyt nien,* nothing. But now, in the supreme reality of the courtly world, to a life without love *tot es niens,* there is no life, all is vanity, nothing. Because without love one has no presence in the world.

In the last strophe the poet makes a technical observation about the versification of his song and praises the melody. Furthermore, whoever best appreciates this song and takes the most pleasure in it, he says, is the man of greatest worth—the most courtly, that is, the most truly noble. The song thus becomes a touchstone for the differentiation of the audience; there are those who will understand it: they are the noble ones, and of these the one who understands it best is the most noble; and, by implication, there are those who will not understand it at all, and they are worth nothing. This claim was made for the old songs too (no. 1, for example). Furthermore, this song is itself one of those *faigz avinens,* one of those graceful and appropriate actions that a courtly man must perform. Now, therefore, when he praises his song, it is not the boast of some phallic master anxious to impress his comrades, but rather a claim to courtliness; he points to the certifying beauty of his song as proof of his right to belong to this great and mighty class—a class that now seeks to justify its privileged station as an ethical reward.

Thus far, the Carnal Man and the Courtly Lover have been two distinct rôles, performed for two different audiences. But

now Guillaume starts to play off one rôle, or one kind of love
against the other. His song, *Farai chansoneta nueva* (no. 7, the
authenticity of which has occasionally been questioned, but for
poor and entirely subjective reasons), starts out with the singer
in the courtly lover's attitude of homage ("She can put my name
down in her charter"). But all of a sudden he changes his
posture and his voice:

> *E no m'en tengatz per yure*
> *s'ieu ma bona dompna am,*

"Now don't go thinking I must be drunk/if I love my virtuous
lady." For in the audience he spots his old companions sitting
there, listening to him and eyeing him. They know him. And he
knows they know him, and knows that when they hear this
roving lecher talk of becoming some virtuous woman's vassal for
love, they must think he is drunk, or crazy, or just a plain liar.
And to deal with them, he has a strategy that is worthy of the
wily old master they know. He does not go on, as though they
weren't there, reading the lines of a timid and submissive courtly
lover, for if he denies their presence and their knowledge of him,
they will drown him out with their jeers. Or at any rate the
song would be cheapened: the worshipful love it celebrates somehow has to originate in the feelings of a carnal man; for otherwise such love would be impossible for men with lusty bodies,
and then it would really be nothing more than the posturing of
a fool and a hypocrite. So, in order to silence them, and to save
his song, he does a brilliant thing: he shows them that he is still
the man they know, their old comrade, the dealer in horseflesh:

> *Morrai, pel cap sanh Gregori—*

"By Saint Gregory's head I'll die/if she doesn't kiss me in a
chamber or underneath the trees . . . I swear, you want to become a nun . . . What will it profit you if I become a monk?"
Dompna conja, he calls her. The accent falls on *con* (compare
no. 2, note 1).

Yes, he says to his comrades, I'm the fellow with Agnes and
Ermessen, only I happen to be after a woman right now who
makes me say this kind of thing before I can have her. So let me

go on. Only, Daurostre, when you sing this one, don't bawl it
out like one of the old songs.

That is enough to silence them. He says nothing about the
accusing heart and the sense of emptiness when love fails. It is
very hard to say just how seriously Guillaume took these senti-
ments. At any rate, they cannot make sense to the companions.
He has said enough to deal with them, and now he can resume
the new song:

> Per aquesta fri e tremble . . .)
> (For this one I shiver and tremble . . .)

The development of the troubadour's dialogue with the audience, which we have been tracing in the poetry of Guillaume IX,
is almost complete. But at this point, before we come to the end,
we ought to look a little more closely at the allusive nature of
Guillaume's language and versification, for that is a part of the
game he plays with his friends.

For example, the song we have just been looking at (no. 7)
imitates, or suggests, the form of a litany, with its careful repeti-
tions: the fourth line of every strophe ends with the verb "love"
—am or amam—which is preceded by the word for "lady,"
dompna, or a pronoun referring to her. (Notice, incidentally,
the words he uses to rhyme with "love.") His questions to the
lady—qual pro y auretz, "what will it profit you"—allude to one
of the most telling biblical passages concerning the vanity of
earthly experience (Matthew 16, 25). Furthermore, the third
and fourth lines of each strophe are built on the fifteen-syllable
trochaic long line (which had a caesura, or pause, after the
eighth syllable), a line as old as the marching songs of the
Roman legions and by Guillaume's time one of the most popular meters in hymns; compare:

> Exaltantes decantemus   deo laudes debitas
> Totz lo joys del mon es nostre,
> Dompna, s'amduy nos aman.

(This is also the basis of the long third line in the strophes of
the song of con, no. 2.) The audience for whom Guillaume wrote
was alive to the effect of such religious echoes in a song like this:
"joy" is a watchword in Christian hymnology, but to the singer
it is del mon, illusory except as a physical experience.

The strophic forms in all but one of Guillaume's songs have been traced (by Spanke, Chailley, and others) to religious sources and analogues. Take the very first song, about the two horses. Each strophe consists of three lines, all on the same rhyme. The first two lines of each strophe contain eleven syllables; the last, fourteen. Finally, in each line, there is a caesura after the seventh syllable. Compare:

> Promat chorus hodie, o contio
> Canticum letitie, o contio,
> Psallite, o contio, psallat cum tripudio!

These are verses in a song composed in the Abbey of St. Martial in Limoges, in Guillaume's domain, where there was a great and famous music school. Shortly before Guillaume was born, songs of this type, called a *conductus,* were being developed at St. Martial as an accompaniment to the liturgy. A *conductus* was a song of any structure, for one or more voices, and, as its name implies, it went along with a procession during the service, or it filled in the time during the preparation for a new part of the mass—it was, in other words, used in the liturgy but was not a part of it. Having this ancillary purpose, it was composed at need; it was a new song—a *novum canticum*—musically independent, an opportunity for the creation of new forms, in contrast to the fixed structure of liturgical music proper. Guillaume's knowledge of this music that flourished in his own realm can certainly be assumed. The following strophe, from a *conductus* of St. Martial, coincides exactly in meter and rhyme with the strophes of the song "about nothing" and of *Pus vezem* (nos. 3 and 6) : six lines, of which four have eight syllables and rhyme, and two have four syllables and rhyme—8a 8a 8a 4b 8a 4b.

> In laudes Innocentium
> qui passi sunt martyrium
> psallat chorus infantium:
>   Alleluia,
> sit decus regi martyrum
>   et gloria!

Other religious music beside the *conductus,* particularly the Ambrosian hymn and the sequence, inspired Guillaume's metri-

cal forms. But at this point enough has been said to suggest that
the songs of Guillaume IX, though they were composed for a
small audience that rejoiced in its exclusiveness, used the substance of far greater and more ancient traditions. Religious verse
forms and vocabulary, as we have seen, feudal conventions, familiar passages of classical literature—anything that might ring
a bell to an aristocratic audience, Guillaume exploits, not only
for purposes of technique, but also to give a certain ironic reso-
nance to the lover's words, or to transfer ancient dignity into
courtly life.

The one song with a metrical structure that cannot be clearly
traced to a source is the song about "joy," *Mout jauzens* (no. 8).
All the lines here are eight syllables long, but the rhyme scheme
divides each strophe into a new and potentially complicated pattern. The first four lines are bound together, the latter two
rhyming in reverse with the first two; then the final two lines
in each strophe repeat the rhymes. So that the strophe divides
like this: ab + ba : ab. It divides into two parts, of which one
subdivides. This is, in rudimentary form, what will prove to be
the most frequent and most characteristic strophic structure in
the courtly lyric all over Europe. We shall see how it was developed by the poets who followed.

In this song, the echoes of Christian hymnology in the celebration of joy are obvious enough; and here again they seem to con-
fer a certain dignity on courtly life and at the same time to give
the singer's carnality an air of defiance. This playfulness depends
on the same easy and direct familiarity with the audience, a
sense of intimacy and exclusiveness which sets the tone of the
language and becomes the context which controls the meaning:

> *Ieu, so sabetz, no·m dey gabar*
> *ni de grans laus no·m say formir.*
> (I, as you know, am not one to boast,
> I do not know how to praise myself.)

The audience whom he speaks to like this has to be familiar with
Guillaume's other songs; has to have heard, before this, his
boasts, his cordial self-congratulation. Here again the singer in-
volves the audience in his song. For the full effect of these words

he needs friends who can appreciate the great disparity between this boisterous and mighty lord, this singer of scurrilous songs, and the respectful, submissive lover he impersonates. As soon as he turns to the audience ("as you know"), he steps out of this new rôle and back into the old one; he reassumes the image they have of him. As you know, he tells them, underneath this mask, it's the old reliable master.

And so, when he says, "I want her for myself,/to refresh my heart,/to renew my flesh," two different meanings keep blinking at us one after the other, like one of those drawings that show two profiles when you look at it once, and an ornate goblet the next time. For in the context of the celebration of joy, the words suggest a revivifying spiritual experience, such as that in the biblical passages they allude to (for example, Isaiah 57, 15: *et vivificet cor contritorum,* "in order to revive the heart of the humble"). But when we hear the echo of those words, we think of the pilgrim and his eight days in the oven.

The relation between the lady and the lover sworn to her service is identical in form to the feudal relation between the lord and his "man," his vassal. Guillaume even refers to her as *Midons,* "My Lord," and he renders himself to her in homage so that she can write his name down in her "charter." These songs which draw on the long tradition of Western poetry and add to it the language of feudal devotion, are a crucial moment, a watershed in the history of literature: the themes, the vocabulary, the techniques that developed over centuries are now set within the context of the court, the traditional language of love is turned to the definition of courtliness. This can be most clearly seen in the secularization of Christian formulas of rapture, jubilation, charity. The idea that love is the supreme ethical condition, and that the joy of love is known through obedience to its "laws," is Christian in origin: *Haec est enim caritas dei ut mandata eius custodiamus, et mandata eius gravia non sunt* (I John 5, 3: "For this is the love of God, that we keep his commandments: and his commandments are not grievous"). But now, in this new song, love is the aspiration to a courtly image, and its "laws" are the rules of deportment in a joyous and fortunate society. The lover's patience and obedience represent the courtly man's self-discipline; the lover's longing and steadfastness re-enact the courtly man's loyalty and his devotion to the glory of his class. In these songs, the meaning of courtliness is made manifest through love.

At least, through the kind of love that Guillaume IX sings about in one of his many rôles. By now it should be clear that it is wrong to call him a man "with two faces," only one of which, the one with the smirk on it, is genuine: he is a singer who takes pride in his mastery of voices and attitudes and who sometimes, in the performance of his songs, switches from one to the other in a game he plays with the audience.

There are at least two other voices in Guillaume's repertory: a voice of truly disciplined, unfaltering renunciation, which needs no comfort; this voice sings in a beautiful song of leave-taking which, regretfully, is not included in this selection. And there is a voice that sings of still another kind of love, a love that Guillaume clearly ranks above the others, above the ridiculousness of lust and above that excessive spirituality which humiliates desire. This voice is heard, with absolute clarity, in *Ab la dolchor del temps novel* (no. 9), one of the most beautiful love songs of the Middle Ages, indeed of all time. Here the love relation is depicted neither as a game of dice nor as vassalage, but as a feast which the man and the woman share together; and their love participates, without bestiality and without transcendence, in the resurrections and devastations of nature. The lady is, in fact, quite distant now, because of a quarrel that is about to end; and yet by that very quarrel she is altogether present in a friendship of desire, being neither an adversary nor a sovereign. The worth of the man is not measured by his performance, for he is here neither a seducer nor a servant. When Guillaume sings in this rôle and praises reciprocal love as the highest, then courtly love has to sound like "strange gibberish," crazy words that boast of the separation of lovers.

All these voices will remain in the repertory of future poets: the *companho* voice, the *chansoneta nueva* voice, the *temps novel* voice. The "strange Latin," the debased language of those who do not know what love is, will become the language of the *fals amadors,* the false lovers, who will prove to be the poet's deadliest enemies. The "companions" will come back as the *gens vilana,* the vulgar element that can never understand why the courtly lover boasts of his fidelity to a lady he cannot embrace. They will all find their place, together with those who praise the poet's love, in the spectrum of the audience. Marcabrun will be the first to coin the terms by which the various segments of the audience, from the most noble to the most vulgar, will be designated. Cercamon, who learned his craft from Marcabrun, will take over the terms and the ethical attitudes of his master. Bernart de Ventadorn will take this whole cast of friends and enemies, and the courtly poet's range of voices, and perfect the essential dialectic of the troubadours: in the performance of the song, the singer's eye will pass through the audience, and as he comes to each part of it, he will put the blindness and revelations of a new perspective into his song. The performance of the troubadour lyric will become more fully what it is already in these songs of Guillaume IX, a kind of game, a kind of play, in the form of a dialogue on love between the singer and the audience.

When we spoke of the change in setting that marks the difference between the old song and the new, we never asked the obvious question: why did the poets, beginning with Guillaume, choose as their great theme the civilizing effect of this courtly setting on sexual behavior? Of course this question can never be answered with any certainty, because so much of the cultural climate in which this poety arose has changed, so many sounds and so many glances that we shall never hear or see. We can only say that the old song and the new song of this poet can suggest something of an answer. In Guillaume's vision of the depravity and unreliability of human behavior, we can sense something of the impulse that led to the development of courtly love as an ethical system. Through this vision of the human race rising and falling with the causes of chance, we can be moved by the invention of a code that required a man's whole life—his random thoughts, the welter of his experience, the accidental succession of his moments—to be reformed into a devoted service. Before this vision of lust and impermanence, we can share in the celebration of longing and steadfastness.

Text: Newly edited for this volume. Base mss.: C (1, 3, 5, 6, 7, 8), E (2), V (4), N² (9). See Alfred Jeanroy, *Bibliographie sommaire des chansonniers provençaux*. Les Classiques français du moyen-âge, 16. Paris, 1916.

1

Companho, faray un vers[1] . . . covinen:
et aura·i mais de foudaz   no·y a de sen,   I
et er totz mesclatz d'amor   e de joy e de joven.

E tenguatz lo per vilan   qui no l'enten
5 o dins son cor voluntiers qui no l'apren;   II
greu partir si fai d'amor   qui la trob'a son talen.

Dos cavalhs ai a ma selha   ben e gen;
bon son e adreg per armas   e valen;   III
e no·ls puesc amdos tener   que l'us l'autre non cos-
      sen.

10 Si·ls pogues adomesjar   a mon talen,
ja no volgra alhors mudar   mon guarnimen,   IV
que miels for' encavalguatz   de nuill home viven.

Laüns fon dels montaniers   lo plus corren;
mas aitan fer' estranhez' a longuamen,   V
15 et es tan fers e salvatges   que del bailar si defen.

L'autre fon noyritz sa jus,   part Cofolen,
et anc no·n vis bellazor,   mon escien;   VI
aquest non er ja camjatz   ni per aur ni per argen.

Qu'ieu doney a son senhor   polin payssen;
20 pero si·m retinc ieu tan   de covenen   VII
que s'elh lo teni' un an   qu'ieu lo tengues mais de cen.

---

[1] A song, of the type that later troubadours would call *canso*.

1

My companions, I am going to make a *vers*[1] that is re-
    fined,
and it will have more foolishness than sense,   I
and it will all be mixed with love and joy and youth.

Whoever does not understand it, take him for a peasant,
5 whoever does not learn it deep in his heart.   II
It is hard for a man to part from love that he finds to
    his desire.

I have two good and noble horses for my saddle,
they are good, adroit in combat, full of spirit,   III
but I cannot keep them both, one can't stand the other.

10 If I could tame them as I wish,
I would not want to put my equipment anywhere else, IV
for I'd be better mounted then than any man alive.

One of them was the fastest of the mountain horses,
but for a long time now it has been so fierce and shy, V
15 so touchy, so wild, it fights off the currycomb.

The other was nurtured down there around Confolens,
and you never saw a prettier one, I know.   VI
I won't get rid of that one, not for gold or silver.

I gave it to its master as a grazing colt;
20 but I reserved the right   VII
that for every year he had it, I got it for more than a
    hundred.

Cavallier, datz mi cosselh   d'un pessamen!
Anc mais no fuy issarratz   de cauzimen: VIII
Gees non sai ab qual mi tengua   de N'Agnes o de
        N'Arsen.²

25 De Gimel ai lo castel   el mandamen,
   E per Niol fauc ergueil   a tota gen,   IX
   C'ambedui me son jurat   e plevit per sagramen.³

2

Companho, tant ai agutz   d'avols conres ¹
qu'ieu non puesc mudar non chan   e que no·m pes;   I
Enpero no vueill c'om sapcha   mon afar de maintas res.

E dirai vos m'entendensa   de que es:
5 no m'azauta cons gardatz   ni gorcs ses peis,   II
  ni gabars de malvatz homes   com de lor faitz non agues.

Senher Dieus, quez es del mon   capdels e reis,
qui anc premiers gardet con   com non esteis?   III
C'anc no fo mestiers ni garda   c'a si dons estes sordeis.

10 Pero dirai vos de con   cals es sa leis,
   com sel hom que mal n'a fait   e peitz n'a pres: IV
   si c'autra res en merma qui·n pana,   e cons en creis.

E silh qui no volran creire   mos casteis
anho vezer pres lo bosc   en un deveis: V
15 per un albre c'om hi tailla   n'i naison dos ho treis.

² *Na* (from *domina*), "Lady." *En* (from *domine*), "Lord."
³ Gimel and Niol are two castles in his domaine, the dwellings of the two
"horses" whose masters are his vassals. Niol is a little more than thirteen
miles from Confolens in the Department of Charente.
¹ "*Conres* provides a pun on *con* and a variety of meanings, 'equipment,
provisioning, hospitality, feast, a course in a meal,' as well as 'company, the
people one frequents.'" (L. T. Topsfield)

You knights, counsel me in this predicament,
no choice ever caused me more embarrassment: VIII
I can't decide which one to keep, Na Agnes or Na
    Arsen.[2]

25 Of Gimel I have the castle and the fief,
and with Niol I show myself proud to everyone,   IX
for both are sworn to me and bound by oath.[3]

2

My companions, I have had so much miserable fare,[1]
I cannot keep from singing and from feeling vexed.   I
Still, I do not want my little doings known in great detail.

And I shall tell you my thoughts:
5 these things do not please me: a cunt under guard, a fish-
    pond without fish,   II
and the boasting of worthless men when there is never to
    be any action.

Lord God, King and Ruler of the universe,
why did he who first set a guard on cunt not perish?   III
For no servant or protector ever served his lady worse.

10 But I shall tell you about cunt, what its law is,
as one who has done badly in this matter and suffered   IV
    worse:
as other things diminish when you take from them, cunt
    increases.

And those who will not believe my advice,
let them go and behold in a private preserve near the   V
    woods:
15 for every tree that gets cut down, two or three grow up in
    its place.

E quam lo bocx es taillatz nais plus espes,
E·l senher no·n pert son comte ni sos ses;   VI
A revers planh hom la tala si·l dampn . . .

Tortz es ca . . . dan noi a . . .   VII

3

Farai un vers de dreyt nien:
non er de mi ni d'autra gen,
non er d'amor ni de joven,   I
ni de ren au,
5 qu'enans fo trobatz en durmen
sobre chevau.

No sai en qual hora·m fuy natz: [1]
no suy alegres ni iratz,
no suy estrayns ni sui privatz,   II
10 ni no·n puesc au,
qu'enaissi fuy de nueitz fadatz,
sobr' un pueg au.

No sai quora·m fuy endurmitz
ni quora·m velh, s'om no m'o ditz.
15 Per pauc no m'es lo cor partitz   III
d'un dol corau;
e no m'o pretz una soritz,
per Sanh Marsau!

Malautz suy e tremi murir,
20 e ren no sai mas quan n'aug dir;
metge querrai al mieu albir,   IV
e non sai tau;
bos metges es qui·m pot guerir,
mas non, si amau.

[1] Which is to say, I do not know what astrological influences determined my character.

And as the wood is cut, the thicker it grows,
and the lord does not lose any property or dues.   VI
A man is wrong to cry damaged goods when there is no
       loss.
It is wrong to cry loss when there's no damaged goods.   VII

3

I will make a *vers* of exactly nothing:
there'll be nothing in it about me or anyone else,
nothing about love or youth   I
or anything else.
5 It came to me before, while I was sleeping
on my horse.

I do not know the hour of my birth.[1]
I am not cheerful or morose,
I am no stranger here and do not belong in these parts,   II
10 and I can't help being this way,
I was turned into this, one night, by some fairy
high on a peak.

I don't know when I slept
or wake, if someone doesn't tell me.
15 My heart is almost broken   III
from the grief in it,
and I swear by Saint Martial, to me the whole thing
isn't worth a mouse.

I am sick and shiver at death
20 and don't know it except when I'm told.
I will look for the doctor I have in mind,   IV
I don't' know who he is.
He's a good doctor if he can make me well,
but not if I get worse.

25 M'amigu' ai ieu, no sai qui s'es,
    qu'anc non la vi, si m'ajut fes;
    ni·m fes que·m plassa ni que·m pes,   V
    ni no m'en cau,
    qu'anc non ac Norman ni Frances
30 dins mon ostau.

    Anc non la vi et am la fort,
    anc no n'aic dreyt ni no·m fes tort;
    quan non la vey, be m'en deport,   VI
    no·m pretz un jau
35 qu'ie·n sai gensor et bellazor,
    e que mais vau.

    No sai lo luec ves on s'esta,
    si es en pueg ho es en pla;
    non aus dire lo tort que m'a,   VII
40 abans m'en cau;
    e peza·m be quar sai rema,
    ab aitan vau.[2]

    Fag ai lo vers, no say de cuy;
    e trametrai lo a selhuy
45 que lo·m trametra per autruy   VIII
    lay vers Anjau,
    que·m tramezes del sieu estuy
    la contraclau.

4

    Farai un vers, pos mi somelh
    e·m vauc e m'estauc al solelh.
    Domnas i a de mal conselh,   I

---

[2] Jeanroy regarded this strophe as "apocryphal" on the grounds that it was flat and merely repeated ideas already expressed; it is not included in the text of his edition. In this case, flatness lies in the eye of the beholder, for other scholars consider it authentic, and even essential. The first word of

25 I have my little friend, I don't know who she is,
   because I've never seen her, so help me God;
   she's done nothing to make me feel good, or bad,   V
   and I don't care,
   because there's never been a Frenchman or a Norman yet
30 inside my house.

   I have never seen her and love her a lot,
   she has never yet done right by me, or wrong.   VI
   When I do not see her, I enjoy myself.
   And I don't care a cock,
35 because I know a nicer one, better looking,
   and worth more.

   I do not know the region where she dwells,
   whether it's in the heights or on the plains.
   I dare not tell how she wrongs me,   VII
40 it hurts me in advance.
   And it pains me to stay on here,
   and so I go.[2]

   I have made this *vers,* I don't know what about;
   and I shall send it to someone
45 who will send it for me with someone else   VIII
   to someone in Anjou there;
   let him send me from his little box the key
   to what we have here.

4

   I shall make a *vers,* since I am sleeping,
   and walking around, and standing in the sun.
   Well, there are ladies who are all wrongheaded,   I

the last line, *ab,* is an emendation for the sake of meter, the manuscript
reading simply *aitan vau.* The word *es* in the second line, also missing in
the manuscript, is a similar emendation.

e sai dir cals:
5   cellas c'amor de cavalier
tornon a mals.

Domna fai gran pechat mortal
qe no ama cavalier leal;
mas si es monge o clergal,   II
10   non a raizo:
per dreg la deuri'hom cremar
ab un tezo.

En Alvernhe, part Lemozi,
m'en aniey totz sols a tapi:
15   trobei la moller d'en Guari   III
e d'en Bernart;
saluderon mi simplamentz
per sant Launart.

La una·m diz en son latin:
20   "E Dieus vos salf, don pelerin;
mout mi semblatz de belh aizin,   IV
mon escient;
mas trop vezem anar pel mon
de folla gent."

25   Ar auzires qu'ai respondut;
anc no li diz ni bat ni but,
ni fer ni fust no ai mentaugut,   V
mas sol aitan:
"Babariol, babariol,
30   babarian."

So diz n'Agnes a n'Ermessen:
"Trobat avem que anam queren.
Sor, per amor Deu, l'alberguem,   VI
qe ben es mutz,
35   e ja per lui nostre conselh
non er saubutz."

and I can say who:
5   the ones who turn down the love of a knight
and treat it badly.

A lady who does not love a loyal knight
commits a great mortal sin.
But if she loves a cleric or a monk   II
10   she is in error:
her they should burn by right
with firebrands.

In Auvergne, beyond Limousin,
I was walking alone, on the sly.
15   I met the wives of En Garin   III
and En Bernard.
They greeted me modestly in the name
of Saint Leonard.

One of them says to me with her high-class speech:
20   "God save you, my lord pilgrim,
you look to me like a gentleman,   IV
as far as I can tell;
but we all see crazy fools too often
walking through the world."

25   Now you are going to hear how I answered them:
I didn't say but or bat to them,
didn't mention a stick or a tool,   V
but only this:
"Babariol, babariol,
30   babarian."

Then Agnes says to Ermessen:
"We've found what we are looking for.
Sister, for the love of God let us take him in,   VI
he is really mute,
35   with this one what we have in mind
will never get found out."

La una·m pres sotz son mantel,
e mes m'en sa cambra, al fornel.
Sapchatz qu'a mi fo bon e bel,   VII
40   e·l focs fo bos,
et eu calfei me volentiers
als gros carbos.

A manjar mi deron capos,
e sapchatz agui mais de dos,
45   e no·i ac cog ni cogastros,   VIII
mas sol nos tres,
e·l pans fo blancs e·l vins fo bos
e·l pebr' espes.

"Sor, aquest hom es enginhos,
50   e laissa lo parlar per nos:
nos aportem nostre gat ros   IX
de mantenent,
qe·l fara parlar az estros,
si de re·nz ment."

55   N'Agnes anet per l'enujos,
e fo granz et ac loncz guinhos:
e eu, can lo vi entre nos,   X
aig n'espavent,
q'a pauc non perdei la valor
60   e l'ardiment.

Qant aguem begut e manjat,
eu mi despoillei a lor grat.
Detras m'aporteron lo gat   XI
mal e felon:
65   la una·l tira del costat
tro al tallon.

Per la coa de mantenen
tira·l gat et el escoissen:

One of them took me under her mantle
and brought me to her chamber, by the fireplace.
Let me tell you, I liked it,   VII
40   and the fire was good,
and I gladly warmed myself
by the big coals.

To eat they gave me capons,
and you can be sure I had more than two,
45   and there was no cook or cook's boy there,   VIII
but just the three of us,
and the bread was white, and the wine was good,
and the pepper plentiful.

"Sister, this man is tricky,
50   he's stopped talking just for us.
Let us bring in our red cat   IX
right now,
it'll make him talk soon enough,
if he's fooling us."

55   Agnes went for that disgusting animal,
and it was big, it had a big long mustache,
and I, when I saw it, among us, there,   X
I got scared,
I nearly lost my courage
60   and my nerve.

When we had drunk and eaten,
I took my clothes off, to oblige them.
They brought the cat up behind me,   XI
it was vicious.
65   One of them pulls it down my side,
down to my heel.

She gets right to it and pulls the cat down
by the tail, and it scratches:

plajas mi feron mais de cen　　　　　　　XII
70　aqella ves;
　　mas eu no·m mogra ges enguers,
　　qui m'ausizes.

　　"Sor, diz n'Agnes a n'Ermessen,
　　mutz es, qe ben es conoissen;
75　sor, del banh nos apareillem　　　　　XIII
　　e del sojorn."
　　Ueit jorns ez encar mais estei
　　en aquel forn.

　　Tant les fotei com auzirets:
80　cen e quatre vint et ueit vetz,
　　q'a pauc no·i rompei mos coretz　　　XIV
　　e mos arnes;
　　e no·us puesc dir lo malaveg,
　　tan gran m'en pres.

85　Ges no·us sai dir lo malaveg,
　　tan gran m'en pres.　　　　　　　　XV

5

Ben vuelh que sapchon li pluzor　　　　1.5
d'est vers si's de bona color,[1]
qu'ieu ai trag de mon obrador:
qu'ieu port d'ayselh mestier la flor,　　　I
5　et es vertaz,
　e puesc en traire·l vers auctor
　quant er lassatz.

Ieu conosc ben sen e folhor,
e conosc anta et honor,
10　et ai ardimen e paor;

---

[1] "*Color* can mean 'manner,' 'kind,' 'quality,' 'brilliance,' 'deception,' but here refers to the images used by Guilhem and to the nuances or levels of

they gave me more than a hundred sores   XII
70   that time;
but I wouldn't have budged an inch
if they killed me.

"Sister," Agnes says to Ermessen,
"he's mute, all right.
75   So, Sister, let us get ourselves a bath   XIII
and unwind."
Eight days and more I stayed
in that oven.

I fucked them, you shall hear how many times:
80   one hundred and eighty-eight times. C.LXXX.VIII.   XIV
I nearly broke my breeching strap
and harness.
And I cannot tell the vexation,
it hurt so bad.

85   No, no, I cannot tell the vexation,   XV
it hurt so bad.

5

I want everyone to tell
whether there's good color to this *vers* [1]
that I have brought out of my workshop:
because I'm the one that gets the flower in this craft,   I
5   and that is the truth,
and I will call this *vers* to witness
when it is all laced up.

I know what wisdom is, and foolishness,
and I know what honor is, and shame,
10   I can tell bravery and fear;   II

meaning given to those images." (L. T. Topsfield)

e si·m partetz un juec d'amor [2]   II
no suy tan fatz
no·n sapcha triar lo melhor
d'entre·ls malvatz.

15 Ieu conosc ben selh qui be·m di,
e selh qui·m vol mal atressi,
e conosc ben selhuy qui·m ri,
e si·l pro s'azauton de mi,   III
conosc assatz
20 qu'atressi dey voler lor fi
e lor solatz.

Mas ben aya sel qui·m noyri,
que tan bo mestier m'eschari
que anc a negu non falhi;
25 qu'ieu sai jogar sobre coyssi   IV
a totz tocatz;
mais en say que nulh mo vezi,
qual que·m vejatz.

Dieu en lau e Sanh Jolia:
30 tant ai apres del juec doussa
que sobre totz n'ai bona ma,
e selh qui cosselh mi querra   V
non l'er vedatz,
ni us mi noa tornara
35 descosselhatz.

Qu'ieu ai nom "maiestre certa":
ja m'amigu' anueg no m'aura
que no·m vuelh' aver l'endema;
qu'ieu suy d'aquest mestier, so·m va,   VI
40 tan ensenhatz
que be·n sai guazanhar mon pa
en totz mercatz.

2 "*Juec d'amor* (11) is a literary term meaning a 'debate on love,' and . . .
serves with its ambiguity to point the way to the two levels of gaming and
sensuality. *Lo melhor* (13) suggests the *summum bonum*, the *mielhs* to be

and set before me a game of love,[2]
I am no such fool
but I can tell the best chances
from the worst.

15 I know which man speaks courteously to me,
yes, and which one seeks my harm,
and I know the one who smiles at me,
and whether valiant men take pleasure in my company;   III
I understand,
20 I too must try to get their trust
and solace.

A blessing on the man who brought me up,
for my portion he gave me such great skill,
I have never disappointed anyone;
25 because I know how to play, on a cushion,   IV
every winning roll;
I know more than anyone around,
this man you see before you.

I praise God for it, and Saint Julian,
30 I have learned that sweet game so well,
I have a winning hand over all the others;
and whoever wants advice from me,   V
I will not deny him,
no one will ever part from me
35 unadvised.

For they call me the old reliable master:
that's right, my little friend will never have me for a
            night
without wanting to have me again next day;
for in this craft—that's right, I boast of it—I am   VI
40 so expert,
I could earn my bread by it
in any exchange.

attained in love, and, looking ahead to the next stanza, 'the better man from
among the wicked,' as well as 'the better side to choose in a debate.' "
(Topsfield)

Pero no m'auzetz tan guabier
qu'ieu non fos rahusatz l'autr'ier,
45 que jogav'a un joc grossier,
que·m fon trop bos al cap primier   VII
tro fuy 'ntaulatz;
quan guardiey, no m'ac plus mestier,
si·m fon camjatz.

50 Mas elha·m dis un reprovier:
"Don, vostre dat son menudier,
et ieu revit vos a doblier."
Dis ieu: "Qui·m dava Monpeslier,   VIII
non er laissatz."
55 E leviey un pauc son taulier,
ab ams mos bratz.

E quant l'aic levat lo taulier,
empeis los datz,   IX
e·lh duy foron cairavallier
60 e·l terz plombatz.

E fi·ls fort ferir al taulier,
E fon joguatz.   X

6

Pus vezem de novel florir
pratz e vergiers reverdezir,
rius e fontanas esclarzir,   I
auras e vens,
5 ben deu quascus lo joy jauzir
don es jauzens.

D'Amor non dey dire mas be.
Quar no·n ai ni petit ni re?
Quar ben leu plus no m'en cove;   II

But, friends, you don't hear me bragging
that I wasn't shaken up the other day.
45 I was playing at a game that was gross
and enjoying it enormously, at first—   VII
till I took my place at the gaming table:
I took one look, and I lost the whole craft,
I was that unnerved.

50 But she gave me this reproach:
"My Lord, your dice are too small,
I challenge you to start again."
I said, "If they gave me Montpellier,   VIII
I shall not fail."
55 And I raised her gaming table a little
with my two arms.

And when I had raised the gaming table
I threw the dice,
and two of them rolled,   IX
60 and the third sank.

And I made them strike that table hard,
and it was played.   X

6

Now when we see the meadows once again
in flower and the orchards turning green,
streams and fountains running clear,   I
the breezes and the winds,
5 it is right that each man celebrate the joy
that makes him rejoice

Now I must not say anything but good of Love.
Why do I get not one bit of it?
Maybe I wasn't meant for more.   II

10 pero leumens
dona gran joy qui be mante
los aizimens.

A totz jorns m'es pres enaissi
qu'anc d'aquo qu'amiey non jauzi,
15 ni o faray ni anc no fi.   III
Qu'az esciens
fas mantas res que·l cor me di:
"Tot es niens."

Per tal n'ai meyns de bon saber
20 quar vuelh so que no puesc aver,
e si·l reproviers me ditz ver   IV
certanamens:
"A bon coratge bon poder,
qui·s ben sufrens."

25 Ja no sera nuls hom ben fis
contr'amor si no·l es aclis,
et als estranhs et als vezis   V
non es consens,
et a totz sels d'aicels aizis
30 obediens.

Obediensa deu portar
a motas gens qui vol amar,
e coven li que sapcha far   VI
faigz avinens,
35 e que·s gart en cort de parlar
vilanamens.

Del vers vos dig que mais en vau
qui ben l'enten e n'a plus lau,
que·l mot son fag tug per egau,   VII
40 comunalmens,
e·l sonetz, qu'ieu mezeis me·n lau,
bos e valens.

10 And yet how freely
it gives great joy to any man who upholds
its rules.

This is the way it has always been with me:
I never had the joy of what I loved,
15 and I never will, as I never did.   III
For I am aware,
I do many things and my heart says,
"It is all nothing."

And so I know less than anyone what pleasure is,
20 because I want what I cannot have.
And yet, one wise saying tells me   IV
the certain truth:
"When the heart is good, its power is good,
if a man knows patience."

25 Surely no one can ever be Love's
perfect man unless he gives it homage in humility
and is obliging to strangers   V
and acquaintances,
and to all the people of that realm
30 obedient.

A man who wants to be a lover
must meet many people with obedience,
and must know how to do   VI
the things that fit in court,
35 and must keep, in court, from speaking
like a vulgar man.

Concerning this *vers* I tell you a man is all the more
                    noble
as he understands it, and he gets more praise;
and all the strophes are built exactly   VII
40 on the same meter,
and the melody, which I myself am happy about,
is fine and good.

Mon Esteve,[1] mas ieu no·i vau,
sia·l prezens　　　　　　　　　　　　　VIII
45　mos vers e vuelh que d'aquest lau
sia guirens.

7

Farai chansoneta nueva
ans que vent ni gel ni plueva;
ma dona m'assai' e·m prueva,　　　　　　　I
quossi de qual guiza l'am;
5　e ja per plag que m'en mueva
no·m solvera de son liam.

Q'ans mi rent a lieys e·m liure,
qu'en sa carta·m pot escriure.
E no m'en tengatz per yure　　　　　　　II
10　s'ieu ma bona dompna am,
quar senes lieys non puesc viure,
tant ai pres de s'amor gran fam.

Que plus etz blanca qu'evori,
per qu'ieu autra non azori.
15　Si·m breu non ai ajutori,　　　　　　　III
cum ma bona dompna m'am,
morrai, pel cap sanh Gregori,
si no·m bayz' en cambr' o sotz ram.

Qual pro y auretz, dompna conja,
20　si vostr' amors mi deslonja?
Par que·us vulhatz metre monja.　　　　　IV
E sapchatz, quar tan vos am,
tem que la dolors me ponja,
si no·m faitz dreg dels tortz qu'ie·us clam.

---

[1] *Mon Esteve* is a cover name, a *senhal* (signal) , for the courtly poet never reveals the lady's real name to the audience. The boastful soldier who names his "mounts" in no. 1 is unaware of this gentle convention; or else he just enjoys astonishing his audience.

Let my *vers,* since I myself do not,
appear before her,   VIII
45 Mon Esteve, and let it be the witness
for my praise.

7

I shall make a new song
before the wind blows and it freezes and rains.
My lady is trying me, putting me to the test   I
to find out how I love her.
5 Well now, no matter what quarrel she moves for that
            reason,
She shall not loose me from her bond.

Instead, I become her man, deliver myself up to her,
and she can write my name down in her charter.
Now don't go thinking I must be drunk   II
10 if I love my virtuous lady,
for without her I have no life,
I have caught such hunger for her love.

For you are whiter than ivory,
I worship no other woman.
15 If I do not get help soon   III
and my lady does not give me love,
by Saint Gregory's holy head I'll die
if she doesn't kiss me in a chamber or under a
            tree.

What shall it profit you, my comely lady,
20 if your love keeps me far away?
I swear, you want to become a nun.   IV
And you better know, I love you so much
I'm afraid the pain will prick me to death,
if you don't do right by me for the wrongs I cry against
            you.

25 Qual pro y auretz, s'ieu m'enclostre
   e no·m retenetz per vostre?
   Totz lo joys del mon es nostre,   V
   Dompna, s'amduy nos amam.
   Lay al mieu amic Daurostre [1]
30 dic e man que chan e (no) bram.

   Per aquesta fri e tremble,
   quar de tan bon' amor l'am;   VI
   qu'anc no cug qu'en nasques semble
   en semblan del gran linh n'Adam.

                        8

   Mout jauzens me prenc en amar
   un joy don plus mi vuelh aizir,
   e pus en joy vuelh revertir   I
   ben dey, si puesc, al mielhs anar,
 5 quar mielhs orna·m, estiers cujar,
   qu'om puesca vezer ni auzir.

   Ieu, so sabetz, no·m dey gabar
   ni de grans laus no·m say formir,
   mas si anc nulhs joys poc florir,   II
10 aquest deu sobre totz granar
   e part los autres esmerar,
   si cum sol brus jorns esclarzir.

   Anc mais no poc hom faissonar
   con's, en voler ni en dezir,
15 ni en pensar ni en cossir;   III
   aitals joy no pot par trobar,
   e qui 'be·l volria lauzar
   d'un an no y poiri' avenir.

[1] Daurostre is probably the *joglar*, the performer who will sing this song; or
else he is one of the "companions." In any case, he has to be cautioned not

25 What shall it profit you if I become a monk shut in
   and you do not keep me for your man?
   All the joy of the world belongs to us,   V
   Lady, if we both love each other.
   Now to my friend down there, Daurostre,[1]
30 I say, I command: sing this nicely, do not bray
          it out.

   For this one I shiver and tremble,
   I love her with such good love;   VI
   I do not think the like of her was ever born
   in the long line of Lord Adam.

8

   I begin, rejoicing already, to love
   a joy that I want most to settle down in;
   and since I want to come back to joy,   I
   I must go, if I can, the best way:
 5 for I am made better by one who is, beyond dispute,
   the best a man ever saw or heard.

   I, as you know, am not one to boast,
   I do not know how to praise myself,
   but if ever any joy has put forth a flower,   II
10 it should, before all other joys, bring forth fruit
   and shine in perfection above them,
   as when a dark day fills with light.

   No man has ever had the cunning to imagine
   what it is like, he will not find it in will or desire,
15 in thought or meditation.   III
   Such joy cannot find its like:
   a man who tried to praise it justly
   would not come to the end of his praise in a year.

to sing this like one of the good old songs.

Totz joys li deu humiliar,
20 et tota ricor obezir
mi dons,[1] per son belh aculhir IV
e per son belh plazent esguar;
e deu hom mais cent ans durar
qui·l joy de s'amor pot sazir.

25 Per son joy pot malautz sanar,
e per sa ira sas morir
e savis hom enfolezir V
e belhs hom sa beutat mudar
e·l plus cortes vilanejar
30 e totz vilas encortezir.

Pus hom gensor no·n pot trobar
ni huelhs vezer ni boca dir,
a mos ops la vuelh retenir, VI
per lo cor dedins refrescar
35 e per la carn renovellar,
que no puesca envellezir.

Si·m vol mi dons s'amor donar,
pres suy del penr' e del grazir
e del celar e del blandir VII
40 e de sos plazers dir e far
e de sos pretz tener en car
e de son laus enavantir.

Ren per autruy non l'aus mandar,
tal paor ay qu'ades s'azir,
45 ni ieu mezeys, tan tem falhir, VIII
no l'aus m'amor fort assemblar;
mas elha·m deu mo mielhs triar,
pus sap qu'ab lieys ai a guerir.

---

[1] *Midons*, "My Lord," a term of feudal courtesy, applied as a *senhal*, or cover name, directly to the lady.

Every joy must abase itself,
20 and every might obey
in the presence of Midons,[1] for the sweetness of her wel-   IV
       come,
for her beautiful and gentle look;
and a man who wins to the joy of her love
will live a hundred years.

25 The joy of her can make the sick man well again,
her wrath can make a well man die,
a wise man turn to childishness,   V
a beautiful man behold his beauty change;
the courtliest man can become a churl,
30 and any churl a courtly man.

Since man cannot discover, nor eye
behold, nor tongue praise anyone more noble,
I want to keep her for myself   VI
to revive the heart within me,
35 and renew my flesh,
that it may never grow old.

If Midons chooses to give me her love,
I am ready to receive it and be grateful,
to keep it secret and pay it compliments;   VII
40 to speak and act only to please her,
to cherish the goodness in her,
to make her praise resound.

I don't dare send her anything with a messenger,
I'm that afraid she might flare up in anger;
45 and I myself, I'm so afraid to fail,   VIII
do not show her a single image of my love.
But she must pick out what is best in me,
because she knows: in her alone I shall be restored.

9

Ab la dolchor del temps novel
foillo li bosc, e li aucel
chanton, chascus en lor lati,   I
segon lo vers del novel chan;
5 adonc esta ben c'om s'aisi
d'acho don hom a plus talan.

De lai don plus m'es bon e bel
non vei mesager ni sagel,
per que mos cors non dorm ni ri,   II
10 ni no m'aus traire adenan,
tro que eu sacha ben de fi
s'el' es aissi com eu deman.

La nostr' amor vai enaissi
com la branca de l'albespi
15 qu'esta sobre l'arbre tremblan,   III
la nuoit, a la ploia ez al gel,
tro l'endeman, que·l sols s'espan
per la fueilla vert e·l ramel.

Enquer me membra d'un mati
20 que nos fezem de guerra fi,
e que·m donet un don tan gran,   IV

sa drudari' e son anel:
enquer me lais Dieus viure tan
c'aia mas manz soz so mantel.

25 Qu'eu non ai soing de lor lati
que·m parta de mon Bon Vezi,

9

In the sweetness of this new season
the woods leaf out, the birds
sing each one in its latin   I
after the verses of the new song.
5 Thus it is right that each man settle down
with what a man wants most.

From over there, where everything to me is good and
        beautiful,
I see no messenger or seal,
and so the heart inside my body knows no sleep, no   II
        laughter,
10 nor do I dare to take a step in that direction   II
until I know for sure about peace,
whether it is such as I ask for.

Our love goes this way,
like a branch of hawthorne
15 on the tree, trembling   III
to the rain, all night, and the frost, all night,
till the next day when the sun spreads out
all through the green leaves and the branches.

It still reminds me of one morning
20 when we made an end to war,
and she gave me so great a gift,   IV

her love and her ring.
God let me live long enough
to get my hands under her mantle;

25 because I do not care for their strange, exquisite gibberish
that keeps me away from my Fair Neighbor;

qu'eu sai de paraulas com van,   V

ab un breu sermon que s'espel,[1]

que tal se van d'amor gaban,

30 nos n'avem la pessa e·l coutel.

---

[1] An alternative translation of this passage (suggested by Dieter Woll): "and
I agree with a little saying that goes:" or, ". . . that is often quoted." In
line 9, *mos cors* means literally, "my body," and is often used by the
troubadours as an equivalent for the first personal pronoun. It could also
mean "my heart," although the word for "heart" in the nominative singular
is usually *cor*; there is, in fact, a variant manuscript reading, *mon cor,*

for I know how it is with words,   v
a short speech goes on and on and on . . .[1]
Such others go around talking and talking big of love,
30 but we have a morsel of its bread, and a knife.

which some editors adopt, correcting *mon* to *mos*. The context demands both
alternatives: the "others" whom the poet mocks in the final strophe, with
their exquisite feelings and endless talk, are like hearts without bodies. The
ending means: these "others" have nothing but talk of love, but we have
the real thing, we sit down together to its feast.

MARCABRU

(fl. 1129–1150)

Marcabru was a Gascon, born in the first decade of the twelfth century. One of the *vidas* makes him a foundling, while he himself says he was the son of a poor woman named Marcabruna. He had many patrons throughout the Midi and Spain, including Guillaume X of Aquitaine, the son of "the first troubadour," and Alfonso VII of Castile and León.

The low birth and noble patronage are reflected in his point of view and in the variety of his style. No one equals him in the furor with which he denounces the effeminacy and depravity of the courtly life and the conventions of courtly love. From this moral urgency and highly idiomatic style arises some of the most difficult poetry in the whole Troubadour canon, the first instance of *trobar clus*, the hermetic style. But these moralizing lyrics are only one mark of his range. At the other end are songs extolling true love; and other songs, such as *A la fontana* and the *pastorela*, which dramatize a profoundly medieval view of right order—they are among the most civilized utterances in Provençal poetry.

His influence was great, not only on the practitioners of the hermetic style, but on others who chose from the wide variety of his forms (compare his *Estornel*, no. 12, with Peire d'Alvernhe's *Rossinhol*, below, no. 29), or who took up his moral stance (compare Peire Cardenal). But no one could ever re-create his irascible and exalted tone. About forty-two lyrics are extant.

The most frequent theme in his songs is the distinction between true love and false love: true love is joyful, intense, in harmony with the welfare of a community and with divine intentions; false love is bitter, dissolute, self-regarding, and de-

structive. He denounces the courtly class for its preciousness and
lust—it is on the way to ruin because it is infested with its own
bastards, the women trick their husbands into raising the children
of others, the men are cuckoos who lay their eggs in someone
else's nest. And pandering to this cupidity are the troubadours, a
vile crowd (*gens frairina*) of liars and madmen who defame love
and glorify lust.

In the songs of Marcabru we see for the first time the figure
of the singer who takes a stand against the "false lovers," the
fals amador, whom he identifies as the other poets of the court.
From this position Marcabru distinguishes different kinds of
people in the society he addresses: they will become the characters whom future poets will identify as their audience—besides
the false lovers, the flatterers, the slanderers, the spies, the envious, the vulgar; and the true lovers, who will be the singer's
"friends."

The poets who followed Marcabru retained all these designa-
tions, though they did not take up Marcabru's religious values
or his prophetic stance. For they were concerned with defining
the values of courtliness in terms of a fictional love relation, and
they stood before their audience as constituents and spokesmen.
The differences between their poetry and Marcabru's reflect the
differences of their poetic task and their performing attitude.

However, these differences are not so great as has sometimes
been made out. What Marcabru means by true love is a secular
experience: it is not *caritas,* or the love of God and of all things
in God; it is love between man and woman. This love is good
because it is involved in a larger life, the life of a society, a noble
class that has a certain ethical and religious mandate, in Marcabru's eyes. True love is of this earth and this life, and it is intense
and full of joy; but in a wonderful way, because the lovers themselves are good and have courtly virtues, like steadfastness and
restraint, their love inevitably realizes a divine intention, the
calling of their class.

This is made very clear in *A la fontana* (no. 10), for example,
where the speaker's voice of carnality is silenced by the young
girl's unanswerable lament. She calls down a curse on King
Louis for commanding the crusade and complains to Jesus that

her sorrow is great because of Him; and in her final words she
brushes aside the very thought of eternal joy in the world to
come: that means nothing to her, because right now her one joy
is far away. Now that is hardly what the Fathers of the Church
meant by charity. And yet, with all her indifference to religion,
she speaks, in the rapture of her loyalty and grief, with the voice
of true love. The narrator is blinded by his carnality and cannot
speak except in carnal terms: too much weeping makes the flesh
grow pale, the color fade; there is no need to despair, God can
provide plenty of joy, he tells her—hoping she will notice him.
But she, in her purity and faithfulness, does not understand his
meaning, she thinks he must be referring to the life in heaven.
Oh, yes, she says, there is that—but that has nothing to do with
me right now. Now this is not *caritas*, and to call it that would
not only degrade divine love, which truly is greater than this,
but also diminish the dignity of her grief. Her love is *Amors*,
good love; the narrator's love is *Amars*, bitter love, the bitterness
of lust, cupidinous and humiliating. And both are of this earth.

The texts of the following songs, unless otherwise noted, are
based on the edition of J.-M.-L. Dejeanne, *Poésies complètes du
troubadour Marcabru* (Toulouse: Privat, 1909); several emendations have been made, most of them suggested by Kurt Lewent,
"Beiträge zum Verständnis der Lieder Marcabrus," *Zeitschrift
für romanische Philologie*, 37 (1913), 313–337; 427–451. The
text of no. 7 has been edited (as noted) by Aurelio Roncaglia,
who for the past several years has been publishing definitive
editions of individual lyrics by Marcabrun, mostly in *Cultura
neolatina*.

10

A la fontana del vergier,
on l'erb' es vertz josta·l gravier,
a l'ombra d'un fust domesgier,
en aiziment de blancas flors   I
5 e de novelh chant costumier,
trobey sola, ses companhier,
selha que no vol mon solatz.

So fon donzelh' ab cors belh
filha d'un senhor de castelh;
10 e quant ieu cugey que l'auzelh
li fesson joy e la verdors,   II
e pel dous termini novelh,
e quez entendes mon favelh,
tost li fon sos afars camjatz.

15 Dels huelhs ploret josta la fon
e del cor sospiret preon.
"Ihesus," dis elha, reys del mon,
per vos mi creys ma grans dolors,   III
quar vostra anta mi cofon,[1]
20 quar li mellor de tot est mon
vos van servir, mas a vos platz.

Ab vos s'en vai lo meus amicx,
lo belhs e·l gens e·l pros e·l ricx;
sai m'en reman lo grans destricx,
25 lo deziriers soven e·l plors.   IV
Ay! mala fos reys Lozoicx
que fay los mans e los prezicx
per que·l dols m'es en cor intratz!

[1] The capture of the Holy City in 1147, the occasion of the crusade led by
Louis VII, King of France.

10

By the fountain in the orchard,
where the grass is green down to the sandy banks,
in the shade of a planted tree,
in a pleasant setting of white flowers   I
5 and the ancient song of the new season,
I found her alone, without a companion,
this girl who does not want my company.

She was a young girl, and beautiful,
the daughter of a castle lord.
10 And just as I reckoned the birds
must be filling her with joy, and the green things,   II
in this sweet new time,
and she would gladly hear my little speech,
suddenly her whole manner changed.

15 Her eyes welled up beside the fountain,
and she sighed from the depths of her heart,
"Jesus," she said, "King of the world,
because of You my grief increases,   III
I am undone by your humiliation,[1]
20 for the best men of this whole world
are going off to serve you, that is your pleasure.

"With you departs my so
handsome, gentle, valiant, noble friend;
here, with me, nothing of him remains but the great dis-
            tress,
25 the frequent desiring, and the tears.   IV
Ai! damn King Louis,
he gave the orders and the sermons,
and grief invaded my heart."

Quant ieu l'auzi desconortar,
30 ves lieys vengui josta·l riu clar:
"Belha," fi·m ieu, "per trop plorar
afolha cara e colors;   v
e no vos cal dezesperar,
que selh qui fai lo bosc fulhar,
35 vos pot donar de joy assatz."

"Senher," dis elha, "ben o crey
que Deus aya de mi mercey
en l'autre segle per jassey,
quon assatz d'autres peccadors;   VI
40 mas say mi tolh aquelha rey
don joys mi crec; mas pauc mi tey [2]
que trop s'es de mi alonhatz."

11

D'aisso lau Dieu [1]
e saint Andrieu
c'om non es de major albir   I
qu'ieu sui, so·m cuig,
5 e no·n fatz bruig
e volrai vos lo per que dir;

C'assatz es lait
s'intratz en plait
don non sabretz a lutz issir,[2]   II
10 e non es bo
jutgetz razo
si non la sabetz defenir.

De gignos sens
sui si manens

[2] Or: "He cares little for me."
[1] Text: Aurelio Roncaglia, *Studi Medievali,* 17 (1951), 46–70. Most of the
following notes are based on Roncaglia's edition, introduction, and notes.
[2] That is, when you can't argue your way to the conclusion. In this case, the

When I heard how she was losing heart,
30 I came up to her beside the clear stream.
   "Beautiful one," I said, "with too much weeping
   your face grows pale, the color fades;   **V**
   you have no reason to despair, now,
   for He who makes the woods burst into leaf
35 has the power to give you joy in great abundance."

   "Lord," she said, "I do believe
   that God may pity me
   in the next world, time without end,
   like many other sinners,   **VI**
40 but here He wrests from me the one thing
   that made my joy increase. Nothing matters now,[2]
   for he has gone so far away."

11

   For this I praise God [1]
   and Saint Andrew:
   no man has more sense   **I**
   than I have, that's what I think,
5 and I'm not just making noise.
   And I'll tell you why.

   It is very unpleasant
   when you get involved in arguing something
   and you can't reach the light at the end,[2]   **II**
10 and it is not good
   to make judgments on any subject
   you can't explain.

   I am so rich
   in brilliant ideas,

speaker's "argument" is that he's the best man around. This entire *gap*
(boasting song) should be compared to Guillaume's *Ben vuelh que sapchon
li pluzor* (no. 5), the obvious model for this song. Compare, for example,
the "two dogs and the third" with Guillaume's "two dice and the third."

15 que mout sui greus ad escarnir; III
   lo pan del fol
   caudet e mol
   manduc, e lais lo mieu frezir: [3]

   Tant quant li dur
20 li pliu e·il jur
   c'om no·m puosca de lui partir, IV
   e quan li faill
   mus e badaill
   e prenda del mieu lo dezir;
25 Qu'ieu jutg'a drei
   que fols follei
   e savis si gart al partir, V
   qu'en dobl'es fatz
   e dessenatz
30 qui·s laiss'a fol enfolletir.

   D'estoc breto
   ni de basto
   no sap om plus ni d'escrimir: VI
   qu'ieu fier autrui
35 e·m gart de lui
   e no·is sap del mieu colp cobrir.

   En l'autrui broill
   chatz cora·m voill
   e fatz mos dos canetz glatir, VII
40 e·l tertz sahus
   eis de rahus
   bautz e ficatz senes mentir.

   Mos alos es
   en tal deves
45 res mas ieu non s'en pot jauzir: VIII

[3] That is, I store mine up (Kurt Lewent).

15 I am very hard to make a fool of; III
   I eat the bread
   of the fool while it is soft
   and warm, and let my own cool down.³

   As long as his bread lasts
20 I swear to him, I pledge
   that nothing could ever make me part from him, IV
   and when he's out of his,
   let him stare at mine with his mouth open
   and long for it;

25 because I think it is right
   that a fool act like a fool
   and a wise man watch out for what he can come away V
       with;
   for he is doubly stupid
   and brainless
30 who lets a fool make a fool of him.

   With a Breton stick
   or any weapon
   or a sword, no one's better: VI
   because I hit the other man
35 and keep him from hitting me,
   and he—he can't take cover from my blow.

   In another man's woods
   I go hunting every time I feel like it,
   and I set my two little dogs barking, VII
40 and my third, my hound,
   thrusts forward,
   all bold and fixed on the prey.

   My own private place
   is so safe
45 no one can enjoy it but me: VIII

aissi l'ai claus
de pens venaus
que nuills no lo·m pot envazir.

Del plus torz fens
50 sui ples e prens,
de cent colors per mieills chauzir; [4]   IX
fog porti sai
et aigua lai
ab que sai la flam' escantir.

55 Cascun si gart,
c'ab aital art
mi fatz a viure e morir;   X
qu'ieu sui l'auzels
c'als estornels
60 fatz los mieus auzellos noirir.[5]

12

Estornel, cueill ta volada:
deman, ab la matinada,
iras m'en un'encontrada,
on cugei aver amia;
5 trobaras
e veiras   I
per que vas
comtar l'as;
e·ill diras
10 en eis pas
per qu'es trasalïa.

No sai s'aissi·s fo fadada
que no m'am e si'amada;
c'ab una sola vegada

---

[4] *Colors:* literally, "colors"; figuratively, "lies, pretexts."
[5] The cuckoo, who lays its eggs in other birds' nests: the nobleman who

I've got it so locked up
and barricaded,
no one can force his way in.

I'm teeming
50 with the snakiest tricks,
with a hundred false colors to choose the best from.[4]   IX
I carry fire here,
water there,
that I can use to put out the flame.

55 Let everyone watch out,
for with such art
I play at living and dying.   X
I am the bird
that gets the starlings
60 to feed my little ones.[5]

12

Starling, take flight:
tomorrow at daybreak
you go to a land
where I thought I'd have a friend.
5 You will find her
and see her—   I
here's' why you go:
you will tell her,
spell out to her,
10 right on the spot
why she goes beyond all bounds.

I don't know, maybe she was fated
to get my love without loving me;
but one single time,

fills the ranks of his class with his bastards.

15 fora grans la matinia,
   si·ll plagues
   ni volgues   II
   qu'o fezes;
   per un mes
20 n'agra tres,
   a qui es
   de sa companhia.

   Ai! com es encabalada
   la falsa razos daurada:
21 "Denan totas vai triada!"
   va! ben es fols qui s'i fia;
   de sos datz
   c'a plombatz   III
   vos gardatz,
30 qu'enganatz
   n'a assatz,
   so sapchatz,
   e mes en la via.

   Per semblant es veziada,
35 plus que veilla volps cassada;
   l'autrier mi fetz far la bada
   tota nueg entruesc'al dia.
   Sos talans
   es volans   IV
40 ab enguans;
   mas us chans
   fa·n enfans
   castians
   de lor felonia.

45 Selui fadet gentils fada
   a cui fo s'amors donada;
   no fo tals crestianada
   de sai lo peiron Elia; [1]

---

[1] Mount Horeb: see I Kings 19, 8–9 (Lewent).

15 what a great day,
   if it pleased her,
   if she wanted   II
   me to do it;
   for one month
20 is worth three,
   to the man
   who breaks bread with her.

   Ai! how convincing it is,
   this falsehood covered with gold:
25 "She is chosen among all women":
   he is crazy who puts his trust there—
   watch out
   for the dice   III
   she has leaded,
30 she has taken
   in so many,
   I tell you,
   and left them on the road.

   You can look at her and tell she has more tricks
35 than an old fox being chased.
   The other day she made me wait around with my mouth
                 open
   the whole night long till day.
   Her desire
   is flighty   IV
40 and full of devices,
   but every child
   makes songs of her,
   punishing such
   women for their cruelty.
45 The man to whom her love was given—
   a pagan fairy marked him out;
   no baptized woman was ever like her
   between here and the cave of Elijah.[1]

vol'e vai   V
50 tot dreit lai,
   e·l retrai
   qu'ieu morrai,
   si no sai
   consi jai
55 nuda o vestia.

   Sa beutatz fon ab lieis nada
   ses fum de creis ni d'erbada;
   de mil amicx es cazada
   e de mil senhors amia.
60 Marcabrus   VI
   ditz que l'us
   non es clus;
   bad e mus
   qui·ll vol plus
65 c'a raüs
   part de la traïa.

   De fin' amor dezirada
   az una flor pic vairada
   plus que d'autruna pauzada.
70 Paucs fols fai tost gran folia.
   Perdo·l grat
   de l'abat
   Saint Privat; [2]   VII
   m'ai pensat
75 ses cujat
   si·m ditz: Mat,
   que l'amors embria.

   Del deslei
   que me fei
80 li fauc drei,
   e·il m'autrei,
   mas sotz mei   VIII
   aplat sei,
   qu'ela·m lass'e·m lia. [3]

[2] An obscene pun.

Fly, go
50 straight there,   V
tell her
I will die
unless I know
how she lies
55 down at night, naked or dressed.

Her beauty was born when she was,
without vapors of cress, or fomentation of herbs.
She has a thousand friends on supply,
and of a thousand lords is the friend.
60 Marcabru
says the door   VI
is never closed.
Let him gape and waste his time
who looks for more in her—
65 he'll back off
and walk away from that treacherous bitch.

She has one many-colored flower, always changing,
of perfect love long desired,
better placed with her than any other woman.
70 A little fool soon commits great foolishness.
I forgive her the thanks
of the Abbot   VII
of St. Privat.[2]
I figured,
75 surely
when she tells me Checkmate,
love will quickly swell forth.

The wrong
she did me
80 I forgive
and hand myself over;   VIII
only, underneath me
let her lie down on her back
and bind me and tie me up.[3]

---

[3] The song of the starling has two parts. The second part follows.

13

Ges l'estornels non s'oblida; [1]
quant ac la razon auzida,
c'ans ha sa vida cuillida
del dreg volar no s'alensa.
5 Tant anet
e volet   I
e seguet,
e trobet
lo devet;
10 orguanet,
a chantar comensa.

Sobr'una branca florida
lo francx auzels brai e crida;
tant ha sa votz esclarzida
15 qu'ela n'a auzit l'entensa.
L'us declui,
lai s'esdui   II
truesc'a lui.
"Auzels, ui
20 ditz, per cui
fas tal brui
o cals amors tensa?"

Di l'estornels: "Part Lerida
a pros es tan descremida,
25 c'anc no saup plus de gandida,
plena de falsa crezensa.
Mil amic
s'en fan ric: III
per l'abric
30 que·us servic,

[1] This is one of Marcabru's most difficult songs, its obscurity increased by a poor manuscript delivery. The following translation owes much to the

13

The starling did not hesitate [1]
once it heard its mission,
didn't even take its food,
just flew straight ahead without stopping,
5 so fast
it flew,   I
it sought
and found
her retreat,
10 twittered
and began to sing.

On a flowering branch
the trusty bird bawls out and cries,
lifts his voice so clear
15 she has heard his great effort,
opens her door,
comes over   II
to him.
"Now, Bird,
20 tell me, what's
the racket for,
or is it love that's driving you?"

The starling says, "There's a valiant man out there
beyond Lérida you've been so vicious to,
25 he never found any defense
against you, you full of bad faith.
A thousand friends
brag about you in public: III
but the discretion
30 with which *he* served you—

ingenious suggestions and reconstructions of Kurt Lewent.

lo meric
del chastic
n'aura ses faillensa."

"Auzels, a tort m'a'nvazida;
35 mas pos amor no·m ressida,
mas qu'ieu no sui sa plevida,
en cug aver m'entendensa.
L'autr'amiu
no vueill ieu,   IV
40 e badiu
ses aisiu
don m'eschiu
tug de briu
ses far contenensa.

45 "Az una part es partida
ma fin'amistatz plevida,[2]
son joc revit, si·l m'envida.
Auzels, per ta conoissensa,
so·l diguatz:
50 qu'en un glatz [3]   V
lev'e jatz
desiratz
er l'a atz
ans asatz
55 que n'ajam lezensa.

"La cambr'er de cel guarnida,
d'un ric jauzir per jauzida,
c'ab dous baizar s'es sentida
desotz se plan de plazensa.
60 Vai e·l di
qu'el mati   VI
si·aisi,
que sotz pi

[2] That is, I do not have such love, I prefer changing partners.

he will get
his reward
for such restraint, make sure of that."

"Bird, this attack of his is unkind.
35 But since your man cannot arouse my lasting love,
and provided I'm not bound to be his alone,
he can count on enjoying my inclination now.
I don't want
some courtly lover,   IV
40 some simpleton
who's no fun—
such a one
I shake off fast
without further ado.

45 "My sworn and loyal love
has taken off somewhere; [2]
but I'll put some life into your man's game, if he wants
                           me to play.
Bird, as you can talk to him,
tell him this:
50 before the shout is over [3]   V
desire
rises and dies;
now calm him down,
go quickly
55 while the moment for our pleasure lasts.

"Our chamber will be furnished with the sky,
a place of rich rejoicing for this joyous woman
who felt herself, once, with a sweet kiss
beneath him, overcome with pleasure.
60 Go, tell him,
be here   VI
in the morning;
under the pine tree

[3] Literally, "in one shout," in an instant.

farem fi,
65 sotz lui mi,
d'esta malvolensa."

Gent ha la razon fenida,
estornels cui l'aura guid'a
son senhor vas cui s'escrida:
70 "Vos ai amor de valensa;
c'als mil drutz
ha rendutz   VII
mil salutz
e pagutz
75 per condutz
ses trautz
de falsa semensa.[4]

S'al mati
l'es aqui
80 on vos di
e·us mandi,   VIII
qu'el ardi
del jardi
e que·us mat e·us vensa!"

14

L'autrier jost' una sebissa
trobei pastora mestissa,
de joi e de sen massissa,
si cum filla de vilana,   I
5 cap' e gonel' e pelissa
vest e camiza treslissa,
sotlars e caussas de lana.

---

[4] Literally, "without tributes of false seed." The bird is telling its poor
master what he wants to hear, that she is faithful and virtuous, not a two-

we will end,
65 I beneath him,
all the bad blood between us."

This mission was handled with great tact
by the starling, now guided by the breeze
to its master, whom it shouts to:
70 "I've got you a precious love:
to a thousand admirers
she has rendered   VII
a thousand greetings,
and sated them
75 with dinners,
never granting
them the rotten fruit they crave.[4]

"In the morning
if you go
80 where she tells
and sends you,   VIII
in the struggle
in the garden
may she checkmate and beat you."

14

The other day, beside a row of hedges,
I found a shepherdess of lowly birth,
full of joy and common sense.
And, like the daughter of a woman of the fields,   I
5 she wore cape and cloak and fur,
and a shift of drill,
and shoes, and woolen stockings.

---

timer, or thousand-timer, with an open door.

Ves lieis vinc per la planissa:
"Toza, fi·m ieu, res faitissa,
10 dol ai car lo freitz vos fissa."
"Seigner, so·m dis la vilana,   II
merce Dieu e ma noirissa,
pauc m'o pretz si·l vens m'erissa,
qu'alegreta sui e sana."

15 "Toza, fi·m ieu, cauza pia,
destors me sui de la via
per far a vos compaignia;
quar aitals toza vilana   III
no deu ses pareill paria
20 pastorgar tanta bestia
en aital terra, soldana."

"Don, fetz ela, qui que·m sia,
ben conosc sen e folia;
la vostra pareillaria,
25 Seigner, so·m dis la vilana,   IV
lai on se tang si s'estia,
que tals la cuid' en bailia
tener, no·n a mas l'ufana."

"Toza de gentil afaire,
30 cavaliers fon vostre paire
que·us engenret en la maire,
car fon corteza vilana.   V
Con plus vos gart, m'etz belaire,
e per vostre joi m'esclaire,
35 si·m fossetz un pauc humana!"

"Don, tot mon ling e mon aire
vei revertir e retriare
al vezoig et a l'araire,
Seigner, so·m dis la vilana;   VI
40 mas tals se fai cavalgaire
c'atrestal deuria faire
los seis jorns de la setmana."

I came to her across the level ground.
"Girl," I said, "beautiful,
10 I am unhappy because the cold is piercing you."
"Lord," this peasant's child said to me,   II
"thanks be to God and the woman who nursed me,
it's nothing to me if the wind ruffles my hair,
because I feel good, and I'm healthy."

15 "Girl," I said, "you're sweet and innocent,
I came out of my way
to keep you company;
for a peasant girl like you   III
should not, without a comrade near by,
20 pasture so many cattle
all alone in such a place."

"Master," she said, "whatever I may be,
I can tell sense from foolishness.
Your comradeship,
25 Lord," said this girl of the fields and pastures,   IV
"let it stay where it belongs,
for such as I, when she thinks she has it
for herself, has nothing but the look of it."

"O you are a girl of noble quality,
30 your father was a knight
who got your mother with you
because she was a courtly peasant.   V
The more I look at you, the more beautiful you are
to me, and I am lit up by your joy,
35 or would be if you had some humanity."

"Master, my whole lineage and descent
I trace all the way back
to the sickle and the plow,
my Lord," said this peasant girl to me;   VI
40 "and such as calls himself a knight
would do better to work, like them,
six days every week."

"Toza, fi·m ieu, gentils fada,
vos adastret, quan fos nada,
45 d'una beutat esmerada
　 sobre tot' autra vilana;　　　　　　　　　　VII
　 e seria·us ben doblada,
　 si·m vezi' una vegada,
　 sobira e vos sotrana."

50 "Seigner, tan m'avetz lauzada,
　 que tota·n seri' enveiada;
　 pois en pretz m'avetz levada,
　 Seigner, so·m dis la vilana,　　　　　　　　VIII
　 per so n'auretz per soudada
55 al partir: bada, fols, bada,
　 e la muz' a meliana."

　 "Toz', estraing cor e salvatge
　 adomesg' om per uzatge.
　 Ben conosc al trespassatge
60 qu'ab aital toza vilana　　　　　　　　　　　IX
　 pot hom far ric compaignatge
　 ab amistat de coratge,
　 si l'us l'autre non engana."

　 "Don, hom coitatz de follatge
65 jur' e pliu e promet gatge:
　 si·m fariatz homenatge,
　 Seigner, so·m dis la vilana;　　　　　　　　X
　 mas ieu, per un pauc d'intratge,
　 non vuoil ges mon piucellatge,
70 camjar per nom de putana."

　 "Toza, tota creatura
　 revertis a sa natura:
　 pareillar pareilladura
　 devem, ieu e vos, vilana,　　　　　　　　　XI
75 a l'abric lonc la pastura,
　 car plus n'estaretz segura
　 per far la cauza doussana."

"Girl," I said, "a gentle fairy
endowed you at birth
45 with your beauty, which is pure
beyond every other peasant girl.   VII
And yet you would be twice as beautiful
if once I saw you
underneath and me on top."

50 "Lord, you have praised me so high,
how everyone would envy me!
Since you have driven up my worth,
my Lord," said this peasant girl,   VIII
"for that you will have as your reward:
55 'Gape, fool, gape,' as we part,
and waiting and waiting the whole afternoon."

"Girl, every shy and wild heart
grows tame with a little getting used to,
and I know that, passing by,
60 a man can offer a peasant girl   IX
like you a fine cash companionship,
with real affection in his heart,
if one doesn't cheat on the other."
"Master, a man hounded by madness
65 promises and pledges and puts up security:
that's how you would do homage to me,
Lord," said this peasant girl;   X
"but I am not willing, for a little
entrance fee, to cash in my virginity
70 for the fame of a whore."

"Girl, every creature
reverts to its nature:
let us become a couple of equals,
you and I, my peasant girl,   XI
75 in the cover there, by the pasture,
you will feel more at ease there
we we do the sweet you know what."

"Don, oc; mas segon dreitura
cerca fols sa follatura,
80 cortes cortez' aventura,
    e·il vilans ab la vilana;   XII
    en tal loc fai sens fraitura
    on hom non garda mezura,
    so ditz la gens anciana."

85 "Toza, de vostra figura
    non vi autra plus tafura   XIII
    ni de son cor plus trefana."

    "Don, lo cavecs vos ahura,
    que tals bad' en la peintura   XIV
90 qu'autre n'espera la mana." [1]

15

Pax in nomine Domini!
Fetz Marcabrus los motz e·l so.
Aujatz que di:
Cum nos a fait, per sa doussor,
5 Lo Seingnorius celestiaus   I
probet de nos un lavador,
c'anc, fors outramar, no·n fon taus,
en de lai deves Josaphas:
e d'aquest de sai vos conort.[1]

10 Lavar de ser e de maiti
   nos deuriam, segon razo,
   ie·us o afi.

[1] These lines have not been clearly explained, but they suggest that the man is wasting his time in false hopes, or that the girl knows where reality is. A. Berry makes the lovely suggestion that at this moment they hear an owl nearby.
[1] This crusade song was written in the court of Alfonso VII of Castile and León, who may be the "emperor" (31). The two *lavador* are the Holy Land and the domain of the Moors in Spain, or the crusades in each place. In the

"Master, yes; but, as it is right,
the fool seeks out his foolishness,
80 a man of the court, his courtly adventure;
and let the peasant be with his peasant girl.   XII
'Good sense suffers from disease
where men do not observe degrees':
that's what the ancients say."

85 "Girl, I never saw another
more roguish in her face   XIII
or more false in her heart."

"Master, that owl is making you a prophecy:
this one stands gaping in front of a painting,   XIV
90 and that one waits for manna." [1]

15

Peace in the name of the Lord!
Marcabru made the words and the melody.
Hear what he says:
how the Lord in heaven
5 has made us, in his gentleness,   I
within our reach, a washing place
such as never was before, except beyond the sea,
way yonder toward the valley of Jehoshaphat:
but for this one near us now, I exhort you.[1]

10 To wash ourselves clean in the evening and the morning
it is right, it is just,
I assure you;

last strophe, the Marquis (55) is Raimon Bérenger IV of Barcelona; the
men of the temple of Solomon are the Knights Templar; the Count is
probably Guillaume VIII of Poitou (d. April 9, 1137), brother of Raimon
of Antioch, though this identification is disputed. The "emperor" has also
been interpreted as a reference to God (Ruggieri), and as the title granted
to the warrior who died for his faith, upon his ascent to Paradise (P.
Groult); the translation reflects this last interpretation.

Chascus a del lavar legor;
domentre qu'el es sas e saus,   II
15 deuri' anar al lavador,
que·ns es verais medicinaus;
que s'abans anam a la mort,
d'aut en sus aurem alberc bas.

Mas Escarsedatz e No-fes
20 part Joven de son compaigno.
Ai! cals dols es,
que tuich volon lai li plusor,
don lo gazaings es enfernaus!   III
S'anz non correm al lavador
25 c'ajam la boca ni·ls huoills claus,
non i a un d'orguoill tant gras
c'al morir non trob contrafort.

Que·l Seigner que sap tot quant es
e sap tot quant er e c'anc fo,
30 nos i promes
honor e nom d'emperador.
E·il beutatz sera,—sabetz caus—   IV
de cels qu'iran al lavador?
Plus que l'estela gauzignaus;
35 ab sol que vengem Dieu del tort
que·ill fan sai, e lai vas Domas.

Probet del lignatge Caï,
del primeiran home felho,
a tans aissi
40 c'us a Dieu non porta honor;
veirem qui·ll er amics coraus;   V
c'ab la vertut del lavador
nos sera Jhesus comunaus;
e tornem los garssos atras
45 qu'en agur crezon et en sort!

every man has a chance to wash himself clean.
While he is yet safe and well   II
15 he must go to the washing place,
it is our true remedy,
for if we go to death before we are washed,
we shall not rise, we shall have our dwelling in Hell.

But Meanness and Faithlessness
20 part Youth from his true companion.
Ai! what grief
that most of them wish to go
where the great reward is the fire of Hell.   III
For if we do not run to the washing place
25 before we have closed our mouth and eyes,
there is not one so swollen with pride of life
but will find, at his dying, a mighty foe.
For the Lord who knows all that is,
knows all that will be and ever was,
30 promised us there
honor and the name of emperor.
And their beauty will be—do you know what it will be,   IV
the beauty of those who will go to the washing place?
Greater than the beauty of the morning star.
35 Only, we must avenge God for the wrong
they are doing to Him here, and over there near Damascus.

In the lineage of Cain,
the first criminal man,
are many like him,
40 not one brings honor to God.
We shall see who will be the friend of God in his heart.   V
For by the power of the washing place
we shall all have Jesus together.
And now let us turn back those brutes
45 who put their faith in divination, in the entrails of
birds.

E·il luxurios corna-vi,
coita-disnar, bufa-tizo,
crup-en-cami,
remanran inz el folpidor;
50 Dieus vol los arditz e·ls suaus   VI
assajar a son lavador;
e cil gaitaran los ostaus;
e trobaran fort contrafort,
so per qu'ieu a lor anta·ls chas.[2]

55 En Espaigna, sai, lo Marques
e cill del temple Salamo
sofron lo pes
e·l fais de l'orguoill paganor,
per que Jovens cuoill avol laus.   VII
60 E·l critz per aquest lavador
versa sobre·ls plus rics captaus
fraitz, faillitz, de proeza las,
que non amon Joi ni Deport.

Desnaturat son li Frances,
65 si de l'afar Dieu dizon no,
qu'ieu sai com es [3]
d'Antiocha, Pretz e Valor
sai plora Guiana e Peitaus.   VIII
Dieus, Seigner, al tieu lavador [4]
70 l'arma del comte met en paus:
e sai gart Peitieus e Niort
Lo Seigner qui ressors del vas!

[2] Or: "that is why, to their shame, I pursue them."
[3] Lines 66–67 of the text have been amended as suggested by Ruggero M.

And all the lustful—the one who toots his horn for
    wine,
the eager eater, the fire blower, the squatter with his
    rump on the road—
all shall be left where the refuse is heaped up for burn-
    ing.
50 God wants to test the brave   VI
and the meek in his washing place,
and these shall keep watch on His dwelling places,
and they shall find a mighty enemy,
and so I hound them on to the place of their humiliation.[2]
55 Here, in Spain, the Marquis
and the men of Solomon's temple
bear the burden
and the weight of the pagans' arrogance:
for this the young must reap disgrace.   VII
60 The wailing for this washing place
pours out upon the mightiest lords,
broken men, failed men, weary of prowess,
who do not love joy and courtliness.

The French are degenerate
65 if they say no to God's task,
for I know how things stand [3]
with Antioch: glory and valor
are wept for in Guyenne and Poitou.   VIII
Lord God, in your holy washing place [4]
70 let the soul of the Count dwell in peace;
and here may Poitou and Niort be safe in the care
of the Lord who rose up from the Sepulcher.

Ruggieri, in *Cultura Neolatina*, 12 (1952), 81–101.
[4] Here, as Ruggieri says, the *lavador* is Paradise.

16

Per savi·l tenc ses doptanssa
cel qui de mon chant devina
so que chascus motz declina,   I
si cum la razos despleia,
5 qu'ieu mezeis sui en erranssa
d'esclarzir paraul' escura.[1]

Trobador, ab sen d'enfanssa,
movon als pros atahina,
e tornon en disciplina   II
10 so que veritatz autreia,
e fant los motz, per esmanssa,
entrebeschatz de fraichura.

E meton en un' eganssa
Falss' Amor encontra fina,
15 qu'ieu dic: que d'Amar[2] s'aizina   III
ab si mezesme guerreia;
c'apres, la bors' a voianssa,
fai fols captenenssa dura.

Per so·n port ir' e pesanssa
20 c'aug dir a la gen frairina
c'Amors engan' e trahina   IV
cellui cui Amar refreia;
menton, que lor benananssa
es Jois, Sofrirs e Mesura.

25 Aitals pareills fai mostranssa,
s'en doas partz non camina,
pois bon' Amors n'es vezina,   V

[1] The original reads, literally: "to clear up, to cast some light on dark,
obscure speech"—period. But the *paraul' escura* refers to the *trobador* in the

16

I say he's a wise man, no doubt about it,
who makes out, word for word,
what my song signifies,   I
and how the theme unfolds:
5 for I myself take pains
to cast some light on the obscurity [1]

of those troubadours with childish minds
who worry honest men:
they scourge and improve   II
10 what Truth itself puts forth,
always taking pains to make their words
tangled up and meaningless.

And they put up that false love of theirs
against true love, as though it were as good.
15 And I say: whoever settles down with Lust [2]   III
wars against himself;
for afterwards, when his wallet is empty,
Lust shows such fools its cruelty.

It fills me with anger and grief
20 to hear that pack of perjurers telling us
that Love deceives and tortures   IV
a man by cooling down his lust.
They are liars, for the happiness of lovers
is Joy, Patience, Restraint.

25 Such lovers, if they don't go off
in two directions, bear witness,
since good Love is their neighbor,   V

second strophe (Lewent).
[2] *Amars:* literally, "bitterness"; see headnote.

ab dos desirs d'un' enveia
ab segurana fianssa
30 blanca cara ver' e pura.

C'Amors a signifianssa
de maracd' e de sardina,[3]
es de Joi cim' e racina,   VI
c'ab veritat seignoreia,
35 e sa poestatz sobranssa
sobre mouta creatura.

Segon dich, faich e semblanssa,
es de veraia corina
car se promet e·s plevina,   VII
40 ab sol que·l dos no sordeia,
e qui vas lieis no s'enanssa
porta nom de follatura.

Sermonars ni predicanssa
non val un ou de gallina,
45 vas cellui ditz qu'es fraïna   VIII
folli' e de cor correia; [4]
qu·ieu sai s'Amars es amanssa,
qu'a mains es fals' e tafura.

Fols, pos tot cant au romanssa,
50 non sec razo, mas bozina,
car s'Amors viu de rapina,   IX
autrei c'Amors s'amoreia
e que Costans es costanssa [5]
e fals usatges dreitura.

55 La defenida balanssa
d'aquest vers e revolina
sobr' un' avol gen canina   X

---

[3] In the *Lapidarium* of Marbod, the emerald is said to restrain lust, the sard
encourages humility, chastity, and restraint (Dimitri Scheludko).
[4] That is, "As surely as a belt is cut from leather, so surely are the things

to the one single longing of two desires,
in trust that is firm,
30 white, precious, true, pure.

   For Love has the meaning
of emerald and sard,[3]
it is the top and root of Joy,   VI
it is a lord who rules with truth,
35 and its power overcomes
every creature.

   By its word, its action, and its look,
it comes from a true heart
when it gives its promise and pledge—   VII
40 if only it does not befoul its gifts;
and whoever does not hasten to it
bears the name of fool.

   No sermon, no preaching
is worth a hen's egg
45 with this fool—they say foolishness   VIII
has to do vile things and belts are made of leather; [4]
for I know, when Lust is the mode of their desiring,
it is false to many men, and full of tricks.

   The fool, since everything he hears he sings to others,
50 does not follow reason, he just makes noise,
for his love lives on what it grabs.   IX
Well, I'll agree: his love really loves,
and Costans is constancy,[5]
and cheating is justice.

55 The end of this *vers*
takes its stand and turns
on a vile people, dogs   X

that foolishness conjures up worthless" (Lewent).
[5] *Costans*, as a proper noun, stands for the talebearers and the false lovers
in Marcabru's songs.

cui malvatz astres ombreia,
c'ab folla cuida bobanssa
60 ses faich de bon aventura.

La cuida per qu'el bobanssa
li sia malaventura.

whom an evil star keeps in the dark,
all pompous with their dumb ideas,
60 barren of the deeds that bring happiness.

May the ideas they're so proud of   XI
make them miserable.

MARCABRU AND UGO CATOLA

17

Amics Marchabrun, car digam
un vers d'amor, que per cor am   I
qu'a l'hora que nos partiram
en sia loing lo chanz auziz.

5 Ugo Catola,[1] er fazam,
mas de faus'amistat me clam,   II
qu'anc pos la serps baisset lo ram
no foron tant enganairiz.

Marcabrun, ço no m'es pas bon
10 que d'amor digaz si ben non;   III
per zo·us en mou eu la tenson,
que d'amor fui naz e noiriz.

Catola, non entenz razon.
Non saps d'amor cum trais Samson?   IV
15 Vos cuidaz e·ill autre bricon
que tot sia vers quant vos diz.

Marcabrun, no·s troban auctor
de Sanso·l fort e de sa uxor   V
qu'ela n'avia ostat s'amor
20 a l'ora que ce fo deliz?

Catola, quar a sordejor
la det e la tolc al meillor,   VI
lo dia perdet sa valor,
que·l seus fo per l'estraing traiz.

[1] Nothing is known about Ugo, or Uc, Catola. One strophe in a dialogue is attributed to him in a unique manuscript, but Dejeanne considers this attribution doubtful.

17

Marcabru, my friend, let us compose
  a *vers* about love, for I have it in my heart,   I
since now we're going to have our dispute,
that our song should be heard far off.

5 Ugo Catola,[1] right, let's do it now,
  but I denounce false love,   II
for never, since the serpent came down from the bough,
have there been so many women full of tricks.

Marcabru, I don't like it
10 when you say anything but good of love;   III
  which is why I have started this debate with you,
for love gave me birth and fostered me.

Catola, you don't listen to reason.
  Don't you know how love betrayed Samson?   IV
15 You think, you and the other fools,
that everything love tells you is true.

Marcabru, aren't there authorities
  who tell us of the mighty Samson and his wife,   V
that she stopped loving him
20 only when he was destroyed, not before?

Catola, she gave her love to the worst,
  and took it away from the best,   VI
and lost her worth that day
she betrayed her husband for a stranger.

25 Marcabrun, si cum declinaz
     qu'amors si' ab engan mesclaz,   VII
     dunc es lo almosna pechaz,
     la cima devers la raïzl

     Catola, l'amors dont parlaz
30 camja cubertament los daz,   VIII
     aprop lo bon lanz vos gardaz,
     ço diz Salomons e Daviz.

     Marcabrun, amistaz dechai,
     car a trobat joven savai;   IX
35 eu n'ai al cor ir' et esclai,
     quar l'en alevaz tan laiz criz.

     Catola, Ovides mostra chai
     e l'ambladura o retrai   X
     que non soana brun ni bai,
40 anz se trai plus aus achaiz.

     Marchabrun, anc non cuit t'ames
     l'amors, ves cui es tant engres,   XI
     ni no fo anc res meinz prezes
     d'aitals joglars esbaluiz.

45 Catola, anc de ren non fo pres
     un pas, que tost no se'n loignes,   XII
     et enquer se'n loigna ades,
     e fera, tro seaz feniz.

     Marcabrun, quant sui las e·m duoill,
50 e ma bon' amia m'acuoill   XIII
     ab un baisar, quant me despuoill,
     me'n vau sans e saus e garitz.

25 Marcabru, if you really mean
that love is involved with deceit,   VII
then giving to the poor is a sin,
and the top of the tree is down with the root.

Catola, this love you're talking about
30 secretly switches the dice: VIII
when you've made a good throw, watch out—
so Solomon and David say.

Marcabru, love declines
because it found Youth empty of valor;   IX
35 there is anger and dread in my heart
for the vile things you have cried against love.

Catola, here Ovid teaches us,
and the way things go confirms it,   X
that love looks down on no one, dark or light,
40 in fact prefers to come to the scum of the earth.

Marcabru, I don't think Love ever loved
you, you're so enraged at it,   XI
nor was there anything it looked down on more
than jongleurs who are out of their minds like this.

45 Catola, it never took one step
closer to anyone without backing off right away,   XII
and love is still playing that trick, backing off,
and always will, till the end of your life.

Marcabru, when I am tired and I feel bad,
50 and my sweet friend welcomes me   XIII
with a kiss, as I undress,
I go from her all well and feeling good again.

Catola, per amor deu truoill
tressaill l'avers al fol lo suoill,   XIV
55 e puois mostra la via a l'uoill
aprop los autres escharniz.[2]

---

[2] That is, a man who loves wine spends all his money; and when it is all
gone, his squandered money shows him the same road followed by the others
who have been made fools of (Lewent). As soon as your money is gone, there
is nothing more to drink and no more love.

Catola, when a fool is in love with the wine press,
his money jumps over the sill,   XIV
55 then shows him the same road to follow
that the other fools have been shown.[2]

CERCAMON

(fl. 1135–1145)

A few details about the life of Cercamon can be gleaned from his songs. He was of Gascon origin. He wrote a lament for the death of Guillaume X of Aquitaine in 1137. Elsewhere he refers to the marriage of Eleanor of Aquitaine with the future Louis VII. It is generally believed that Marcabru was his teacher (instead of the other way around, as Marcabru's *vida* asserts) , or at least a powerful influence. Only seven of his songs survive; an eighth song (*Per fin' amor m'esjauzira*) is of uncertain authorship.

Text: Newly edited for this voume. Base ms.: C.

18

Quant l'aura doussa s'amarzis
e·l fuelha chai de sul verjan
e l'auzelh chanton lor latis,   I
et ieu de sai sospir e chan
5 d'Amor que·m te lassat e pres,
qu'ieu encar no l'aic en poder.

Las! qu'ieu d'Amor non ai conquis
mas las trebalhas e l'afan,
ni res tant greu no·s covertis   II
10 com so que·m plus vau deziran;
ni tal enveja no·m fai res
cum fai so qu'ieu non posc aver.

Per una joja m'esjauzis
fina, qu'anc re non amiey tan;
15 quan suy ab lieys si m'esbahis   III
qu'ieu no·ill sai dire mon talan,
e quan m'en vauc, vejaire m'es
que tot perda·l sen e·l saber.

Tota la genser qu'anc hom vis
20 encontra lieys no pretz un guan;
quan totz lo segles brunezis,   IV
lai on ylh es aissi resplan.
Dieus mi respieyt tro que l'agues
o que la vej'anar jazer.

25 Totz trassalh e bran e fremis
per s'amor, durmen o velhan.
Tal paor ai qu'ieu mesfalhis   V
no m'aus pessar cum la deman,
mas servir l'ai dos ans o tres,
30 e pueys ben leu sabra'n lo ver.

18

When the sweet breeze turns bitter
and the leaf falls down from the branch
and the birds change their language,   I
I, here, sigh, and sing
5 of Love, who holds me bound and captured,
Love, whom I never have had in my power.

I am weary, for I have won nothing from love
but toil and torture,
for nothing is so hard to get   II
10 as the thing I desire;
and nothing fills me with such longing
as the thing I cannot have.

I rejoice in a jewel
so precious that I never loved another thing so much;
15 when I am with her I am struck so dumb,   III
I cannot tell her my desire,
and when I go away from her I think
I lose my mind completely, and everything I know.

The most beautiful lady a man ever saw
20 is not worth a glove next to *her;*
when the whole world grows dark,   IV
where she is—see, there is light.
God let me live long enough to have her,
or see her going to bed.

25 I start, I burn, I tremble, all over,
sleeping and waking, for love of her.
I am so afraid of dying,   V
I dare not think of asking her;
however, I shall serve her two years or three,
30 and then, maybe, she will know the truth.

Ni muer ni viu ni no guaris,
ni mal no·m sent e si l'ai gran,
quar de s'amor no suy devis,   VI
non sai si ja l'aurai ni quan,
35 qu'en lieys es tota la merces
que·m pot sorzer o descazer.

Bel m'es quant ilh m'enfolhetis
e·m fai badar e·n vau muzan;
et es me belh si m'escarnis   VII
40 o·m gaba dereir'o denan,
qu'aprop lo mal me venra bes
ben tost, s'a lieys ven a plazer.

S'elha no·m vol, volgra moris
lo dia que·m pres a coman;
45 ai, dieus! tan suavet m'aucis   VIII
quan de s'amor me fetz semblan,
que tornat m'a en tal deves
que nuill' autra no vuelh vezer.

Totz cossiros m'en esjauzis,
50 car s'ieu la dopti o la blan,
per lieys serai o fals o fis,   IX
o drechuriers o ples d'enjan,
o totz vilas o totz cortes,
o trebalhos o de lezer.

55 Mas, cui que plass' o cui que pes,
elha·m pot, si·s vol, retener.   X

Cercamons ditz: greu er cortes
hom qui d'amor se desesper.   XI

I neither die, nor live, nor get well,
I do not feel my suffering, and yet it is great suffering,
because I cannot tell the future of her love,   VI
whether I shall have it, or when,
35 for in her is all the pity,
which can raise me up, or make me fall.

I am pleased when she maddens me,
when she makes me stand with my mouth open, staring;
I am pleased when she laughs at me,   VII
40 or makes a fool of me right to my face or behind my
                    back,
for after this bad time the good will come,
very quickly, if such is her pleasure.

If she does not want me, I would have liked to die
that day, when she took me as her servant;
45 oh lord, how gently she slew me   VIII
when she showed me the look of her love,
and locked me in such an enclosure,
I never want to see another.

I am full of worries and yet I enjoy it,
50 for if I fear my lady and court her,
I will be false or true, it all depends on her,   IX
faithful or full of tricks,
a vulgar or a courtly man,
full of torment or at my ease.

55 It may please some and annoy others,
but she can retain me, if that's what she wants.   X

Cercamon says: a man will hardly belong in court
if he despairs of love.   XI

JAUFRÉ RUDEL

(*fl. mid-twelfth century*)

Only a few details of Jaufré Rudel's life are fairly certain. In 1148 Marcabru sent one of his songs "to Lord Jaufré Rudel beyond the sea." Jaufré, in fact, announces his intention of joining a crusade in at least one passage, and it is generally believed that he did so, in 1147, and that he never returned. He was probably a lord of Blaye (Gironde).

Beginning toward the end of the thirteenth century, long after the best days of the troubadour lyric, many manuscripts provide brief biographies of the poets and explanations of their songs. These biographies, called *vidas*, "lives," have little historical value, for they are based almost entirely on the contents of the songs. Whoever wrote them made up a "life" by embroidering on certain references in the troubadour's work and by taking his figurative expressions literally. They are wonderful to read, the stories they tell are perfect miniature romances. The explanations of the songs, called *razos*, which tell of the conditions in which the songs were composed and the events they refer to, are no less exciting, imaginative, and inaccurate.

The *vida* of Jaufré Rudel is clearly inspired by certain images in his songs. The story of Jaufré Rudel and the lady of Tripoli (in Syria) is very famous; it appears in the work of Petrarch, Heine, Browning, and many others:

> Jaufré Rudel of Blaye was a most noble man, the prince of Blaye; and he fell in love with the countess of Tripoli, without seeing her, for the good that he heard of her from the pilgrims who came from Antioch; and he made many songs about her, with good melodies and simple words. And from the desire to see her he took the cross and put out to sea; and illness seized him on the boat and

he was taken as a dead man to an inn in Tripoli. And it was made known to the countess, and she came to him, by his bed, and took him in her ams; and he knew that she was the countess, and he recovered his hearing and the sense of smell; and praised God and thanked Him that He sustained his life until he might see her. And that way he died in her arms, and she had him buried with great honor in the house of the Templars. And then, on that day, she became a nun, because of the grief that she had from his death.

Text: Newly edited for this volume.

Quan lo rius de la fontana [1]
s'esclarzis, si cum far sol,
e par la flors aiglentina,
e·l rossinholetz el ram   I
5 volf e refranh ez aplana
son dous chantar e l'afina,
dreitz es qu'ieu lo mieu refranha.

Amors de terra lonhdana,
per vos totz lo cors mi dol;
10 e no·n puesc trobar mezina
si non au vostre reclam   II
ab atraich d'amor doussana
dinz vergier o sotz cortina
ab dezirada companha.

15 Pus totz jorns m'en falh aizina,
no·m meravilh si·m n'aflam,
quar anc genser crestiana
non fo, ni Dieus non o vol,   III
Juzeva ni Sarrazina;
20 ben es selh pagutz de mana,
qui ren de s'amor guazanha.

De dezir mos cors no fina
vas selha ren qu'ieu pus am;
e cre que volers m'enguana
25 si cobezeza la·m tol;   IV
que pus es ponhens qu'espina
la dolors que per joi sana;
don ja non vuelh qu'om m'en planha.

[1] Base ms.: C.

When the waters of the spring
run clear once more,
and the flower comes forth on the eglantine,
and on the branch the nightingale   I
5 turns, modulates, softens
his sweet song, and refines it,
it is right that I modulate mine.

Love of a far-off land,
for you my whole heart aches;
10 and I cannot find the remedy
if I do not listen to your call,   II
drawn by the sweetness of love,
in a garden, or behind curtains,
with a friend I desire.

15 Since I am always denied any chance for that,
it is no wonder I am on fire,
for there never was a gentler woman,
Christian, Jew, or Saracen—   III
God does not want it:
20 he is fed on manna
who wins a little of her love.

My heart does not come to the end of desire
for the one I love most;
and I think my will misleads me
25 if lust takes her away from me;   IV
far more piercing than a thorn
is the pain only joy can cure;
therefore let no man pity me.

Senes breu de parguamina
30 tramet lo vers, que chantam
en plana lengua romana,
a·n Hugo Bru per Filhol; [1]   v
bo·m sap quar gens Peitavina
de Berri e de Guïana
35 s'esgau per lui e Bretanha.

20

Lanquan li jorn son lonc en may [1]
m'es belhs dous chans d'auzelhs de lonh,
e quan mi suy partitz de lay
remembra·m d'un' amor de lonh: I
5 vauc, de talan embroncs e clis
si que chans ni flors d'albespis
no·m platz plus que l'yverns gelatz.

Be tenc lo senhor per veray
per qu'ieu veirai l amor de lonh;
10 mas per un ben que m'en eschay
n'ai dos mals, quar tan m'es de lonh.   II
Ai! car me fos lai pelegris,
si que mos fustz e mos tapis
fos pels sieus belhs huelhs remiratz!

15 Be·m parra joys quan li querray,
per amor Dieu, l'amor de lonh:
e, s'a lieys platz, alberguarai
pres de lieys, si be·m suy de lonh: III
adoncs parra·l parlamens fis
20 quan drutz lonhdas er tan vezis
qu'ab bels digz jauzirai solatz.

[1] Base: C.

Without any letter of parchment
30 I send this *vers*, which we sing
in our plain romance tongue,
to En Hugo Brun, by Filhol; [1]   v
it makes me glad that the people of Poitou,
Berry, and Guyenne,
35 and Brittany too, rejoice in him.

20

When days are long in May,
I enjoy the sweet song of the birds far away,
and when I am parted from their song,
the parting reminds me of a love far away: I
5 I go bent with desire, head bowed down;
then neither the song nor the hawthorn's flower
pleases me more than the winter's ice.

I shall consider him my lord, in truth, the man
who lets me see this love far away;
10 but for one good thing that falls to me,
I get two evils, for this love is far away.   II
Ai! I wish I were a pilgrim there,
my staff and my cloak
reflected in her beautiful eyes.

15 My joy will come forth, when I entreat her
for the love of God, the love far away,
and, if it pleases her, I shall lodge
close to her, though now I am far away.   III
Then what fine conferring will come forth,
20 when the lover come from afar will be so close
I shall know the comfort of her sweet words.

[1] Hugo Brun: Jeanroy thinks this is Hugues VII, who took the Cross in
1146. Filhol: the jongleur who will perform Rudel's song.

Iratz e gauzens m'en partray,
quan veirai cest amor de lonh:
mas non sai quoras la veyrai,
25 car trop son nostras terras lonh: IV
assatz hi a pas e camis,
e per aisso no·n suy devis . . .
mas tot sia cum a Dieu platz!

Ja mais d'amor no·m jauziray
30 si no·m jau d'est'amor de lonh,
que gensor ni melhor no·n sai
vas nulha part, ni pres ni lonh;   V
tant es sos pretz verais e fis
que lay el reng dels Sarrazis
35 fos ieu per lieys chaitius clamatz!

Dieus que fetz tot quant ve ni vai
e formet sest'amor de lonh
mi don poder, que·l cor ieu n'ai,
qu'ieu veya sest'amor de lonh,   VI
40 verayamen, en luecs aizis,
si que la cambra e·l jardis
mi resembles tos temps palatz!

Ver ditz qui m'apella lechay
ni deziran d'amor de lonh,
45 car nulhs autres joys tan no·m play
cum jauzimens d'amor de lonh.   VII
Mas so qu'ieu vuoill m'es tant ahis,
qu'enaissi·m fadet mos pairis
qu'ieu ames e nos fos amatz.

50 Mas so q'ieu vuoill m'es tant ahis.
Totz sia mauditz lo pairis
qe·m fadet q'ieu non fos amatz!   VIII

Sad and rejoicing I shall part from her,
when I have seen this love far away:
but when I shall see her I do not know,
25 our lands are very far away: IV
there are many ways and roads,
and I am no prophet . . .
but as it pleases God!

I shall have no pleasure in love
30 if it is not the pleasure of this love far away,
for I do not know a gentler or a better one
anywhere, not close by, not far away: V
her worth is true, and perfect, so
that there, in the kingdom of the Saracens,
35 I wish I were a prisoner for her.

God, who made everything that comes and goes
and formed this love far away,
give me the power—for I have the heart—
to see this love far away VI
40 face to face, in such pleasant dwellings
that the chamber and the garden
would all the while be a palace to my eyes.

He speaks the truth who says I crave
and go desiring this love far away,
45 for no other joy pleases me more
than the rich enjoyment of this love far away. VII
But the path is blocked to my desire,
for my godfather gave me this fate:
I must love and not be loved.

50 But the path is blocked to my desire,
a great curse on this godfather
who doomed to to be unloved. VIII

BERNART DE VENTADORN

(fl. 1150–1180)

Nothing certain is known about Bernart's life. The absence of any verifiable biographical information has spurred the invention of many stories about him, beginning with the *vida*. According to these stories, he rose from his low birth as the son of a serf and a baker in the castle of Ebles II of Ventadour to become the great lover of three noble ladies, including Eleanor of Aquitaine; and, after the death of his protector, ended his days in the monastery of Dalon. It is clear that these stories originated in a literal-minded response to a strophe in Peire d'Alvernhe's playful poem about the troubadors (see below, no. 31), and to some passages in Bernart's lyrics. The only certain fact about him is that he was one of the most popular poets of his own day, judging from the numerous manuscripts of his songs, and from the many poets who allude to, or imitate, his work. He wrote songs about love exclusively; apart from three *tensos,* all his poems are *cansos.*

With Bernart, the troubadour technique of playing on the perspectives of an audience reaches a level that was never to be surpassed. What began to take shape in the songs of Guillaume IX is now completely developed.

We have seen how Guillaume, in his new song, continually acknowledges the powerful presence of his old companions, and thus of his own carnality, all during his lyric vow of service to the lady. That was how he saved his song from the jeers and snickers of those who had Agnes and Ermessen in their minds. The lyric audience of Bernart de Ventadorn contains this same element: the *gens vilana,* the vulgar ones. They keep their place, for no poet, especially one who values refinement, would ever want to dislodge them.

But Bernart's audience is more variously populated than Guillaume's. There are many other kinds of dangerous people threatening to destroy his song. There are slanderers, and flatterers, and spies. And of all these enemies the deadliest ones are the *fals amador,* the "false lovers," for they are the only ones before whom he is completely disarmed. They are the ones who, in Guillaume's song, go talking and talking of love without ever knowing a thing about it. Guillaume is able to brush them off without any trouble in his song of reciprocal love—"We have love's bread and knife." He already has what these empty-hearted rivals, with all their courteous formulas, would like to deprive him of: the lady's love, the assurance that she distinguishes him from all those others in court who dress and speak as he does. But it is just this distinctiveness in his lady's eyes that Bernart longs for: for she does not really see him yet. The love he sings about is not reciprocal; or if it is, then the love the lady returns is not the same as the love her "vassal" gives. He is an aspirant, perpetually struggling to be recognized by her, dreaming of the moment when her eyes will rest, or remembering the moment when her eyes once rested, on him alone, singling him out for his noble worth, for the purity of his love, for his courtliness.

Bernart's obsessive concern is to get the lady to spot him in a crowd, but that is so very difficult when everyone, by convention, looks alike. Courtliness as a moral condition is invisible; as a form of behavior it can be aped by anyone, including those rivals from whom the poet wants to be distinguished. The poet and his enemies all talk alike and act alike; and these enemies are, by birth, entitled to enter the lady's field of vision and pay homage to her. How can she, judging from the distance of her perfection, distinguish the one sincere Tweedledum from all those phony Tweedledees? It would be hard to do in any circumstance, but it is nearly impossible when all one has to judge by is the poet's song. For the conventions of the troubadour lyric were not such as to encourage what we would call a personal style.

For it had to be put together out of a very limited range of themes and motifs; and so all these songs, to a casual hearing at least, sound as much alike as the lovers who compose them are required to look alike. However, one should not misjudge the conventionality of these songs. "To infer from this basic uniformity a want of creative power or a lack of originality on the part of the troubadours is to reason badly. It is much more natural to think that the troubadours really had in mind a kind of ideal *canso*, which all the laws written into the structure of this genre made perfectly real. It is no less legitimate to suppose that this ideal was equally present in the mind of the public who set themselves to hear a song, and any composition was all the more appreciated the more it approached this ideal. It was in the nature of this idea not to be capable of any one realization, and to be capable of multiple realizations, for its essence resided in the variability that its structural tension conferred on it" (Erich Köhler). Then (putting aside the question of structure and variability for the moment) let us say that all that could be recaptured of this supreme song were the separate bits and pieces of it, the themes and motifs cherished by all who were dedicated to the ideal of courtliness: the singer's whole life is devoted to trying to put it all back together again for his friends. But all these formulas of the perfect song were in the public domain, even parrots (as Heinrich von Morungen called his enemies) could repeat them and sound convincing, or as convincing as it was possible to sound using forms of expression that sound like platitudes.

It was said of Jaufré Rudel that his lyrics were *ab pobres motz;* as we would say, he had a small vocabulary. But the same might be said of many troubadours in this early period. The ladies they praise are all blond, universally esteemed, unreliable, and distant; the lovers are all sincere and inadequate—their sincere avowal of their inadequacy, with a few words about the lady's heartbreaking monumentality, comprising the substance of their praise. The "poverty" of the words in the songs of the troubadours is all the more striking in comparison with the great variety of their metrical forms. For they did not cultivate the beautiful line, the oracular utterance big with meaning. That kind of show-stopping brilliance was hardly esteemed in any medieval art; but it would have been especially crude in the courtly lyric, for it would have ruined the integrity of the song's performance. The great troubadours were, indeed, brilliant and original, but not on the verbal surface.

By the very nature of his song, the poet had to follow a common pattern. One of the formulas in that pattern was a prayer to the lady to believe that the poet, her lover, was really being sincere when he spoke all the other formulas. The tantalizing result was that when he made this prayer, the true lover could only succeed in sounding exactly like the false ones, for whom it was just another thing that one is supposed to say. It was a nightmarish predicament, and the horror of it can only be truly savored when one thinks of who these "false lovers" were. Their identity is still implicit in the songs of Guillaume, but Marcabru names them out loud: they are the other poets of the court. All of them sing to the poet's lady, she hears them all. And if, in the severity of her virtue, she should think he is as insincere as they; or if, in her female vanity, she should think they are as sincere as he, then, as the poet often says, he has to stop singing altogether. There is no reason, no chance, to sing any more.

In fact, the poet never does stop, he only sings a song about not singing any more. He must never really stop. He would betray those whom he calls his friends if he ever deprived them of his song. For these friends, who comprise one of the many sectors in the audience, believe in the poet's love. They are the truly courtly, and they listen to the story of this love as the truest image of their dignity. Whatever it means to be courtly, it will never be so clear as in this story of a man who has trained all the forces of his body to the service of a noble lady; a lady so great, no ordinary passion is adequate to her, for she is the perfection and arbiter of courtliness. He is a courtly poet, and bound to his office among these friends: it is for them that he sings, it is by his song that they know he is one of them, it is in the circle of their recognition that he is truly situated, redeemed from exile, named and valued. That realizing look is what he longs to see in the lady's eyes, and he struggles to make his song of praise so nearly adequate to her worth that that look will shine there. He rarely succeeds, for the greatness he can imagine far surpasses any song he can compose. But he does get one re-

ward: in his continual service of song he gets to see that look
in the eyes of his friends. And that is reward enough, in a way.
The lady is distant, and her aspect continually changes; but these
friends form a circle in which he has some significance.

The poet stands under the gaze of his friends and enemies.
The friends demand his song; the enemies, by their hypocrisy,
deprive him of his language. He has to find a way not to be
silent. He does have one way out, as we have seen, and it works
for a while: he can sing about not singing. That will give him
a chance to tell about all the things he suffers and at the same
time to reaffirm his devotion to the lady. In this tested loyalty
he will show the friends an image of true courtliness and so fulfill his bond with them. Then things go very well, and the more
he complains of his torment the more inspiring that image will
be; for the courtly lover's famous complaints are really boasts
of steadfastness.

But this will not work forever, and besides, it is just another
formula, and the false lovers use it too. So there he is, in the
same bind: everybody says the same things, and the only difference between him and all the others is that he really means the
things he says. He cannot prove his sincerity by praising the lady,
for that is precisely when he sounds just like the others, who are
all hypocrites.

The only way to save the song was to give every part of the
audience a share in it, both the friends who cherish his song and
the enemies who want to destroy it. That was Guillaume's way,
only now the poet has a greater variety of enemies to accommo-
date and disarm. The singer scans the audience, and he sees: a
sector of gross carnality occupied by those old companions who
think, lacking all imagination and being absolutely right, that a
lover sworn to service and renunciation is a fool, or else that a
man who claims to be so dedicated is a liar; another sector,
perverse and vicious, in which a host of spies and slanderers find
their places, looking for proof that this man with all his precious
affectations really conceals an ordinary affair, waiting for the
chance to blow the whole thing wide open, and hoping he will
drop the lady's name so that they can deprive him of her company for good; another sector containing those infamous col-

leagues of his, false poets and false lovers, who have no doubt
that this song of his is part of a campaign of seduction, and who
listen to see whether he is a better parrot than they are. And
facing him as well, interspersed among these enemies whom he
has to disarm, are the truly noble friends, all set to contemplate
the perfect image of exaltation and subservience. And facing all
of them is the singer, committed to familiar themes, not to say
clichés, and required to tell, movingly, of his sufferings and joys
in love, though everyone knows that none of it could possibly
have happened.

The singer begins, his eye resting on one group or another. As
he sings, his eye moves. In the course of the performance, it
passes through the whole moral spectrum of the audience, from
the companions to the friends. And as his vision passes through
each sector, he justifies its point of view, proves that what these
people see when they look at him is really there, for he carefully
takes on the image they have of him. Now to do all that he has
to play a very tricky rôle. He impersonates "the courtly lover"
for the entire audience, but his appearance continually changes,
according to what each group, enemies included, would expect.
When his eye lights on the enemies, he acts like the fool they
think he is, and his song turns into self-mockery; a moment
later, when his eye lights on the friends, he puts on their dignity.
But that is only half the trick. He also steps out of this rôle
altogether and talks flat out like his enemies, impersonates *them*
and shares the moral values implicit in their point of view.
Clearly the singer has to be a great performer, for if these quick
changes are not done well, the game is lost. Bernart runs through
his repertory of attitudes sometimes with amazing speed, but
always fluently and with a certain rhythm that he plays off
against the metrical, strophic rhythm of the song.

We can trace the movement of the singer's eye in the songs
included here. For example, in *Lancan vei la folha* (no. 27), the
singer begins with his attention focused on the friends, and so
he speaks like a courtly lover: there he is, suffering the pains of
love and not showing it, for he sings, and he does the right
things in court, acts full of joy though wracked with longing.
Then his eye begins to move toward a hostile sector: the image

of the mirror in the fourth strophe is completely ambiguous; it can signify the lady's moral perfection or her vain sensuality, the mirror having both meanings in medieval literature. It all depends on the point of view: the friends see the beautiful reflection of the courtly ideal, the companions see a sister of Agnes and Ermessen, all wrapped up in herself, and primping. The neatest turn of all is the poet's outburst against "the man who invented the mirror"—who turns out to be none other than himself.

Once his eye sets on the companions, he reveals in his own person the image they behold. They know that any man who says he wants nothing more from a woman than the joy of serving her, if he isn't a rank liar, must be the worst kind of fool, a woman's slave. This is what he promptly becomes: "Let her kill me, if it pleases her, I wouldn't complain." But the singer's eye does not dwell on them, it returns to where it began, and resuming the part of the courtly lover before the regard of his friends, he frees himself from the prison of the enemies' carnality: those who try to make him happy with another woman are mad, vulgar, presumptuous. And so he reaffirms his devotion to the one woman, to whom he sends his heart as messenger.

Or in *Be m'an perdut* (no. 23), he says three times over that his lady does not have a single fault; a few lines later he is leaving her because of her vicious nature. It was for this "inconsistency" that this lyric was criticized by one of those several mediocre poets of a later generation who tried to catch the spirit of these early troubadours by pinning it down in poetic manuals (the first one appears late in the thirteenth century). Now let us suppose that Bernart did deliberately what these critics with their latecomer's sense of correctness, regarded as a lapse. Again he begins with his eye on the friends: nothing, not even his lady's cruelty, can stop him from loving . . . Then his eye lights on the companions, and the verb "to love" immediately takes a carnal complement: no one can stop him from loving any woman he wants to love, provided she is easy to get; and so he is ready for all comers now. This change in attitude is effected in the fourth strophe through an outrageous parody of reasoning: if anyone wants to see the logic of lust in action, let him look there.

Of course, the singer's declaration—Ladies, I'm available—

is excruciatingly ridiculous, even on the vulgar level of those he is reacting to. This bold promiscuity of his has nothing to work on but the images of passing women. In announcing his decision to become a great lover, he tries to sound like the companions, but he only succeeds in confirming their opinion of the courtly lover, that stationary fool.

One last example, *Can l'erba fresch'* (no. 24). Once more the starting point is in the sector of the friends. It is for them that he sings his praise of "joy," for this word, *joi,* is the watchword of courtliness. Hardly a song does not praise it or lament the lack of it, for this "joy" is the great reward of the dedicated man. It denotes his whole courtly reality: his outward bearing, his personal grace, and his self-esteem, his awareness of his own worth, tested and proved in loyal service.

The singer continues in this vein for several strophes, with quick alternations of self-mockery (robbers could steal him) and carnality (her body is so suited for "the work of love"). At the end of the fourth strophe he expresses his submission to the will of the lady and his concern for her reputation.

This last remark, concerning his fear of the slanderers, indicates that the singer's attention has moved to the carnal sector; and that whole array—companions, talebearers, spies, false lovers —comes forward in the following strophes. Now he has something for every one of them: he would do what the companions would do and what the spies are sure he does do (at the end of strophe vi he puts the spies on notice). And just as he sees the lady from their perspective (she makes believe she is sleeping; the mark of his kiss would last for a month), so he sees the courtly lover—that is, himself (he would steal a kiss because he isn't worth enough to demand it). In the last strophe there is an incredible movement through every single perspective, the courtly lover's words falling right next to those of the false lovers ("Let us nobly lie"), the singer denouncing all tricks and proposing one of his own all in the same breath. At the very last minute, in the *tornada,* he quickly resumes his initial stance, just before the song ends.

In other songs, the singer really does take up with another lady and brags about the joy he has found, now that he has abandoned that ridiculous posture of entreaty. In still others, he comes all the way around again, denounces his error, reaffirms his devotion to the first lady, as he does at the end of *Lancan vei* (no. 27). Wherever he is when the lyric ends—vowing his life long service to his emblematic lady, beneath the gaze of his friends; boastful, in the sight of his enemies, of the simple lust he enjoys with his simple lady, or cringing before her devouring power—depends on where he is when the song begins, and on the movement of his gaze through the audience. In the whole series of his songs he says all that he has to say about love, about the different ways in which a noble man can choose to love, and the different moments in the life of love. What each strophe is to the song, so is each lyric to a larger continuing song, the entire music of the poet's career. Each lyric, performed before an audience that has accompanied the poet through his career, adds to the fullness of this encompassing song.

Now this is the maneuver by which the singer saves his song and redeems the language of poetry from those who debase it. He silences his enemies by sharing their point of view for a while and proving that he can see all the things they see. He can see a woman as they do, as a creature of some sexual use provided she is under a man's complete domination (for the lady he complains of and the lady he enjoys, and all the others he mentions, are aspects of one single lady perceived from various perspectives). And he can see the courtly lover as they do, as a groveling servant in search of a master to mistreat him. The result of this maneuver is that he enlists all those who would destroy his song into the service of its defense. And he does this just by acknowledging their presence and, for a moment or two, taking a stand in their midst.

In fact, he really has no choice: he must acknowledge their point of view, for he cannot deny what is true in their vulgar ideas about love. He needs these enemies. The new love he celebrates cannot have any dignity apart from the body and its plain desires, for otherwise this glorious love would be for angels, not men. The pride of the courtly lover is that he can control his lust by allowing it no other object than this lady who is too great for it. Thus his very lust becomes a force of his integrity, moves as

an ally with his love of virtue and courtliness. The price he must
pay for this triumph is prolonged, if not perpetual, frustration.
But then even this frustration becomes a positive value: it becomes the rock of his self-esteem, his *joi,* his certainty that no
chance appetite, no natural "law," can bring down the edifice of
his devotion.

This personal pride would be impossible and of little significance were it not also experienced as pride of class. That is the
bond between the lover and the friends: the lover stands as proof
that the ethical rules of their society can withstand every riotous
appetite, can teach restraint and the forms of courtesy to lust.
The churl does not know any higher "law" than genital rule. But
the courtly man, feeling the force of the same desires, will not
let it erase, or disguise, the look that distinguishes him, but instead he will make it enrich the quality that the others of his
class can recognize. It is just for this recognition that the lover
sings, and that the friends demand his song. For in these songs,
love is the supreme condition of courtliness.

This courtly love could not bear such dignity unless it moved
with the dignity of choice. The singer has to prove that he chooses
this way to love, and that other ways are open to him, especially
that common, dreary round of tension and release in which his
enemies tread. In fact, he and his enemies share a common way
before he separates himself from them: his love is lust hemmed
in by esteem and loyalty. And so it is a love that continually
demands to be put to the test—this testing is precisely the subject of his song. Therefore, he needs his enemies, not simply to
oppose them, but to share a common ground with them. He cannot sing of this new love unless he can prove that the force of
desire is strong in him, urging him to love the nearest woman
instead of the best one, or urging him to see this woman as someone just to have some fun with, instead of glorifying her beyond
the body's approach.

This is the great benefit of the dialectical technique, which
enables him to represent the continual tension in his love. It
proves that he really chooses to see the lady as the worthiest goal
of all his striving, though he could, if he wanted to, see her as
just an ordinary creature. The play of perspectives acts out the

singer's freedom of choice, and though this technique is most
often used for a comic effect—and you have to laugh when you
listen to most of these songs—it is capable of the most moving
seriousness, for it continually confronts the lover with the consequences of his choice, and forces him continually to acknowledge the willfulness, the unreality of his vision. Bernart's most
famous song, *Can vei la lauzeta* (no. 26), portrays the courtly
lover grieving over the carnality of his lady.

By this dialectical play of perspectives the poet finally distinguishes himself from all the liars, slanderers, flatterers, hypocrites, and debased poets who ape the courtly style. They all
recite the same formulas of adoration, but only he can say: I
see these things the way you do, I see love the way you see it.
The moment he can say that, he proves he can see these things
in a way that they cannot imagine, that he has in mind a love
that realizes the idea of courtliness.

Of course, that idea is "realized" only in a certain way: it is
made real to the imagination by a performer who impersonates
a rôle. For everyone knows what the enemies know: no one in
this world can really love that way. No one can appoint his beloved as his judge. No human being can so spiritualize his daily
desires and transform experience into service; and no human
object of desire can survive such exaltation. That is one more
reason why the singer needs his enemies. Their incomprehension
is the clearest proof that courtly love has nothing to do with
real experience. Or we can say: that is one more reason why the
troubadours needed the dialectical technique for their songs. The
courtly lover has to be identified as a made-up character, a part
of a dream. He is a figment of an imagination shaped by courtly
life, an absolute representation of courtly refinement. To those
who are proud of their nobility, this figure is pleasant to contemplate, but only as an ideal; that is, as someone who is not
real, and who therefore cannot demand that they actually do
the things he does and judge themselves by his purity.

The courtly lover can excite the admiration of the audience
provided that he comes forth only in play. His love has to be
confined to a space and a time marked off from the daily round,
to the space occupied by the singer, and the time occupied by the

song. Now this assurance that the singer's love will never be
taken for real experience is provided by the play of perspectives:
the singer goes from one rôle to another, his song is a pattern
of impersonations, of which "the courtly lover" is but one. To
protect this play from being spoiled, the best bulwark against
the invasion of ordinary life is the enemies and their redeeming
disbelief. They do not have the faintest idea that there is a great
game going on, from which they are excluded. They listen to the
song standing on ordinary ground: they cannot enter into that
exalted play of courtliness in which the singer and his friends
alone are initiates. The enemies can only judge what they see
and hear from the perspective of common experience, and so
their disbelief is the clearest sign that the singer's love has nothing to do with real life, the life of bodies. The courtly love relation is a representation, a work of art; and the enemies, with
their massive incomprehension, are the frame that separates it
from mortal space.

The great game first played in the songs of Guillaume IX now
has all its rules complete. The audience has become a more complicated instrument for the poet to sound. He plays on the
rhythm of their perspectives and sets it going against the absolute and mechanical rhythm of the metrical form. The lines
count off the syllables, the rhymes recur in an ideal pattern, the
motifs fall into place, materializing the theme . . . And the
singer looks from person to person before him, greets them all,
for he and they have been long acquainted; and as he speaks of
his loneliness "here" and the end of all his desires "there," he
gestures, meaning for them to look where he points, for his love,
though it is pure play, is set in the places they inhabit; and
when he refers to other songs he sang on similar occasions, or
when he makes fun of his enemies or of some jealous boor of a
husband, then they all enter the game by playing the part of the
friends and assigning faces to the enemies, and then they know
the great pleasure of seeing their own images enclosed in a frame:
never was any song so absolute in its form and so immediate in
its reference. Thus, when we hear a troubadour song we keep
changing our minds about it, being conscious of it now as a

prescribed rhetorical utterance, now as a kind of patter, full of instantaneous reactions to a live audience; and this continual alternation in our consciousness is the joy it was meant to give. That joy will bring us close to its original audience, to those in attendance, who knew the pleasure of hearing their own ordinary life, the people they knew, the settlement they saw from their windows and the wilderness beyond the walls, the very chamber in which they were together, become the subject of an elevated, formulary, cadenced language—like the language of ritual—the chanted language reserved for perpetuation. It is hard to say to what extent they found it comic to see their routine rendered in a glorious image, though it is impossible to believe they took every bit of it seriously. At any rate, this performance situation produced the most distinctive feature of the troubadour lyric, its tension. Every song is held together by an inherent opposition between formality and casualness, ceremoniousness and spontaneity, modality and self-consciousness, affirmation and play.

These moments of the performance revealed the true meaning of the song. For the length of its verses and its melody the members of the audience were united in a common esteem, and their intimacy was intensified, rather than spoiled, by their awareness of the destructive elements in their midst, lust, selfishness, hypocrisy, the mean conformity of the unaspiring. These enemies of the community created by the song were turned into champions and protectors by the performer, and their voices enriched the whole chorus that sang through him. The performance thus became an image of courtly life, a ceremonious enactment of its essential experience, and a celebration of the courtly man's character: this privileged and glorious life is dedicated to the loftiest ideals of devotion and behavior, and its raw appetites are so controlled by discipline and skill that they reinforce its effort toward moral perfection.

Because the troubadour lyric is so involved in this play of perspectives, it absolutely requires a performance situation to achieve its full effect—even if today that situation can only exist in the imagination of the reader. On paper, and read, the courtly love lyric is a form filled with clichés, lacking in coherence; and it has raised the question of "sincerity" even in the minds of those who swear this question is aesthetically irrelevant. But when this lyric is played—not just performed in the sense that every song needs a performance to realize the harmony of its words and music—when it is set in motion before an attending audience, then it takes on a life that no other body of lyric poetry has ever shared. Then it even becomes a kind of life itself, uniting the poet and his audience into one joyful community inspired by this play of love and courtliness.

It was a great game, and it reached a wonderful stage of complication in the hands of Bernart de Ventadorn and the others of his generation, and in the hands of the Minnesänger beginning with Heinrich von Veldeke. Still, the number of moves was limited, and it was bound to play itself out.

Whenever it comes time to account for the decline and disappearance of the troubadour lyric, one usually mentions the Albigensian Crusade, which began in 1208 and ended in 1229 with the King of France in possession of Toulouse. The Albigenses were a heretical Manichaean sect that flourished in southern France, and when the long attempt to convert them proved unsuccessful, a crusade against them was proclaimed by Innocent III. Simon de Montfort descended with an army from the north and wiped out many of the southern courts, particularly around Toulouse. Thus it is said that the troubadours lost their patrons and their audience at once, and the social and cultural atmosphere in which such songs as theirs could flourish.

This cannot be denied, but it is not altogether an adequate explanation, either historically or critically. The history of troubadour poetry, as Henri Davenson says, is indeed brief: ". . . two centuries, let us say, and the second already the period of decadence. Their vein was quickly used up: it is not the Albigensian Crusade, nor the French conquest (neither of which subjugated Provence or Limousin), nor the terror nor the anxieties of the Inquisition that killed it, as has been said; it died of its own exhaustion." It is true that the later lyrics in France, Germany, and Italy are no longer dominated by the court setting. Though there are some pertinent historical reasons for this—the stilnovisti did not even have a court, though they longed for one; and the courts of the later German poets were impoverished—the only adequate explanation must be sought in the nature of the courtly love lyric itself, in the limitations that were the necessary result of its strengths.

Because it was confined in a performance situation, its possibilities were indeed limited. The range of its expression had to coincide with the range of the audience, of which the highest level was determined by an exclusive and interested notion of courtliness. The situation was what effectively prevented this poetry from speaking to the human longing for transcendence; and, except for versification, it kept poetic resources in a state of poverty. The language had to be appropriate for a performance, and the experience of love could not be explored beyond the point where it ceased to have a communal significance. Figurative language was frozen stiff: it had to stay strictly representational, it could not make many associations outside the facts of courtly life—the heavens themselves were framed by the windows of the court. Thus the basic poetic means of exploring experience, namely, the exploration of language, was practically unavailable. The moment poets sought to create a lyric that would not require the perspectives of an audience, that would be free to examine the consequences of its own figures of speech— that is the moment when the troubadour tradition changed forever. This moment came somewhere around the middle of the thirteenth century, earlier in some places, later in others. The history of the later lyric can be surmised from the introductory notes to Burkart von Hohenvels, Guido Guinizelli, Guido Cavalcanti, and Thibaut de Champagne.

Thus, in addition to historical reasons, there was an inherent cause for the playing out of the troubadour lyric. Its range of expression could never be as large as one that does not depend on external perspectives but rather on the possibilities of language itself. And this narrowness in its technique naturally limited the experience it could evoke.

Let us say first, however, that the highest "joy" the troubadours could sing about was high indeed: the union in love with a beautiful, wise, virtuous lady, full of tutelary concern, whose look and smile of recognition confirmed her lover's essential courtliness and transported him to an even greater union, his reception into the exalted community of his class. And when, in the course of the song, the perspective that had this joy in view was changed, as it had to be, and this perfect union was undone by the enemies, before whose gaze the lady turned into a woman like all the others, and the lover became a fool, that only made the precious moment yet more precious: this was the extraordinary triumph of the dialectical technique, which resolved destructive force into a protective frame. Now that was very good indeed, but it was still not everything a human being could wish for. How easily this kind of thing could sink to municipal art, as it did in German-speaking areas with the Meistersingers. That was because the love that the troubadours celebrated wants to soar, and they could not let it.

When love is as good as human beings can imagine, the two lovers feel that somehow they now belong to a community of love, and no mortal fact, like time and circumstance, can keep them from loving all others, the long dead and the unknown living, who have loved with such love as theirs. The troubadours and their audience knew this very well, but they wanted to make everything too clear, and that was when they set very narrow limits to the language of poetry.

For these "others," though they have a certain presence, cannot have familiar faces: only one such face can be loved, all others being the victims of time and mirrors of all those conditions that love escapes. And besides, if ordinary people loved like this, how could this love be extraordinary? "Who else ever knew this?" the lovers wonder, and they have to feel that others have, for they will not let their perfect love banish them to a wilderness. And so the lovers love these certain others, who cannot be their ordinary friends, and in their world apart they somehow find other inhabitants who would recognize them.

In the troubadour lyric, this community of lovers was supposed to be courtly society, the audience of friends. So complete and so trusting an involvement with an earthly community has always been a human dream. But in the courtly lyric, one vital part of that dream has to be left out, because the troubadours, bound to their technique, were incapable of expressing it: the Being which is greater than the dream community and which holds it together. We say "being" rather than "idea" or "purpose," because no matter what a community is sworn to, even if it is some nationalistic image, it must always take on some aura of personality in order to be experienced and loved. No matter what this universal beloved may be, it has to be of longer standing than the present moment and of greater magnitude than the circle of one's accidental friends.

For lovers, this greater being is love itself, which they feel must transcend their moment and join them with all other lovers. But when this imperishable community of love is made to coincide with an actual group of people, a social class in fact, then it loses its transcendency and love is deprived of its aspiration. That was what was wrong with courtly love. It could never go as high as human longing: it had to stay within the vision of an audience whose perspectives were limited to the collective concerns and aspirations of a class. It could never reach that transcendent "Being," it was grounded in conditions. The courtly love lyric soon played itself out because it was bound to the dimensions of the audience and to its utilitarian purpose of class congratulation. It was superb for evoking that sense of solidarity that the poets called *cortezia*, meaning not simply "courtesy" but "courtliness"; but its technique made it inadequate for the celebration of love. Later poets, whose task was different, who did not have to take the courtliness of their audiences as their supreme theme, would have to develop a different technique.

It was just this conflict between the representation demanded by the audience and the richness of individual experience that many poets, especially the German poets—and among them especially Heinrich von Morungen and Walther von der Vogelweide —took for their theme. And it was because of the limitedness of its aspiration that some poets, for example Hartmann von Aue, sometimes reject courtly love. Hartmann calls his fellow poets "poor," "pathetic," because of the trap they were in. "The 'poorness' of the love servants of a courtly lady does not stem simply from the fact that the beloved does not listen to their plea. They are poor because all their suffering of 'love from afar' does not suffice to force an answer from the highest partner, because, in short, they cannot love high enough for a union with the transcendently real being of the partner" (Hugo Kuhn).

The troubadours who came last, for example Giraut Riquier and Folquet de Marseille, dispensed with the audience altogether and took love away from its intimate setting: they ended the game. They sang of their love for the one Lady in whom all perspectives agree, who could be loved and venerated and would never fail her lover. Sometimes there is deep and touching piety in these songs, but they always make one think of the moment that has passed forever, for the language of their piety comes from the songs of the courtly circle. In fact, from that brief moment and that small circle came the customary language of devotion in our world ever since, down to the present moment.

Text: *Bernart von Ventadorn, seine Lieder, mit Einleitung und Glossar,* ed. Carl Appel. Halle: Max Niemeyer, 1915; with occasional changes in punctuation. A recent edition has been published by Moshé Lazar: *Bernard de Ventadour, troubadour du XIIe siècle, Chansons d'amour.* Paris: Klincksieck, 1966.

21

Non es meravelha s'eu chan
melhs de nul autre chantador,
que plus me tra·l cors vas amor
e melhs sui faihz a so coman.   I
5 Cor e cors e saber e sen
e fors' e poder i ai mes.
Si·m tira vas amor lo fres
que vas autra part no·m aten.

Ben es mortz qui d'amor no sen
10 al cor cal que dousa sabor;
e que val viure ses valor
mas per enoi far a la gen?   II
Ja Domnedeus no·m azir tan
qu'eu ja pois viva jorn ni mes,
15 pois que d'enoi serai mespres
ni d'amor non aurai talan.

Per bona fe e ses enjan
am la plus bel' e la melhor.
Del cor sospir e dels olhs plor,
20 car tan l'am eu, per que i ai dan.   III
Eu que·n posc mais, s'Amors me pren,
e las charcers en que m'a mes
no pot claus obrir mas merces,
e de merce no·i trop nien?

25 Aquest' amors me fer tan gen
al cor d'una dousa sabor:
cen vetz mor lo jorn de dolor
e reviu de joi autras cen.   IV
Ben es mos mals de bel semblan,
30 que mais val mos mals qu'autre bes;
e pois mos mals aitan bos m'es,
bos er lo bes apres l'afan.

Of course it's no wonder I sing
better than any other troubadour:
my heart draws me more toward love,
and I am better made for his command.   I
5 Heart body knowledge sense
strength and energy—I have set all on love.
The rein draws me straight toward love,
and I cannot turn toward anything else.

A man is really dead when he does not feel
10 some sweet taste of love in his heart;
and what is it worth to live without worth,
except to irritate everyone?   II
May the Lord God never hate me so
that I live another day, or even less than a day,
15 after I am guilty of being such a pest,
and I no longer have the will to love.

In good faith, without deceit,
I love the best and most beautiful.
My heart sighs, my eyes weep,
20 because I love her so much, and I suffer for it.   III
What else can I do, if Love takes hold of me,
and no key but pity can open up
the prison where he has put me,
and I find no sign of pity there?

25 This love wounds my heart
with a sweet taste, so gently,
I die of grief a hundred times a day
and a hundred times revive with joy.   IV
My pain seems beautiful,
30 this pain is worth more than any pleasure;
and since I find this bad so good,
how good the good will be when this suffering is done.

Ai Deus! car se fosson trian
d'entrels faus li fin amador,
35 e·lh lauzenger e·lh trichador
portesson corns el fron denan!   V
Tot l'aur del mon e tot l'argen [1]
i volgr'aver dat, s'eu l'agues,
sol que ma domna conogues
40 aissi com eu l'am finamen.

Cant eu la vei, be m'es parven
als olhs, al vis, a la color,
car aissi tremble de paor
com fa la folha contra·l ven.   VI
45 Non ai de sen per un efan,
aissi sui d'amor entrepres;
e d'ome qu'es aissi conques,
pot domn' aver almorna gran.

Bona domna, re no·us deman
50 mas que·m prendatz per servidor,
qu'e·us servirai com bo senhor,
cossi que del gazardo m'an.   VII
Ve·us m'al vostre comandamen,
francs cors umils, gais e cortes!
55 Ors ni leos non etz vos ges,
que·m aucizatz, s'a vos me ren.

A Mo Cortes, lai on ilh es,
tramet lo vers, e ja no·lh pes   VIII
car n'ai estat tan lonjamen.

22

Tant ai mo cor ple de joya,
tot me desnatura.

---

[1] Literally, "I would like to have given . . ." Appel remarks that this tense
reflects the poet's impatience and anger.

Ah, God! if only true lovers
stood out from the false;
35 if all those slanderers and frauds
had horns on their heads.
I'd give all the gold in the world,[1]   V
and all the silver, if I had it to give,
just so that my lady knew
40 how I love her with the love of a courtly man.

Whenever I see her, you can see it in me,
in my eyes, my look, my color,
because I shake with fear
like a leaf in the wind.   VI
45 I don't have the good sense of a child,
I am so taken over, ruled by love;
and when a man is overcome like this,
a lady may let herself feel great pity.

Good lady, I ask you for nothing
50 but to take me for your servant,
for I will serve you as my good lord,
whatever wages come my way.   VII
Behold me at your command, a man to rely on,
before you, o noble, gentle, courteous, and gay.
55 You are not, after all, a bear or a lion,
you would not kill me if I give myself to you.

To Mon Cortes, down there, where she dwells,
I send this song, and let her not be vexed   VIII
that I have been so far away.

22

My heart is so full of joy
it changes every nature.

Flor blancha, vermelh' e groya
me par la frejura,
5 c'ab lo ven et ab la ploya
me creis l'aventura,   I
per que mos chans mont' e poya
e mos pretz melhura.
Tan ai al cor d'amor,
10 de joi e de doussor,
per que·l gels me sembla flor
e la neus verdura.

Anar posc ses vestidura,
nutz en ma chamiza,
15 car fin' amors m'asegura
de la freja biza.
Mas es fols qui·s desmezura,
e no·s te de guiza.   II
Per qu'eu ai pres de me cura,
20 deis c'agui enquiza
la plus bela d'amor,
don aten tan d'onor,
car en loc de sa ricor
no volh aver Piza.[1]

25 De s'amistat me recizal
Mas be n'ai fiansa,
que sivals eu n'ai conquiza
la bela semblansa.
Et ai ne a ma deviza
30 tan de benanansa,   III
que ja·l jorn que l'aurai viza,
non aurai pezansa.
Mo cor ai pres d'Amor,
que l'esperitz lai cor,
35 mas lo cors es sai, alhor,
lonh de leis, en Fransa.

---

[1] "The city of Pisa around 1180 was at the height of its power and wealth.
And yet one may well ask whether one should not hold rather to the reading *frisa* . . . and to the unpublished suggestion of A. Hilka that this should

The winter that comes to me
is white red yellow flowers;
5 my good luck grows
with the wind and the rain,
and so my song mounts up, rises,
and my worth increases.
I have such love in my heart,
10 such joy, such sweetness,
the ice I see is a flower,
the snow, green things that grow.

I could walk around undressed,
naked in my shirt,
15 for perfect love protects me
from the cold north wind.
But a man is a fool when he does things out of measure
and doesn't hold himself with courtesy.
Therefore I have kept a watch upon myself
20 ever since I begged her,
my most beautiful, for love,
and I await such honor
that in place of her riches
I don't want Pisa.[1]

25 Let her make me keep my distance from her love—
there's still one thing I'm sure of:
I have conquered nothing less
than her beautiful image.
Cut off from her like this I have
30 such bliss,
that the day I see her again,
not having seen her will not weigh on me.
My heart stays close to Love,
my spirit runs to it there,
35 but my body is here, in another place,
far from her, in France.

I

II

III

be identified with Phrygia, the land of legendary wealth." (Hamlin, Ricketts, and Hathaway) Lines 7 and 8 follow an alternative version in the manuscripts; Appel has *pretz* in 7 and *chans* in 8.

Eu n'ai la bon'esperansa.
Mas petit m'aonda,
c'atressi·m ten en balansa
40 com la naus en l'onda.
Del mal pes que·m desenansa,
no sai on m'esconda.   IV
Tota noih me vir' e·m lansa
desobre l'esponda.

45 Plus trac pena d'amor
de Tristan l'amador,
que·n sofri manhta dolor
per Izeut la blonda.

Ai Deus! car no sui ironda,
50 que voles per l'aire
e vengues de noih prionda
lai dins so repaire?
Bona domna jauzionda,
mor se·l vostr' amaire!   V
55 Paor ai que·l cors me fonda,
s'aissi·m dura gaire.
Domna, per vostr' amor
jonh las mas et ador!
Gens cors ab frescha color,
60 gran mal me faitz traire!

Qu'el mon non a nul afaire
don eu tan cossire,
can de leis au re retraire,
que mo cor no i vire
65 e mo semblan no·m n'esclaire.
Que que·m n'aujatz dire,   VI
si c'ades vos er vejaire
c'ai talan de rire.
Tan l'am de bon' amor
70 que manhtas vetz en plor
per o que melhor sabor

I get good hope from her;
but that does me little good,
because she holds me like this, poised
40 like a ship on the wave.
I don't know where to take cover
from the sad thoughts that pull me down.   IV
The whole night long I toss and turn
on the edge of the bed.
45 I bear more pain from love
than Tristan the lover,
who suffered many sorrows
for Isolt the blonde.

Ah, God! couldn't I be a swallow
50 and fly through the air
and come in the depths of the night
into her dwelling there.
O gentle lady, o joyful,
your lover dies.   V
55 I fear the heart will melt within me
if this lasts a little longer.
Lady, for your love
I join my hands and worship.
Beautiful body of the colors of youth,
60 what suffering you make me bear.

For in this world no enterprise
so draws my thought,
that when I hear any talk of her
my heart does not turn to it
65 and my face light up,
so that no matter what you hear me saying,   VI
you will always think
I want to laugh.
I love her so with such good love,
70 that many time I weep for it,
because for me the sighs

m'en an li sospire.
Messatgers, vai e cor,
e di·m a la gensor   VII
75 la pena e la dolor
que·n trac, e·l martire.

23

Be m'an perdut lai enves Ventadorn
tuih mei amic, pois ma domna no m'ama;
et es be dreihz que ja mais lai no torn,
c'ades estai vas me salvatj' e grama.   I
5 Ve·us per que·m fai semblan irat e morn:
car en s'amor me deleih e·m sojorn!
Ni de ren als no·s rancura ni·s clama.

Aissi co·l peis qui s'eslaiss' el cadorn
e no·n sap mot, tro que s'es pres en l'ama,
10 m'eslaissei eu vas trop amar un jorn,
c'anc no·m gardei, tro fui en mei la flama,   II
que m'art plus fort, no·m feira focs de forn;
e ges per so no·m posc partir un dorn,
aissi·m te pres s'amors e m'aliama.

15 No·m meravilh si s'amors me te pres,
que genser cors no crei qu'el mon se mire:
bels e blancs es, e frescs e gais e les
e totz aitals com eu volh e dezire.   III
No posc dir mal de leis, que non i es;
20 qu'e·l n'agra dih de joi, s'eu li saubes;
mas no li sai, per so m'en lais de dire.

have a sweeter taste.
Go, messenger, run,
and tell her, the one most beautiful,   VII
75 of the pain and the sorrow
I bear for her, and the willing death.

23

Down there, around Ventadorn, all my friends
have lost me, because my lady does not love me;
and so, it is right that I never go back there again,
because always she is wild and morose with me.   I
5 Now here is why the face she shows me is gloomy and
        full of anger:
because my pleasure is in loving her, and I have settled
        down to it.
She is resentful, and complains, for no other reason.

Like a fish that rushes to the bait
suspecting nothing till it is caught on the hook,
10 I rushed into too much loving one day
and took no care till I was in the middle of the flame   II
that burns me now more hotly than a furnace fire;
and for all that I can't move away the width of a hand,
that's how her love holds me captive, puts me in chains.

15 I do not wonder that love of her holds me bound,
because I do not think you can see a nobler body in the
        world:
she is beautiful and white, young and gay and soft,
altogether as I want her, long for her.   III
I cannot say anything bad about her, because nothing
        bad is in her—
20 if I knew of anything, I would tell it with joy,
but I do not know one bad thing about her, and so I say
        nothing.

Totz tems volrai sa onor e sos bes
e·lh serai om et amics e servire,
e l'amarai, be li plass' o be·lh pes,
25 c'om no pot cor destrenher ses aucire.   IV
No sai domna, volgues o no volgues,
si·m volia, c'amar no la pogues.
Mas totas res pot om en mal escrire.

A las autras sui aissi eschazutz;
30 la cals se vol me pot vas se atraire,
per tal cove que no·m sia vendutz
l'onors ni·l bes que m'a en cor a faire;   V
qu'enoyos es preyars, pos er perdutz;
per me·us o dic, que mals m'en es vengutz,
35 car traït m'a la bela de mal aire.

En Proensa tramet jois e salutz
e mais de bes c'om no lor sap retraire;
e fatz esfortz, miracles e vertutz,
car eu lor man de so don non ai gaire,   VI
40 qu'eu non ai joi, mas tan can m'en adutz
mos Bels Vezers e'n Fachura, mos drutz,
e'n Alvernhatz, lo senher de Belcaire.[1]

Mos Bels Vezers, per vos fai Deus vertutz
tals c'om no·us ve que no si' ereubutz   VII
45 dels bels plazers que sabetz dir e faire.

24

Can l'erba fresch' e·lh folha par
e la flors boton' el verjan,
e·l rossinhols autet e clar

---

[1] Each name is a *senhal,* probably designating persons in the court of Toulouse. *Bel Vezer* means belvedere, something beautiful to look at. *Fachura* means sorcerer.

I shall always desire her honor and her good,
and I shall be her man, and her lover, and her servant,
and I shall love her whether it pleases her or grieves her,
25 for no one can constrain a heart without killing it.   IV
I don't know one woman that I could not love,
if I wanted to, whether she wanted it or not.
But anything can be set down as a bad thing.

And so I have now become available to all other women—
30 anyone who wants to can get me to come to her,
on one condition: let her not sell me at too dear a price
the honor and the good she has it in her heart to do me;   V
for it is wearisome to beg, if it all turns out for noth-
        ing.
I tell you this from my own case, because much suffering
        has come my way,
35 that beautiful lady there, with that vicious nature,
        has betrayed me.

To Provence I send joy and well-being
and a greater blessing than I can specify;
and thus I do heroic deeds, miracles, prodigies,
for I send them in abundance what I scarcely have myself,   VI
40 for I have no joy except what comes
from my Bel Vezer, and from En Fachura, my friend,
and En Auvergnat, the lord of Beaucaire.[1]

My Bel Vezer, for your sake God performs this miracle:
no man beholds you without getting carried away   VII
45 by the pleasant things you know how to do and say.

24

When the new grass and the leaves come forth
and the flower burgeons on the branch,
and the nightingale lifts its high

leva sa votz e mou so chan,   I
5 joi ai de lui, e joi ai de la flor
e joi de me e de midons major;
daus totas partz sui de joi claus e sens,
mas sel es jois que totz autres jois vens.

Ai las! com mor de cossirar!
10 Que manhtas vetz en cossir tan:
lairo m'en poirian portar,
que re no sabria que·s fan.   II
Per Deu, Amors! be·m trobas vensedor:
ab paucs d'amics e ses autre senhor.
15 Car una vetz tan midons no destrens
abans qu'eu fos del dezirer estens?

Meravilh me com posc durar
que no·lh demostre mo talan.
Can eu vei midons ni l'esgar,
20 li seu bel olh tan be l'estan: III
per pauc me tenh car eu vas leis no cor.
Si feira eu, si no fos per paor,
c'anc no vi cors melhs talhatz ni depens
ad ops d'amar sia tan greus ni lens.

25 Tan am midons e la tenh car,
e tan la dopt' e la reblan
c'anc de me no·lh auzei parlar,
ni re no·lh quer ni re no·lh man.   IV
Pero ilh sap mo mal e ma dolor,
30 e can li plai, mi fai ben et onor,
e can li plai, eu m'en sofert ab mens,
per so c'a leis no·n avenha blastens.

S'eu saubes la gen enchantar,
mei enemic foran efan,
35 que ja us no saubra triar
ni dir re que·ns tornes a dan.   V
Adoncs sai eu que vira la gensor

pure voice and begins its song,   I

5. I have joy in it, and joy in the flower,
and joy in myself, and in my lady most of all;
on every side I am enclosed and girded with joy,
and a joy that overwhelms all other joys.

Ah, weary, how I die from thinking—
10 for many times I am so lost in thought of her,
robbers could come and carry me away,
and I wouldn't even know what they were doing.   II
By God, love, you find me an easy victim,
a man with few friends and no other lord.
15 Why don't you press on my lady like this one time,
before I am destroyed by my desiring?

It makes me wonder, how I can go on
not letting her know what I want.
When I see my lady, when I gaze on her,
20 her beautiful eyes become her so well,   III
I can hardly keep myself from running to her;
and I would do it, if I weren't so afraid,
for I never saw a body so well cut and colored
for the work of love be so slow and hard to move.

25 I love her and cherish her so much,
fear her and attend to her so much,
I have never dared to speak to her of myself,
and I ask her for nothing, and I send her nothing.   IV
But she knows my sorrow and my pain,
30 and when it pleases her, she gives me comfort and hon-
              ors me,
and when it pleases her, I make do with less,
so that no blame should touch her.

If I only knew how to put a spell on people,
my enemies would turn into babies,
35 so that none of them could pick us out
and say anything to hurt us.   V
I know I would see my most noble then,

e sos bels olhs e sa frescha color,
e baizera·lh la bocha en totz sens,
40 si que d'un mes i paregra lo sens.

Be la volgra sola trobar,
que dormis, o·n fezes semblan,
per qu'e·lh embles un doutz baizar,
pus no valh tan qu'eu lo·lh deman.   VI
45 Per Deu, domna, pauc esplecham d'amor;
vai s'en lo tems, e perdem lo melhor!
Parlar degram ab cubertz entresens,
e, pus no·ns val arditz, valgues nos gens!

Be deuri'om domna blasmar,
50 can trop vai son amic tarzan,
que lonja paraula d'amar
es grans enois e par d'enjan,   VII
c'amar pot om e far semblan alhor,
e gen mentir lai on non a autor.
55 Bona domna, ab sol c'amar mi dens,
ja per mentir eu no serai atens.

Messatger, vai, e no m'en prezes mens,
s'eu del anar vas midons sui temens.   VIII

25

Era·m cosselhatz, senhor,   4
vos c'avetz saber e sen:
una domna·m det s'amor,
c'ai amada lonjamen;   I
5   mas eras sai de vertat
qu'ilh a autr' amic privat,
ni anc de nul companho
companha tan greus no·m fo.

her beautiful eyes, her young color,
and I would kiss her mouth in all directions,
40 so that for a month the mark of it would show.

I would like to find her alone,
sleeping, or pretending to,
so I could steal a soft kiss off her,
because I am not worth enough to ask for it.   VI
45 By God, lady, we get little loving done,
times passes, and we lose the best of it.
Let us talk in secret signs,
and, since being direct can't help us, let our cunning
     help us.

A lady deserves blame
50 when she makes her lover wait too long,
for endless talk of love
is a great vexation, and seems like a trick,   VII
because one can love, and pretend to everyone else,
and nobly lie when there are no witnesses.
55 Sweet lady, if only you would deign to love me,
no one will ever catch me when I lie.

Messenger, go, and may she not think less of me,
if I am afraid to go to her.   VIII

25

Lords, counsel me now,
you who have experience and understanding:
a lady I have long loved
gave me her love;   I
5   but now I know beyond all doubt
she keeps another lover close,
and never yet has a companion's
companionship been so hard to bear.

De una re sui en error
10   e·n estau en pensamen:
que m'alonje ma dolor,
s'eu aquest plaih li cossen,   II
e s'aissi·l dic mon pessat,
vei mo damnatge doblat.
15   Cal que·n fassa o cal que no,
re no posc far de mo pro.

E s'eu l'am a dezonor,
esquerns er a tota gen;
e tenran m'en li pluzor
20   per cornut e per sofren.   III
E s'aissi pert s'amistat,
be·m tenh per dezeretat
d'amor, e ja Deus no·m do
mais faire vers ni chanso.

25   Pois voutz sui en la folor,
be serai fols, s'eu no pren
d'aquestz dos mals lo menor;
que mais val, mon essien,   IV
qu'eu ay' en leis la meitat
30   que·l tot perda per foldat,
car anc a nul drut felo
d'amor no vi far son pro.

Pois vol autre amador
ma domn', eu no lo·lh defen;
35   e lais m'en mais per paor
que per autre chauzimen;   V
e s'anc om dec aver grat
de nul servizi forsat,
be dei aver guizerdo
40   eu, que tan gran tort perdo.

Li seu belh olh traïdor,
que m'esgardavon tan gen,

One thing torments me
10   and makes me pause for thought:
if I acquiesce in this little arrangement
I just prolong my suffering,   II
but if I tell her exactly what I think,
I see myself with a double loss.
15   Thus no matter what I do, or don't do,
I can't do myself any good.

And if I love her in dishonor,
I shall be a man whom everyone scorns,
nearly all these people will take me for a cuckold,
20   a man who really doesn't mind his horns.   III
But, on the other hand, if I lose her friendship,
I hold myself disowned
by love, and then God never let me
write a *vers* or *canson* again.

25   Since I am involved in madness,
I would really be mad if I did not choose
of these two evils the lesser one;
for it is better—I see it clearly now—   IV
to have a half of her
30   than lose her altogether by my raging,
for I never saw a lover full of rancor
do himself any good in love.

Since she wants another lover,
my lady, well, I won't say anything against it,
35   and I go along with it more from fear
than by choice;   V
and if ever a man deserved gratitude
for some involuntary service,
then I should have some reward,
40   I who pardon so great a wrong.

Her beautiful traitor eyes
that once looked on me with much gentleness,

s'atressi gardon alhor,
mout i fan gran flahimen;   VI
45   mas d'aitan m'an mout onrat
que, s'eron mil ajostat,
plus gardon lai on eu so,
c'a totz aicels d'eviro.

De l'aiga que dels olhs plor,
50   escriu salutz mais de cen,
que tramet a la gensor
et a la plus avinen.   VII
Manhtas vetz m'es pois membrat
de so que·m fetz al comjat:
55   que·lh vi cobrir sa faisso,
c'anc no·m poc dir oc ni no.

Domna, a prezen amat
autrui, e me a celat,   VIII
si qu'eu n'aya tot lo pro
60   et el la bela razo.

Garsio, ara·m chantat
ma chanso, e la·m portat   IX
a mo Messager, qu'i fo,[1]
qu'e·lh quer cosselh qu'el me do.

26

Can vei la lauzeta mover
de joi sas alas contral rai,
que s'oblid' e·s laissa chazer
per la doussor c'al cor li vai,   I
5 ai! tan grans enveya m'en ve
de cui qu'eu veya jauzion,

---

[1] Garsio is the *joglar*, Messenger the *senhal* for a friend or patron.

if they look like that elsewhere
they do wrong, great wrong;   VI
45   yes, but they have done me this great honor:
when a thousand people were gathered together,
there—they look to where I am
more than to all the others around.

With the water I weep from my eyes
50   I write more than a hundred love letters
and send them to the most beautiful,
the courtliest.   VII
Many times it reminds me afterwards
of what she did when we parted:
55   I saw her cover her face,
so that she could not tell me yes or no.

Lady, in public love
the other one, and me in private,   VIII
so that I get all the good of it,
60   and he the edifying conversation.

Garsio, now sing my song
for me, and take it   IX
to my Messenger, who was there.[1]
I ask what counsel he would give.

26

When I see the lark moving
its wings in joy against the light,
rising up into forgetfulness, letting go, and falling
for the sweetness that comes to its heart,   I
5 alas, what envy then comes over me
of everyone I see rejoicing,

meravilhas ai, car desse
lo cor de dezirer no·m fon.

Ai, las! tan cuidava saber
10 d'amor, e tan petit en sai,
car eu d'amar no·m posc tener
celeis don ja pro non aurai.   II
Tout m'a mo cor, e tout m'a me,
e se mezeis e tot lo mon;
15 e can se·m tolc, no·m laisset re
mas dezirer e cor volon.

Anc non agui de me poder
ni no fui meus de l'or' en sai
que·m laisset en sos olhs vezer
20 en un miralh que mout me plai.   III
Miralhs, pus me mirei en te,
m'an mort li sospir de preon,
c'aissi·m perdei com perdet se
lo bels Narcisus en la fon.

25 De las domnas me dezesper;
ja mais en lor no·m fiarai;
c'aissi com las solh chaptener,
enaissi las deschaptenrai.   IV
Pois vei c'una pro no m'en te
30 vas leis que·m destrui e·m cofon,
totas las dopt' e las mescre,
car be sai c'atretals se son.

D'aisso's fa be femna parer
ma domna, per qu'e·lh o retrai,
35 car no vol so c'om voler,
e so c'om li deveda, fai.   V
Chazutz sui en mala merce,
et ai be faih co·l fols en pon; [1]

---

[1] A proverb states that a wise man always dismounts before he crosses a narrow bridge; he never rides his horses across it.

it makes me wonder that my heart,
right then, does not melt with desire.

I, weary, how much I thought I knew
10   about love, and how little I know,
     because I cannot keep myself from loving
     one from whom I shall get no favor.   II
     She has it all: she took my heart, and me,
     and herself, and the whole world.
15   And when she took herself away from me, she left me
                    nothing
     but desire and a heart still wanting.

     I have never had the power of myself,
     I have not been my own man since that moment
     when she let me look into her eyes,
20   into a mirror that gives great pleasure, even now.   III
     Mirror, since I beheld myself in you,
     the sighs from my depths have slain me,
     and I have lost myself, as fair Narcissus
     lost himself in the fountain.
25   I give up all hope in women.
     I shall not put my faith in them again;
     as much as I used to hold them up,
     now I shall let them fall,   IV
     because I do not see one who is of any use to me
30   with her, who destroys me and brings me down.
     I shall fear and distrust them all,
     because they are all alike, I know it well.

     This is how she shows herself a woman indeed,
     my lady, and I reproach her for it:
35   she does not want what one ought to want,
     and what she is forbidden to do, she does.   V
     I have fallen in evil grace,
     I have acted like the madman on the bridge,[1]

e no sai per que m'esdeve,
40 mas car trop puyei contra mon.

Merces es perduda, per ver,
et eu non o saubi anc mai,
car cilh qui plus en degr'aver,
no·n a ges, et on la querrai?   VI
45 A! can mal sembla, qui la ve,
qued aquest chaitiu deziron
que ja ses leis non aura be,
laisse morrir, que no l·aon.

Pus ab midons no·m pot valer
50 precs ni merces ni·l dreihz qu'eu ai,
ni a leis no ven a plazer
qu'eu l'am, ja mais no·lh o dirai.   VII
Aissi·m part de leis e·m recre;
mort m'a, e per mort li respon,
55 e vau m'en, pus ilh no·m rete,
chaitius, en issilh, no sai on.

Tristans,[2] ges no·n auretz de me,
qu'eu m'en vau, chaitius, no sai on.   VIII
De chantar me gic e·m recre,
60 e de joi e d'amor m'escon.

27

Lancan vei la folha
jos dels albres chazer,
cui que pes ni dolha,
a me deu bo saber.
5 No crezatz qu'eu volha
flor ni folha vezer,   I
car vas me s'orgolha

[2] Tristan, in the *tornada*, is a *senhal*.

and how this came about I cannot say,
40 except that I climbed too high on the mountain.

In truth, kindness is lost from the world,
and I never knew it;
for she who ought to have the most of it
has none, and where shall I look?   VI
45 Ah, you would never guess, when you look at her,
that she would let this man, miserable with desire,
who can never be well without her,
just die, just let him die and not help him.

Since these things do me no good with my lady,
50 prayer, pity, the rights I have,
and since it is no pleasure to her
that I love her, I shall not tell her again.   VII
Thus I part from her, and I give it all up.
She has given me death, and I will answer her with
                death,
55 and I am going away, because she does not retain me,
a broken man, in exile, I know not where.

Tristan,² you will have nothing more from me,
for I go away, a broken man, I know not where;   VIII
I shall withdraw from singing, I renounce it,
60 far from joy and love, I hide myself away.

27

When I see the leaves
falling down from the trees,
it may upset someone else,
but it has to suit me.
5 Don't think I want
to see a flower or a leaf,   I
when the one I want most

so qu'eu plus volh aver.
Cor ai que m'en tolha
10 mas no·n ai ges poder,
c'ades cuit m'acolha,
on plus m'en dezesper.

Estranha novela
podetz de me auzir,
15 que, can vei la bela
que·m soli' acolhir,
ara no m'apela
ni·m fai vas se venir.   II
Lo cor sotz l'aissela
20 m'en vol de dol partir.
Deus que·l mon chapdela,
si·lh platz, m'en lais jauzir,
que s'aissi·m revela,
no·i a mas del morir.

25 Non ai mais fiansa
en agur ni en sort,
que bon' esperansa
m'a confondut e mort,
que tan lonh me lansa
30 la bela cui am fort,   III
can li quer s'amansa,
com s'eu l'agues gran tort.
Tan n'ai de pezansa
que totz m'en desconort;
35 mas no·n fatz semblansa,
c'ades chant e deport.

Als non sai que dire
mas: mout fatz gran folor
car am ni dezire
40 del mon la belazor.
Be deuri' aucire
qui anc fetz mirador!   IV

is cold with pride.
I have the heart to break away
10 but not the strength,
because I always think, maybe she'll receive me yet,
exactly when I most despair.

There's strange news
you can hear about me:
15 when I see my beautiful lady
who used to receive me,
she does not call me now,
or send for me to come to her.   II
The heart inside my breast
20 wants to break with the grief of that.
God, who rules the world,
if it please Him, may He let me have some joy of her,
for if she keeps on opposing me,
there is nothing left but to die.

25 I have no more faith
in augury, reading the marks of the future,
because good hope
has destroyed me, killed me,
for she thrusts me so far away,
30 the beautiful lady I love,   III
every time I ask for her love,
as if I had done her some great wrong.
This weighs me down,
I become all dispirited.
35 But I do not show any of this,
I go on singing, I play the game.

I cannot say anything
but this: I am crazy
to love and desire
40 no one but the most beautiful in the world.
I would have gladly murdered
the man who first made the mirror.   IV

Can be m'o cossire,
no·n ai guerrer peyor.
45 Ja·l jorn qu'ela·s mire
ni pens de sa valor,
no serai jauzire
de leis ni de s'amor.
Ja per drudaria
50 no m'am, que no·s cove;
pero si·lh plazia
que·m fezes cal que be,
eu li juraria
per leis e per ma fe,   v
55 que·l bes que·m faria,
no fos saubutz per me.
En son plazer sia,
qu'eu sui en sa merce.
Si·lh platz, que m'aucia,
60 qu'eu no m'en clam de re!

Ben es dreihz qu'eu planha,
s'eu pert per mon orgolh
la bona companha
e·l solatz c'aver solh.
65 Petit me gazanha
lo fols arditz qu'eu colh,   vi
car vas me s'estranha
so qu'eu plus am e volh.
Orgolhs, Deus vos franha,
70 c'ara·n ploron mei olh.
Dreihz es que·m sofranha
totz jois, qu'eu eis lo·m tolh.

Encontra·l damnatge
e la pena qu'eu trai,
75 ai mo bon uzatge:
c'ades consir de lai.
Orgolh e folatge
e vilania fai   vii

When I think about it,
I don't have a worse enemy.
45 The second she looks at herself
and realizes how much she's worth,
it won't be me who enjoys
her or her love.

Let her by no means love me
50 with her body, that doesn't fit.
But if, perhaps, it should please her
to do me some kind of good,
I'd swear to her,
by her and by my honor,   V
55 the good she'd do me
would never get found out, not through me.
Let it all be as she pleases,
I am at her mercy.
If she pleases, let her kill me,
60 I would not complain about a thing.

But I would be right to lament
if I, through my presumption, lost
that good company,
that sweet conversing I used to enjoy.
65 That crazy rushing in of mine
has won me nothing,   VI
for she stands like a stranger to me,
and I love her and want her most.
O Presumption, God break you to pieces,
70 for now, because of you, my eyes weep.
It is right that I lack every joy,
for I alone deprive myself of every joy.

Against the loss
and pain I suffer
75 I have my own good way:
I always think about *there,* where she is.
It is presumption, madness
and vulgarity   VII

qui·n mou mo coratge
80 ni d'autra·m [1] met en plai,
car melhor messatge
en tot lo mon no·n ai,
e man lo·lh ostatge
entro qu'eu torn de sai.

85 Domna, mo coratge,
·l melhor amic qu'eu ai,   VIII
vos man en ostatge
entro qu'eu torn de sai.

28

Lo tems vai e ven e vire
per jorns, per mes e per ans,
et eu, las! no·n sai que dire,
c'ades es us mos talans.   I
5 Ades es us e no·s muda,
c'una·n volh e·n ai volguda,
don anc non aic jauzimen.

Pois ela no·n pert lo rire,
e me·n ven e dols e dans,
10 c'a tal joc m'a faih assire
don ai lo peyor dos tans,   II
—c'aitals amors es perduda
qu'es d'una part mantenguda—
tro que fai acordamen.

15 Be deuri' esser blasmaire
de me mezeis a razo,
c'anc no nasquet cel de maire
que tan servis en perdo;   III
e s'ela no m'en chastia,

___
[1] Appel: *d'alre·m.*

when anyone distracts my heart
80 or entangles me with some other woman,
for the best messenger I have
in the world is my heart,
and I send it hostage to her
till I return from here.

85 Lady, my heart,
the best friend I have,   VIII
I send you hostage
till I return from here.

28

Time comes, and turns, and goes,
in days, in months, in years,
and I, weary, know not what to say of it,
for my desire is always one.   I
5 It is always one, and does not change,
for I desire and have desired one,
with whom I never knew rejoicing.

Since she does not waste any laughter over this,
grief and injury come over me,
10 for she made me sit down to a game
such that I get the worst of it two times—   II
because love is always lost
sustained by only one—
until she comes to some accord with me.

15 I ought to be a censurer
of myself, by right,
for no man ever born of woman
served so much for nothing,   III
and if she does not punish me for that,

20 ades doblara·lh folia,
   que: "fols no tem, tro que pren."
   Ja mais no serai chantaire
   ni de l'escola N'Eblo,[1]
   que mos chantars no val gaire
25 ni mas voutas ni mei so;   IV
   ni res qu'eu fassa ni dia,
   no conosc que pros me sia
   ni no·i vei melhuramen.

   Si tot fatz de joi parvensa,
30 mout ai dins lo cor irat.
   Qui vid anc mais penedensa
   faire denan lo pechat?   V
   On plus la prec, plus m'es dura;
   mas si'n breu tems no·s melhura,
35 vengut er al partimen.

   Pero ben es qu'ela·m vensa
   a tota sa volontat,
   que, s'el' a tort o bistensa,
   ades n'aura pietat;   VI
40 que so mostra l'escriptura:[2]
   causa de bon'aventura
   val us sols jorns mais de cen.

   Ja no·m partrai a ma vida,
   tan com sia sals ni sas,
45 que pois l'arma n'es issida,[3]
   balaya lonc tems lo gras.   VII
   E si tot no s'es cochada,
   ja per me no·n er blasmada,
   sol d'eus adenan s'emen.

50 Ai, bon' amors encobida,
   cors be faihz, delgatz e plas,

---

[1] The existence of such a "school" has been a subject of much conjecture. See Moshé Lazar, *Amour Courtois et Fin'Amors dans la littérature du* XIIe *siècle* (Paris, 1964), pp. 49-52.
[2] Cf. Psalm 84 (Vulgate 83), verse 10.
[3] Literally, "When the *soul* of it is gone." Compare Hamlin, Hathaway, and

20 my foolishness will quickly double,
   because, "The fool has no dread, till he feels it on the
                  head."

   I shall be a singer no more,
   nor of the school of Lord Ebles,[1]
   for my song does not avail me,
25 neither my melody nor my refrains;   IV
   I do not know a thing that I can do
   or say that would help me,
   and I see no getting better in it.

   Though I put on the likeness of joy,
30 there is a heavy grievance in my heart.
   Who ever saw a penance
   being done before the sin?   V
   The more I pray, the more she hardens her heart;
   but if, in a short time, she does not reform,
35 I shall come to the parting.

   And yet it is good that she subdues me
   to her entire will,
   because if she does wrong, or makes me wait,
   she will soon feel pity for it;   VI
40 because the Scriptures set it forth: [2]
   in the courts of rejoicing
   one single day is worth more than a hundred.

   I shall never go away from her in my life,
   as long as I am all in one piece;
45 for when the heart of it is gone,[3]
   the straw stands a long time wavering.   VII
   And if she does not rush forth at once,
   I shall not censure her for that,
   as long as, sometime, she makes up for it in full.

50 Ah, sweet love long desired,
   body gently made and narrow,

Ricketts: "'For after the soul has departed, the flesh continues to live . . .
for a long time; and, although she . . . is not distressed over this, she will
not be blamed by me—provided she reforms from now on.'" The translation
takes *gras* as the nominative of *gran* (wheat, grain). Hamlin, Hathaway, and
Ricketts take *gras* (flesh) as opposed to *arma* (soul).

frescha chara colorida,
cui Deus formet ab sas mas!
Totz tems vos ai dezirada,
55 que res autra no m'agrada.
Autr' amor no volh nien!

VIII

Dousa res ben ensenhada,
cel que·us a tan gen formada,
me·n do cel joi qu'eu n'aten!

IX

brightly colored face of youth,
that God formed with His hands!   VIII
In every time I have desired you,
55 for I have no pleasure in another thing,
I want no other love but the one.

Creature of sweet breeding,
the One who formed you so nobly,   IX
may He give me the joy I await.

PEIRE D'ALVERNHE

(*fl. 1150–1180*)

Little is known of the life of Peire d'Alvernhe. The *vida* says he was from the diocese of Clermont, in Auvergne, and a contemporary poet says that he had been a canon of the Church and broke his vows in order to become a troubadour. He was in several courts in southern France and in Spain. Strongly influenced by Marcabru, he often composed in a hermetic style (*trobar clus*), and he himself makes fun of the obscurity of his verses in his most famous and most original production, the satire on the troubadours (no. 31). He wrote the first religious songs in Occitan. He was highly esteemed in his day, and he is cited by Dante, in the *De vulgari eloquentia,* as a venerable and learned poet.

Text: *Peire d'Alvernha: liriche,* ed. A. Del Monte. Turin: Loescher-Chiantore, 1955; with slight alterations in spelling.

29

"Rossinhol, el seu repaire
m'iras ma dona vezer,
e digas li·l mieu afaire
e ilh diga·t del sieu ver,
5   e man sai   I
com l'estai,
mas de mi·ll sovenha,
que ges lai
per nuill plai
10 ab si no·t retenha,

"Qu'ades no·m tornes retraire
son star e son captener,
qu'ieu non ai paren ni fraire
don tant o vueilla saber."
15 Ar s'en vai   II
l'auzels gai
dreit vas on ilh renha,
ab essai
ses esglai,
20 tro qu'en trob l'ensenha.

Quan l'auzeletz de bon aire
vi sa beutat aparer,
dous chant comenset a braire,
si com sol far contra·l ser;
25 pueis se tai,   III

que non brai,
mas de liei s'engenha,
co·l retrai
ses pantai
30 so qu·ilh auzir denha.

"Nightingale, you will go for me
to see my lady in her residence,
and tell her how things go with me,
and let her tell you truly of herself,
5 and send here   I
how she fares,
but let her think of me,
let her not
for any reason
10 keep you there with her,

so that you do not soon return to tell
me how she is and how she acts,
for I have no brother and no kin
I so long to hear about."
15 Now gaily   II
goes the bird
straight to where she rules,
thrusting forth
unafraid,
20 until it finds her banner.

When this bird of noble lineage
saw the beauty of her come forth,
it commenced its sweet song,
as it is wont to do toward evening,
25 then falls silent,   III

sings no more,
strains its wits,
how to tell,
without confusion,
30 the things she might deign to hear.

"Sel que·us es verais amaire,
volc qu'ieu en vostre poder
vengues sai esser chantaire,
per so que·us fos a plazer;
35   e sabrai,   IV
quan veirai,
de vos l'entresenha,
que·il dirai.
Si ren sai,
40   per qu'el lai s'en fenha,

"E si·l port per que·s n'esclaire,
gran gaug en devetz aver,
qu'anc om no nasquet de maire,
tan de be·us puesca voler;
45   ie·m n'irai   V
e·m mourai
ab gaug, on que·m venha;—
no farai,
quar non ai
50   dig qual plag en prenha.

"D'aisso·m farai plaidejaire:
qui·n amor a son esper,
no·s deuria tardar gaire,
tan com l'amors n'a lezer;
55   que tost chai   VI
blancs en bai,
com flors sobre lenha;
e val mai
qui·l fag fai,
60   ans qu'als la·n destrenha." [1]

---

[1] The song of the *rossinhol* has two parts. The second part follows.

"The one who is a faithful lover to you
made me come
to your domain to be his singer here,
to bring you pleasure
35   I shall know   IV
when I see
some sign from you
what I shall tell him.
Now if I hear anything
40   that tells him to act with discretion,

"if I bring something back to rejoice him,
you should have great joy for that,
for no man ever born of mother
could ever wish such good for you.
45   I shall fly away,   V
shall soar
with joy wherever I come—
No, I shall not,
I have not yet
50   said how I would judge in this.

"For this I shall be an advocate:
whoever has her hope in love,
she must never feel unrushed
while there is still a chance for love.
55   The white turns quick-   VI
ly into dark,
like the flower on the branch;
and a woman is nobler
who acts
60   before other things compel her." [1]

30

Ben a tengut dreg viatge
l'auzels lai on e·l tramis,
et ill envia·m messatge
segon que de mi formis:
"Molt mi platz,   I
so sapchatz,
vostra parladura;
et aujatz,
que·l digatz,
so don mi pren cura.

"Fort mi pot esser salvatge
quar s'es lonhatz mos amis,
qu'anc joi de negun linhatge
no vi que tan m'abelis;
trop viatz   II
fo·l comjatz,
mas s'ieu fos segura,
mais bontatz
n'agr' assatz,
per qu'ieu n'ai rancura.

"Que tan l'am de bon coratge,
qu'ades, s'eu entredormis,
ab lui ai en guidontage
joc e joi e guag e ris;
e·l solatz   III
qu'ai em patz
no sap creatura,
tan quan jatz
e mos bratz,
tro que·s trasfigura.

30

The bird has held a straight, true
path there, where I sent it,
and she sends me a message
to answer what he said of me.

5   "Your sweet discourse   I
be assured,
has given me much pleasure.
Now you must listen,
for you must tell him

10   the things that lie in my heart.

"It is cruel pain to me
that my friend took himself away,
for I never knew another joy
that gave me so much pleasure.

15   Too quick   II
was the parting.
But if I were confident,
he would get
more kindness yet;

20   so there is regret in me.

"For I love him so with my whole heart,
that always, when I go between sleeping and waking
I have one guide with him together:
play and pleasure and joy and laughter.

25   The content I have   III
in silence and peace
no creature knows,
while he lies
in my arms,

30   till his whole figure changes.

"Tostems mi fo d'agradatge,
pos lo vi et ans que·l vis,
e ges de plus ric linhatge
no vuelh autr' aver conquis;
35   mos cuidatz   IV
es bos fatz;
no·m pot far tortura
vens ni glatz
ni estatz
40   ni cautz ni freidura.

"Bon' amors a un uzatge
co·l bos aurs, quan ben es fis,
que s'esmera de bontatge,
qui ab bontat li servis;
45   e crezatz   V
qu'amistatz
cascun jorn melhura,
melhuratz
et amatz
50   es cui jois s'aura.

"Dous auzels, vas son estatge
m'iretz, quan venra·l matis,
e digatz l'en dreg lengatge
de qual guiza l'obedis."
55   Abrivatz   VI
n'es tornatz,
trop per gran mesura,
doctrinatz,
emparlatz
60   de bon' aventura.[1]

---

[1] The song of the *rossinhol* should be compared with Marcabru's *estornel* (Nos. 12 and 13).

"He was always my pleasure,
since I saw him and before I saw him,
and I do not wish that I had won
another man of greater lineage.
35   My mind is   IV
firm.
They cannot cause me pain,
wind, nor ice,
nor summer, nor heat,
40   nor yet the cold again.

"Honest love has a way
like honest gold, when it is pure,
its virtue is refined
when there is worth in the one intent on it.
45   And have faith   V
that friendship
perpetually exalts,
exalted
and beloved
50   is he of whom joy is foretold.

"Sweet bird, you will go for me
to his dwelling, when the morning comes,
and tell him with an honest tongue
how I wait on his desire."
55   Sped on,   VI
it returned,
extraordinarily
instructed,
eloquent
60   with good news.[1]

31

Cantarai d'aquestz trobadors
que canton de maintas colors
e·l pieier cuida dir mout gen;   I
mas a cantar lor er alhors
5 qu'entrametre·n vei cent pastors,
qu'us non sap que·s mont'o·s dissen.

D'aisso mer mal Peire Rotgiers,
per que n'er encolpatz primiers,
car chanta d'amor a presen;   II
10 e valgra li mais us sautiers
en la glieis' o us candeliers
tener ab gran candel' arden.[1]

E·l segonz, Girautz de Bornelh,
que sembl' oire sec al solelh
15 ab son chantar magre dolen,   III
qu'es chans de velha porta-selh;
que si·s mirava en espelh,
no·s prezari' un aiguilen.

E·l tertz, Bernartz de Ventedorn,
20 qu'es menre de Bornelh un dorn;
en son paire ac bon sirven   IV
per trair' ab arc nanal d'alborn,
e sa mair' escaldava·l forn
et amassava l'issermen.

25 E·l quartz, de Briva·l Lemozis,[2]
us joglars qu'es plus querentis
que sia tro qu'en Beniven,   V
e semblari' us pelegris
malautes, quan chanta·l mesquis,
30 qu'a pauc pïetatz no m'en pren.

---

[1] Like Peire d'Alvernhe, Peire Rogier (fl. last quarter of the twelfth century) began in the Church and broke away to seek a career as a troubadour.

31

I shall sing about those troubadours
who sing in many fashions, and all praise
their own verses, even the most appalling;   I
but they shall have to sing elsewhere,
5 for a hundred competing shepherds I hear,
and not one knows whether the melody's rising or falling.

In this Peire Rogier is guilty,
thus he shall be the first accused,
for he carries tunes of love in public right now,   II
10 and he would do better to carry
a psalter in church, or a candlestick
with a great big burning candle.[1]

And the second: Giraut de Bornelh,
who looks like a goatskin dried out in the sun,
15 with that meager voice of his, and that whine,   III
it is the song of an old lady bearing buckets of water;
if he saw himself in a mirror,
he would think himself less than an eglantine.

And the third: Bernart de Ventadorn,
20 a hand's breadth smaller than Bornelh;
a fellow who worked for a wage was his father,   IV
he shot a laburnum handbow well,
and his mother heated the oven
and gathered the brushwood together.

25 And the fourth, from Brive, the Limousin,[2]
a jongleur, and the most beggarly man
between Benevento and here;   V
and he looks like a sick
pilgrim when he sings, the wretch,
30 so that I nearly pity him myself.

[2] Zenker identifies him with the Limousin in a *tenso* with Bernart de Ventadorn, *Bernart de Ventadorn, del chan.*

E'n Guilhems de Ribas lo quins,[3]
qu'es malvatz defors e dedins,
e ditz totz sos vers raucamen,   VI
per que es avols sos retins
35 qu'atretan s'en fari' us chins;
e l'uolh semblan de vout d'argen.[4]

E·l seises, Grimoartz Gausmars,[5]
qu'es cavalliers e fai joglars;
e perda Dieu qui·l o cossen   VII
40 ni·l dona vestirs vertz ni vars,
que tals er adobatz semprars
qu'enjoglarit s'en seran cen.

Ab Peire de Monzo son set,[3]
pos lo coms de Tolosa·l det,
45 chantan, un sonet avinen,   VIII
e cel fon cortes que·l raubet,
e mal o fes quar no·il trenquet
aquel pe que porta penden.

E l'oites, Bernatz de Saissac,[3]
50 qu'anc un sol bon mestier non ac
mas d'anar menutz dons queren;   IX
et anc puois no·l prezei un brac
pois a'n Bertran de Cardalhac
ques un vielh mantel suzolen.

55 E·l novens es En Raembautz,[6]
que·s fai de son trobar trop bautz;
mas eu lo torni en nïen,   X
qu'el non es alegres ni chautz;
per so pretz aitan los pipautz
60 que van los almosnas queren.

[3] We know little or nothing about Guillem de Ribas, Peire de Monzon,
Bernart de Sayssac, Bertran de Cardalhac, Elbes de Sagna, Gonzalo Roïtz,
the Lombard "Cossezen."
[4] I.e., an image of Christ crucified. Zenker paraphrases: "He rolls up his
eyes when he sings, so that you only see the whites."

En Guillem de Ribas is the fifth,[3]
who is bad outside and in,
he recites all his verses with a raucous voice,   VI
so his singing sounds like hell,
for a dog would sing as well,
and his eyes roll up like Christ in silver.[4]

And the sixth, Grimoart Gausmar,[5]
a knight who tries to pass for a jongleur,
and whoever agrees to let him could not do worse,   VII
40 God damn whoever gives him clothing of motley
            and green,
for once his costume has been seen,
a hundred more will want to be jongleurs.

And Peire de Monzó makes seven,[3]
since the Count of Toulouse sang him
45 a charming song, though he himself never sang;   VIII
and whoever stole it from him is to be respected,
except it was a pity he neglected
to amputate the little foot that hangs.

And the eighth, Bernart de Sayssac,[3]
50 who never knew any other work
but going around begging little gifts;   IX
and I have not thought him worth a piece of mud
since he begged En Bertran de Cardalhac
for an old cloak that stank of sweat.

55 And the ninth is En Raimbaut,[6]
who thinks so highly of his poetry;
but I think nothing of his rhymes,   X
they have neither warmth nor cheer,
therefore I rank him with the pipers
60 who come up to you and beg for dimes.

[5] Probably the author of *Lanquan lo temps renovela* (Pillet, 190, 1), his only extant song. (Del Monte)
[6] Probably Raimbaut d'Aurenga.

E n'Ebles de Sanha·l dezes,[3]
a cui anc d'amor non venc bes,
si tot se chanta de coinden: XI
us vilanetz enflatz plages,
65 que dizen que per dos poges [7]
lai se loga e sai se ven.

E l'onzes, Gonzalgo Roïtz,[3]
que·s fai de son chant trop formitz,
per qu'en cavallaria·s fen;   XII
70 et anc per lui non fo feritz
bos colps, tan ben non fo garnitz,
si doncs no·l trobet en fugen.

E·l dotzes, us velhetz lombartz,[3]
que clama sos vezins coartz,
75 et ilh eis sent de l'espaven;   XIII
pero sonetz fai mout galhartz
ab motz maribotz e bastartz,[8]
e lui apel' om Cossezen.[9]

Peire d'Alvernhe a tal votz
80 que canta de sus e de sotz,
e lauza·s mout a tota gen;   XIV
pero maïstres es de totz,
ab qu'un pauc esclarzis sos motz,
qu'a penas nulhs om los enten.

85 Lo vers fo faitz als enflabotz   XV
a Puog-Vert, tot jogan rizen.

---

[7] *Poges:* a coin of low value made at Le Puy. *Almo nas,* 1. 60: literally, "alms."

[8] Zenker traces the word *marabotz* from *Marrabais,* marrano, a Jew or Mohammedan who pretended to be a Christian during the Spanish Inquisition but secretly adhered to his native faith—in other words, not entirely one thing or the other (cf. *bastartz*).

[9] That is, "Suitable," "Fitting," "Convenient." This poet is thus the oldest

En Ebles de Sagna is the tenth,[3]
who never had any luck in love,
though he sweetly sings his little air;   XI
a vulgar puffed-up shyster
65 who, they say, for two cents [7]
rents himself here, and sells himself there.

And the eleventh, Gonzalgo Roïtz,[3]
who vaunts his skill in song
and thus presumes to call himself a knight;   XII
70 no strong blow was ever struck
by him, he was never that well armed,
unless, of course, he got off in flight.

And twelfth is an old Lombard,[3]
who calls his friends all cowards,
75 and he himself is terrified;   XIII
and yet the songs he writes are valiant,
with bastard phrases neither Occitan nor Italian,[8]
and he is known to all as Cossezen,[9] "Just Right."

Peire d'Alvernhe, now he has such a voice
80 he sings the high notes, and the low (and the in-between),
and before all people gives himself much praise;   XIV
and so he is the master of all who here convene;
if only he would make his words a little clearer,
for hardly a man can tell what they mean.

85 This vers was made to the noise of bagpipes
at Puivert, with much laughter and play.   XV

troubadour of Italian birth to whom any reference has been made. (Del
Monte)

RAIMBAUT D'ORANGE

(*fl. c. 1150–1173*)

Raimbaut, Count of Orange, was the heir to large domains in the regions of Montpellier and Vaucluse. He is the first troubadour native to the area properly called Provence. His thirty-nine extant songs show his great technical skill and the variety of his styles. His early compositions, heavily influenced by Marcabru, are written in that difficult, allusive language known as *trobar clus*—the "closed style," full of intricate and baffling imagery and unusual words, impenetrable to all but a few initiates. In the course of his career, however, and perhaps under the influence of Guiraut de Bornelh (see below, no. 36), he composed in a more direct style *(trobar leu)*; and in the latter part of his life devoted himself to the development of ornamentation, especially the rare rhymes and the complex rhyme patterns which characterize the style known as *trobar ric*. His technical skill was equaled only by few other troubadours.

Text: *The Life and Works of the Troubadour Raimbaut d'Orange,* ed. Walter T. Pattison. Minneapolis: The University of Minnesota Press, 1952.

32

Escotatz, mas no say que s'es
senhor, so que vuelh comensar.
Vers, estribot, ni sirventes
non es, ni nom no·l sai trobar;   I
5 ni ges no say co·l mi fezes
s'aytal no·l podi' acabar,
que ia hom mays non vis fag aytal ad home ni a femna en
est segle ni en l'autre qu'es passatz.[1]

Sitot m'o tenetz a foles
per tan no·m poiria layssar
10 que ieu mon talan non disses:
no m'en cujes hom castiar;   II
tot cant es non pres un pojes
vas so c'ades vey et esgar,
e dir vos ay per que. Car si ieu vos o avia mogut, e no·us
o trazia a cap, tenriatz m'en per fol. Car mais
amaria seis deniers en mon punh que mil sols
el cel.[2]

15 Ja no·m tema ren far que·m pes
mos amicx, aisso·l vuelh prejar;
s'als obs no·m vol valer manes
pus m'o profer' ab lonc tarzar;   III
pus leu que selh que m'a conques
20 no·m pot nulh autre galiar.
Tot ayso dic per una domna que·m fay languir ab belas
paraulas et ab lonc respieg, no say per que.
Pot me bon' esser, senhors?

[1] "This work is obviously humorous, falling into the genre of the *gap*
[compare nos. 5 and 11]. But in addition to the general humor brought about
especially by the introduction of prose lines into the poetic composition,
there is a more specific parody of the work of Guillaume de Poitiers. The
latter begins a poem [no. 3], then proceeds to tell us that it is dedicated to
an unknown lady . . . Raimbaut merely shifts from an unknown lady to

32

Listen, Lords . . . but I don't know what
to call this thing I'm about to declaim.
Vers? Estribot? Sirventes? It's none
of these. I can't think up a name,   I
5 and don't know how I'd compose such a thing
if I could not finish it and claim
that no one ever saw the like of it made by any man or
        woman in our century or in the other which
        has passed.[1]

Call me a madman if you like,
it would not make me leave my vow,
10 Lords, to tell you what I feel.
Let no one blame me. I would not set
a penny on this whole Creation,
compared to what I see right now,
and I'll tell you why: because if I started this thing for
        you and did not bring it off, you'd take me for
        a fool: because I prefer six cents in my fist to
        a thousand suns in the sky.[2]

15 Let my friend never fear he may have done
a thing that weighs on me, I pray:
if he will not help me in my need at once,
let him offer me help after long delay.   III
But she that conquered me alone
20 deceives me as though it were child's play.
I say all this because of one lady who makes me pine
        away with beautiful words and a long expec-
        tation, I don't know why—Lords, can she be
        good to me?

an unknown and nameless verse form, from *no sai qui s'es* to *no sai que s'es*
. . . Then Raimbaut's long prose line makes fun of the long final verse of
some of Guillaume's archaic and outmoded compositions [see nos. 1 and 2]."
(Pattison)
[2] *Sol* means both "sun" and "sou."

Que ben a passatz quatre mes,
  (oc! e mays de mil ans so·m par)
que m'a autrejat e promes
25 que·m dara so que m'es pus car.   IV
Dona! Pus mon cor tenetz pres
adossatz me ab dous l'amar.
Dieus, aiuda! *In nomine patris et filii et spiritus sancti!*
    Aiso, que sera, domna?

Qu'ieu soy per vos gays, d'ira ples;
30 iratz-jauzens me faytz trobar;
e so m'en partitz de tals tres
qu'el mon non a, mas vos, lur par;   V
e soy fols cantayre cortes
tan c'om m'en apela ioglar.[3]
35 Dona, far ne podetz a vostra guiza, co fes n'Ayma de
    l'espatla que la estujet lay on li plac.[4]

Er fenisc mo no-say-que-s'es,[5]
c'aisi l'ay volgut batejar;
pus mays d'aital non auzi jes
be·l dey enaysi apelar;   VI
40 e diga·l, can l'aura apres,
    qui que s'en vuelha azautar.
E si hom li demanda qui l'a fag, pot dir que sel que
    sap be far totas fazendas can se vol.

[3] *Joglar* is a frequent *senhal* in Raimbaut's songs, designating both himself and his lady.
[4] An obscure but undoubtedly obscene reference.
[5] Literally, "I don't know what it is."

It's been a good four months—that's more
than a thousand years to me, yes,
since she promised me and swore
25 to give me what I long for most.   IV
Lady, my heart is your prisoner,
therefore sweeten my bitterness.
Help me, God, *in nomine Patris et Filii et Spiritus
sancti!* Madam, how will it all turn out?

You make me frolic in my wrath,
30 you make me sing with joyful rage;
and I have left three such as have
no peer, save you, in our age.   V
Joglar they call me, I go singing
mad with love, in courtly ways.[3]
35 Lady, you can do as you please about it, as Na Ayma
did with the shoulder bone, she stuck it where
she liked.[4]

Now I conclude my Whatdoyoucallit,[5]
for that is how I've had it baptized;
since I've never heard of a similar thing,
I use the name that I devised;   VI
40 whoever likes it, let him sing,
once he has it memorized,
and if anyone asks him who made it, he can say: one who
can do anything, and do it well, when he
wants to.

LA COMTESSA DE DIA

(fl. c. 1160)

Nothing is known about the Countess of Die, the most important and probably the oldest of the *trobairitz,* the female composers. There is no basis for assigning her the first name Beatritz, as many editors have done. The *vida* says she was in love with En Raimbaut d'Aurenga—a statement that is probably as fanciful as most of the others in the *vidas* and, in any case, as Pattison has shown, could not be true of the famous troubadour of that name. Five songs are extant, including a *tenso* (a dispute between two poets who compose alternate strophes) with the lover (compare nos. 17 and 36).

Text: *Chrestomathie provençale,* ed. K. Bartsch and E. Koll-witz. 6th edition. Marburg, 1904.

A chantar m'er de so qu'eu no volria,
tant me rancur de lui cui sui amia;
car eu l'am mais que nuilla ren que sia:
vas lui no·m val merces ni cortezia   I
5 ni ma beltatz ni mos pretz ni mos sens;
c'atressi·m sui enganad' e trahia
Com degr' esser, s'eu fos dezavinens.

D'aisso·m conort, car anc non fi faillensa,
amics, vas vos per nuilla captenensa;
10 ans vo am mais non fetz Seguis Valensa,[1]
e platz mi mout que eu d'amar vos vensa,   II
lo meus amics, car etz lo plus valens;
mi faitz orgoil en digz et en parvensa
et si etz francs vas totas autras gens.

15 Meraveill me cum vostre cors s'orgoilla,
amics, vas me, per qui'ai razon que·m doilla;
non es ges dreitz c'autr' amors vos mi toilla,
per nuilla ren que·us diga ni acoilla.   III
E membre vos cals fo·l comensamens
20 de nostr' amor! Ja Dompnedeus non voilla
qu'en ma colpa sia·l departimens.

Proeza grans, qu'el vostre cors s'aizina
e lo rics pretz qu'avetz, m'en ataïna;
c'una non sai, loindana ni vezina,
25 si vol amar, vas vos no si' aclina;   IV
mas vos, amics, etz ben tant conoissens
que ben devetz conoisser la plus fina;
e membre vos de nostres partimens.[2]

[1] Lovers in a lost romance.
[2] Some have interpreted *partimens* as referring to the *tensos* she composed
with her lover.

It will be mine to sing of that which I would not desire,
I am so aggrieved by the one to whom I am the friend,
for I love him more than anything than can be.
Pity does not help me toward him, nor courtliness,   I
5 nor my beauty, nor my good name, nor my wit;
and so I am cheated and betrayed as much
as I'd deserve to be if I were ugly.

I draw strength from one thing, I never did wrong,
my friend, toward you, by any act,
10 no, I love you more than Seguin loved Valensa,[1]
and I am most pleased that I could conquer you in love,   II
my friend, for you are worth more than everyone.
You display such arrogance to me in your words and your
                             bearing,
and yet you are open with everyone else.

15 It makes me wonder how you are cold with pride,
my friend, to me, I have reason to lament;
it is not right that another love take you away from me,
no matter what things she says to you, or how she makes
                             you welcome.
And remember what was the beginning   III
20 of our love. May the Lord God never want
that in my fault lies the parting.

The great manliness at home in you
and your ringing merit, they disquiet me,
for I do not know one woman, far or near,
25 who, desiring to love, does not lean toward you.   IV
But, friend, you have judgment,
you can tell who is more true:
remember our sharing.[2]

Valer mi deu mos pretz e mos paratges
30 e ma beutatz e plus mos fins coratges;
   per qu'eu vos man lai on es vostr' estatges
   esta chanson, que me sia messatges,   V
   e voill saber, lo meus bels amics gens,
   per que vos m'etz tant fers ni tant salvatges;
35 no sai si s'es orgoills o mals talens.

   Mais aitan plus voill li digas, messatges,   VI
   qu'en trop d'orgoill an gran dan maintas gens.

My name and high descent should help me,
30 and my beauty, and the purity of my heart most of all;
therefore I send this song to you down there,
to your dwelling, let it be my messenger,   V
and I wish to know, my fair gentle friend,
why are you so barbarous and cruel to me,
35 is it pride, or wishing ill?

And also I want you to tell him, messenger,   VI
many people suffer for having too much pride.

GIRAUT DE BORNELH

(fl. 1165–after 1211)

Born in the region of Excideuil (Dordogne), Giraut ranged widely and served several patrons in southern France and Spain. He accompanied one of them, Adémar V of Limoges, to Jerusalem. The *vida* reflects the great esteem he enjoyed among his contemporaries, and the gravity of his moral tone:

> Giraut de Bornelh . . . was a man of low estate, but wise in learning and natural understanding. And he was the best troubadour of all those who came before or after him; wherefore he was called the Master of the Troubadours, and is so to this day among all those who truly understand subtle words, well arranged, concerning love and wisdom . . . And his life was such that all winter long he was in school and studied letters, and all summer he went from court to court and took two singers with him, who sang his songs. He never desired a wife, and everything he earned he gave to his poor relatives and to the church of the village where he was born, which church was called, then as now, Saint-Gervais.

Dante, quoting from no. 36, cites him as an illustrious poet who composed in the vernacular on the theme of moral rectitude (*De vulgari eloquentia*, II, 2). Some eighty of his songs are extant, of great variety in form and style. Giraut alternated between *trobar clus* and *trobar leu*—the deliberately obscure, and the very plain style—explaining at different times why each one was preferable to the other.

Text: Adolf Kolsen, *Sämtliche Lieder des Trobadors Giraut de Bornelh*. 2 vols. Halle: Max Niemeyer, 1910 (I) & 1935 (II).

Can lo glatz e·l frechs e la neus [1]
s'en vai e torna la chalors
e reverdezis lo pascors
et auch las voltas dels auzeus,
5 m'es aitan beus
lo dolz tems a l'issen de martz
que plus sui salhens que leupartz   I
e vils non es chabrols ni cers.
Si la bela cui sui profers
10 me vol onrar
d'aitan que·m denhe sofertar
qu'eu sia sos fis entendens,
sobre totz sui rics e manens.

Tan es sos cors gais et isneus
15 e complitz de belas colors
c'anc de rozeus no nasquet flors
plus frescha ni d'altres brondeus,
ni anc Bordeus
non ac senhor fos plus galhartz
20 de me, si n'era coltz ni partz   II
tan que fos sos dominis sers,
e fos apelatz de Bezers,[2]
can ja parlar
m'auziri' om de nulh celar
25 qu'ela·m disses, celadamens,
don s'aïres lo seus cors gens!

Bona domna, lo vostr'aneus
que·m donetz, me fai gran socors;
qu'en lui refranhi mas dolors,

[1] The following text is that printed in: Frank R. Hamlin, Peter T. Ricketts, and John Hathaway, *Introduction à l'étude de l'ancien Provençal* (Geneva: Droz, 1967). The editors emend Kolsen's text following suggestions by Kurt Lewent, "Zum Text der Lieder des Giraut de Bornelh," *Biblioteca dell'archivum romanicum*, 26 (1938), 12.

34

When the ice and the cold and the snow [1]
retreat and the warmth returns
and the spring regreens
and I hear the birds' melismas,
5 I am so pleased
by that sweet season at the going-out of March,
I am more bounding than the leopard,   I
quicker than the goat or the stag.
If the beautiful lady I want to belong to
10 wants to honor me
just so much that she agrees to let
me be her faithful lover,
I am mighty and rich above all men.

Her body is so gay and quick
15 and fulfilled in beautiful colors,
no flower ever came forth more pure
on rose tree or other branches.
Nor did Bordeaux ever
get a lord as full of life as I
20 would be if I were with her—or away from her   II
but still her own requited man.
And may I be called a man of Bedlam [2]
if any heard me
speak one secret thing
25 she told me under cover, in confidence,
it would fill that gentle one with rage.

Good lady, this ring of yours,
this ring you gave me helps me greatly:
it sweetens my sorrow

[2] Literally, Béziers: to come from Béziers = to be a fool.

30 e can lo remir, sui plus leus
c'us estorneus
e sui per vos aissi auzartz
que no tem que lansa ni dartz   III
me tenha dan n'acers ni fers.
35 E d'altra part sui plus despers
per sobramar
que naus, can vai torban per mar
destrecha d'ondas e de vens;
aissi·m destrenh lo pensamens.

40 Domna, aissi com us chasteus
qu'es assetjatz per fortz senhors,
can la peirer' abat las tors
e·l chalabres e·l manganeus
et es tan greus
45 la guerra devas totas partz
que no lor te pro genhs ni artz   IV
e·l dols e·l critz es aitan fers
de cels dedins quez an grans gers,
sembla·us ni·us par
50 que lor ai' obs merce clamar,
aissi·us clam merce umilmens,
bona domna pros e valens.

Domna, aissi com us anheus
non a forsa contr' ad un ors,
55 sui eu, si la vostra valors
no·m val, plus frevols c'us rauzeus,
et er plus breus
ma vida que de cartel chartz,
s'oimais me pren negus destartz,   V
60 que no·m fassatz drech de l'envers.
E tu, fin' amors, que·m sofers,
que deus garar
los fis amans de foleiar,
sias me chabdeus e guirens
65 a ma domna, pos aissi·m vens!

30 when I gaze on it, I become lighter
   than a starling;
   and then, because of you, I become so brave
   I never fear any arrow or lance
   can harm me; no iron or steel can touch me.   III
35 A moment later and I am more lost,
   through too much loving,
   than a ship whirled round by the sea,
   pulled apart by waves and winds.
   So I am racked with thought.

40 Lady, like a castle
   besieged by powerful lords,
   perrier, catapult, and mangonel
   knock the towers down,
   and war bears down so

45 heavily, from all directions,
   no device, no cunning can help the besieged,   IV
   the anguish and the shrieks are tremendous and wild
   of those inside, who are in terror,
   then you see
50 they have nothing left but to call out for mercy—
   that is how I beg you for mercy, in great humility,
   my lady, my good and gentle and kind.

   Lady, as a lamb
   is powerless against a bear,
55 so am I, wanting
   your strength, weaker than a reed.
   And my life will be
   briefer than the fourth part of an instant
   now if any harm should come my way   V
60 and you still deny me justice for all this neglect.
   And you, True Love, bear me up,
   preserve
   true lovers from doing foolish things,
   be my guide and witness
65 with my lady, see now how she conquers me.

35

Reis glorios, verais lums e clartatz,
Deus poderos, Senher, si a vos platz,
al meu companh sïatz fizels ajuda,　　　　　　　　　　I
qu'eu non lo vi pos la nochs fo venguda,
5　　e ades sera l'alba.[1]

Bel companho, si dormetz o veillatz?
Non dormatz plus, suau vos ressidatz,
qu'en orïent vei l'estela creguda　　　　　　　　　　II
qu'amena·l jorn, qu'eu lai ben coneguda,
10　　e ades sera l'alba.

Bel companho, en chantan vos apel:
non dormatz plus, qu'eu aug chantar l'auzel
que vai queren lo jorn per lo boscatge,　　　　　　　III
et ai paor que·l gilos vos assatge,
15　　e ades sera l'alba.

Bel companho, eissetz al fenestrel,
et esgardatz las ensenhas del cel;
conoisseretz si·us sui fizels messatge:　　　　　　　IV
si non o faitz, vostres n'er lo damnatge,
20　　e ades sera l'alba.

Bel companho, pos mi parti de vos,
eu non dormi ni·m moc de ginolhos,
ans preguei Deu, lo filh Santa Maria,　　　　　　　V
que·us mi rendes per lejal companhia,
25　　e ades sera l'alba.

[1] This *alba* (dawn song) is sung by the lover's friend, who has watched all
night and now warns him to leave the side of his beloved, for the night is
over.

35

Glorious King, true Light and Splendor,
Almighty God, Lord, if it please You,
stand faithfully by my companion,   I
for I have not seen him since the night came on,
5   and soon the dawn will rise.[1]

Fair friend, are you asleep or awake?
Sleep no longer, rise up quietly,
for in the east I see the star grown big   II
that spurs on the day, I knew it clearly,
10 and soon the dawn will rise.

Fair friend, this singing is to call to you:
sleep no more, I hear the bird who sings now
searching the woods, looking for day,   III
and I fear the jealous one will fall on you,
15 and soon the dawn will rise.

Fair friend, go up to the window,
look at the stars in the sky:
you will know whether I am your faithful messenger—   IV
do this, or yours is the harm that will come,
20 and soon the dawn will rise.

Fair friend, since I left you
I have not slept or risen from my knees
but prayed God, blessed Mary's son,   V
to give you back to me in true companionship,
25 and soon the dawn will rise.

Bel companho, la foras als peiros
me prejavatz qu'eu no fos dormilhos,
enans velhes tota noch tro al dia;   VI
aras no·us platz mos chans ni ma paria,
30   e ades sera l'alba.

36

Per solatz revelhar,
que s'es trop endormitz,
e per pretz, qu'es faiditz,
acolhir e tornar,
5   me cudei trebalhar;   I
mas er m'en sui gequitz!
Per so m'en sui falhitz,
car non es d'achabar;
c'on plus m'en ve volontatz e talans,
10   plus creis de lai lo destorbers e·l dans.

Greu es de sofertar.
A vos o dic c'auzitz
com era jois grazitz
e tuch li benestar.
15   Mais no podetz jurar   II
qu'egas de fust no vitz [1]
ni vilas, velhs, fronitz
esters grat chavalgar.
Lachs es l'afars e fers e malestans,
20   don om pert Deu e rema malanans!

Vos vitz torneis mandar
e segre·ls gen garnitz
e pois dels melhs feritz
una sazo parlar;
25   er' es pretz de raubar   III
e d'ebranchar berbitz.

[1] This line is not understood.

Fair friend, how you begged me not to fall
asleep outside there on the steps
but watch all night till daybreak; now   VI
you wish my song away, and me,
30   and soon the dawn will rise.

36

To reawaken courtly pleasure,
which had too long slept,
and to welcome glory,
to bring it back from exile,
5 I thought to give myself some pains;   I
but now I have renounced all that.
And so I failed to do it,
because the thing cannot be done.
Where the will to restore our courtliness most comes
                    on me,
10 there the damage and the loss get worse.

It is hard to bear.
I say this to you who heard
joy commended in your youth
and every noble thing.
15 But now you cannot swear   II
you have not seen wooden mares [1]
and lowborn, old and broken wrecks
sitting on horses against their will.
An ugly, gross, indecent time,
20 where man loses God and dwells in misery.

You saw tournaments proclaimed,
nobility attending, well equipped,
and then for some while the talk
of those who fought and struck the best.
25 Now the glory lies in robbing   III
and stealing sheep.

Chavalers si' aunitz
que·s met en domneiar,

pos que tocha dels mas moltos belans
30 ni que rauba gleizas ni viandans!

E vitz per cortz anar
de joglaretz formitz
gen chaussatz e vestitz
sol per domnas lauzar;
35 er no n'auzem parlar,   IV
tan es lor pretz delitz!—
Don es lo tortz issitz
d'elas malrazonar,
no sai—De cals, d'elas o dels amans?
40 Eu dic de totz, que·l pretz n'a trach l'engans!

On son gandit joglar
que vitz gen acolhitz?
C'a tal a mester guitz
que solia guidar,
45 e pero ses reptar   V
vai er tals escharitz,
pos fo bos pretz falhitz,
que solia menar
50 gen en arnes e bels e benestans.

Qu'eu eis que solh sonar
totz pros, om eissernitz,
estauc tan esbaïtz
que no·m sai conselhar;
55 qu'en loc de solassar   VI
auch er'en cortz los critz

c'aitan leu s'er grazitz
de l'aucha de Bretmar

Shame to the knight
who presumes to court a lady

after he has touched bleating sheep with his hands
30 or stolen from churches or robbed travelers on the road.

And you saw the faultless singers,
handsomely booted and dressed,
going from court to court
for the one purpose of praising ladies.
35 Now you hear no talk of them,   IV
how their glory lies in ruins!
Where this perversion started
of speaking ill of ladies
I cannot say.   Whose fault was it?   the ladies? the
                lovers?
40 I say both, for trickery robbed them of their worth.

Where have they fled, the singers
you saw so gently welcomed?
For every lord who leads must have
a man who guides the leader.
45 But now, making no reproaches,   V
such a man wanders all alone
—now that the glory has faded—
who used to lead
companions, I cannot say how many,
50 exalted in their accouterments, and brave, and standing
                well.

For I myself, a man distinguished,
who used to celebrate all valiant men,
am so bewildered
I cannot seek counsel with myself.
55 For where there was courtly conversation,   VI
now I hear in these societies guffaws,
so that they love
the dirty story of Bretmar's

lo comtes [2] entre lor com us bos chans
60 dels rics afars e dels tems e dels ans.

Mas a cor afranchar,
que s'es trop enduritz,
no deu om los oblitz
ni·ls velhs fachs remembrar?
65 Que mals es a laissar   VII
afars, pos es plevitz,
e·l mal don sui garitz
no·m chal ja mezinar;
mas so c'om ve, volv'e vir e balans
70 e prend' e lais e forse d'ams los pans! [3]

D'aitan me posc vanar
c'anc mos ostals petitz
no fo d'els envazitz;
que·l vei per totz doptar
75 ni no·m fetz mas onrar   VIII
lo volpils ni l'arditz,
don mos senher chauzitz
se deuria pensar
que no l'es ges pretz ni laus ni bobans
80 qu'eu, que·m laus d'els, sia de lui clamans.

Era no m'ais! Per que? No m'o demans;   IX
car planchs sera, s'aissi rema mos chans.

So di·l Dalfis que conois los bos chans. [4]   X

[2] This story is not known.
[3] "Because one courageously reveals the abuses he witnesses, speaks in every
direction and continually stigmatizes, he helps toward the removal of those
abuses." (Kolsen)
[4] Dauphin d'Auvergne, a troubadour.

goose [2] as much as a well-made song
60 about the old nobility, the times, the years.

But to free the heart
grown hard,
should we not recall
the forgotten things, the old deeds?
65 For it is bad to forget   VII
the life that men have sworn to.
I need no medicine
for the sickness I am cured of;
but what a man sees, let him turn and spin and balance
70 and grasp and release and lay hold of at both ends.[3]

This much I can boast of:
they have never broken into
my own little house;
for I see how they hold it in awe
75 and do me nothing but honor,   VIII
cowards and brave men alike;
and so let my lord, who is in everyone's eye,
reflect on this:
it does not redound to his glory, praise, magnificence
80 if I, declaring myself content with them, complain of
           him.

Right now I do not complain. Why? Do not ask.   IX
It will be a pity if my song ends on such a note.

So says the Dauphin, who understands what good songs   X
           are.[4]

GIRAUT DE BORNELH AND RAIMBAUT D'AURENGA

37

Ara·m platz, Giraut de Borneill, [1]
que sapcha per c'anatz blasman
trobar clus, ni per cal semblan.
Aiso·m digaz,   I
5 si tan prezatz
so que es a toz comunal;
car adonc tut seran egual.

Seign'en Lignaura,[2] no·m coreill
si qecs s'i trob'a son talan.
10 Mas eu son jujaire d'aitan
qu'es mais amatz   II
e plus prezatz
qui·l fa levet e venarsal;
e vos no m'o tornetz a mal.

15 Giraut, non voill qu'en tal trepeil
torn mos trobars; que ja ogan
lo lauzo·l bon e·l pauc e·l gran.
Ja per los faz   III
non er lauzatz,
20 car non conoisson (ni lor cal)
so que plus car es ni mais val.

Lingnaura, si per aiso veil
ni mon sojorn torn en affan
sembla que·m dopte del mazan.[3]

---

[1] Text: Walter T. Pattison, *The Life and Works of the Troubadour Raimbaut d'Orange.* Minneapolis: The University of Minnesota Press, 1952.
[2] Adolf Kolsen first identified Lignaura as Raimbaut d'Orange.

37

Now, Giraut de Bornelh, I would like [1]
to know why you go denouncing
our difficult style, on what pretext.
Tell me whether
5 you esteem   I
what is common to everyone,
for then all will be equal.

En Lignaura,[2] I have no complaint
if each man writes the kind of song that suits him,
10 but it seems to me
the song is better loved   II
and more applauded
when you make it easy and open to all . . .
Do not look down on me for saying this.

15 Giraut, I do not want my songs turned
into such a lot of noise; from now on
let the good and the little and the great never praise
        them.
Fools will never   III
be able to praise them,
20 for such have no taste and no concern
for the worthiest and most precious things.
Lignaura, if I give up my nights for that
and turn my repose into taking pains,
then I seem to fear their riotous applause.[3]

---

[3] Kolsen: "If I exerted myself to write poetry just for a small circle of
connoisseurs and not for the multitude, it would seem as though I disdained
universal applause; but this is just what I want to strive for." (Kolsen,
Giraut de Bornelh, I, p. 377, n. 1)

25 A que trobatz   IV
   si non vos platz
   c'ades o sapchon tal e cal?
   Que chanz non port'altre cabtal.

   Giraut, sol que·l miels appareil
30 e·l dig'ades e·l trag'enan,
   mi non cal sitot non s'espan.
   C'anc granz viutaz   V
   non fon denhtatz:
   per so prez'om mais aur que sal,
35 e de tot chant es atretal.

   Lingnaura, fort de bon conseill,
   etz fis amans contrarian,
   e per o si n'ai mais d'affan.
   Mos sos levatz,   VI
40 c'us enraumatz
   lo·m deissazec e·l diga mal,
   que no·l deing ad home sesal.[4]

   Giraut, per cel ni per soleil
   ni per la clardat que resplan,
45 non sai de que·ns anam parlan,
   ni don fui natz,[5]   VII
   si soi torbatz
   tan pes d'un fin joi natural.
   Can d'als cossir, no·m es coral.

50 Lingnaura, si·m gira·l vermeil
   de l'escut cella cui reblan,[6]

[4] That is, worthy of a man of rank and noble standing. The translation follows Pattison's elucidation of this difficult strophe.
[5] Pattison's interpretation of this line ("or from what parents I was born").
[6] That is, the front side: she is hostile.

25 But why do you compose   IV
     if you don't want
     this one and that one to understand you right away?
     For the song brings no other reward

     Giraut, as long as I compose my song well
30 and always speak it and bring it forth,
     I do not care if it is not widespread;
     cheap abundance never   V
     had great worth:
     that is why you set a higher price on gold than salt,
35 and it is the same with any song.

     Lignaura, strong in good advice,
     you are a true lover and full of arguments,
     and so, as you see, I am more dismayed.
     Let some poor singer   VI

40 with a head cold
     mangle my lofty song as his hoarse voice cracks,
     I know it's not worthy of one who pays a property tax.[4]

     Giraut, by heaven and by the sun
     and by the light that shines,
45 I don't know what we are talking about,
     or what parents I was born to,[5]   VII
     I am so muddled,
     lost in the thought of a certain soaring joy, the best in
               the world—
     when I think of anything else, it is not from my heart.

50 Lignaura, she whom I serve in courtly fashion
     turns the red side of the shield toward me,[6]

qu'eu voill dir "a Deu mi coman."
Cals fols pensatz   VIII
outracuidatz!
55 M'a mes doptanza deslial!
No·m soven com me fes comtal? [7]

Giraut, greu m'es, per San Marsal,   IX
car vos n'anatz de sai nadal.

Lingnaura, que ves cort rial   X
60 m'en vauc ades ric e cabal.[8]

---

[7] Here Giraut refers to one of his own songs, no. 27, L. 74 in Kolsen's edition
(Pattison).
[8] Probably in Spain; perhaps, as Kolsen suggests, the court of Alfonso II of
Aragón.

it makes me feel like crying out, "God help me now."
What a crazy   VIII
reckless thought!
55 It has set disloyal doubt on me . . .
Do I not remember how she made me like a count? [7]

Giraut, by Saint Martial, it weighs on me   IX
that you are leaving here at Christmas.

Lignaura, yes, soon, for a royal court,   X
I am leaving for a rich and noble court.[8]

ARNAUT DANIEL

(*b. 1150–1160; fl. 1180–1200*)

According to the *vida*, Arnaut came from Ribérac (Dordogne) in the bishopric of Périgueux, and was of noble birth. He thus came from an area close to the residences of Bertran de Born and Giraut de Borneil, with both of whom he was probably well acquainted. He claims that he attended the coronation of Philippe-Auguste in 1180 and that he was present in many courts and entourages, perhaps including that of Richard Lion-Heart.

With a few exceptions he composed in a style characterized by brilliant ornamentation, particularly by elaborate rhyming and by the use of rare words chosen for their sound effects, the sense falling where it may: the *vida* says his songs were hard to understand and learn. As a master craftsman he was greatly admired by Dante, who cites him several times in the *De vulgari eloquentia* and who tried his own hand at a form that Arnaut seems to have invented, the *sestina* (no. 40). In a famous passage in *Purgatorio*, xxvi, 115 ff, an Italian poet revered by Dante, Guido Guinizelli, points to Arnaut and hails him as *miglior fabbro del parlar materno*, a better craftsman of the mother tongue. Arnaut speaks to Dante in Occitan verses, a moving gesture of reverence on Dante's part and at the same time a demonstration of his own self-esteem and devotion to the glory of the "mother tongue" (Arnaut addresses him with the honorifice *vos*).

Text: *Canzoni*, ed. Gianluigi Toja. Florence: Sansoni, 1960.

L'aur' amara
fa·ls bruoills brancutz
clarzir
qe·l dous' espeis' ab fuoills,
5   e·ls letz
becs
dels auzels ramencs
ten balps e mutz,
pars
10   e non pars;
per q'eu m'esfortz
de far e dir
plazers
a mains, per liei
15   que m'a virat bas d'aut,
don tem morir
si·ls afans no m'asoma.

                                 I

Tant fo clara
ma prima lutz
20   d'eslir
lieis don cre·l cors los huoills,
non pretz
necs
mans dos aguilencs,
25   d'autra s'es dutz
rars

                                 II

mos preiars:
pero deportz
m'es ad auzir
30   volers,
bos motz ses grei
de liei, don tant m'azaut

38

The rough wind
traces out the ramify-
ing trees
that the sweet breeze weights with leaves,
5   and makes the joyful
beaks
of the birds in the branches
stammering and mute,
the paired   I
10   and the unpaired.
And so I force myself
in word and deed to bring
pleasures
to many, for the one
15   who has made me come down from the heights,
and now I fear death
if she does not end the sum of my afflictions.

So clarifying,
my first light when
20   I chose
her whose eyes my heart fears,
I prize
another
woman's secret messages
25   two thorns; my prayer
never   II
gets out of my mouth;
but it transports
me to hear
30   desires,
sweet words without vexation,
from her who is so to my liking,

qu'al sieu servir
sui del pe tro c'al coma.

35   Amors, gara,
        sui ben vencutz,
        c'auzir
        tem far, si·m desacuoills,
        tals d'etz
40   pecs
        que t'es mieills qe·t trencs;
        q'ieu soi fis drutz,
        cars   III
        e non vars,
45   ma·l cors ferms fortz
        mi fai cobrir
        mains vers;
        c'ab tot lo nei
        m'agr' ops us bais al chaut
50   cor refrezir,
        que no·i val autra goma.

        Si m'ampara
        cill cui·m trahutz,
        d'aizir,
55   si q'es de pretz capduoills,
        dels qetz
        precs
        c'ai dedinz a rencs,
        l'er for rendutz
60   clars   IV
        mos pensars:
        q'eu fora mortz,
        mas fa·m sofrir
        l'espers,
65   qe·ill prec qe·m brei,
        c'aisso·m ten let e baut;

I am in her service
from my foot to my hair.

35   Love, take note:
I am clearly conquered,
for I fear
I would tell, if you turn me away,
some of those
40   sins
of yours you'd be better off curtailing;
true, I am an honest lover,
rare,   III
unwavering;
45   but staid and steady, my heart
makes me cover
many truths,
to wit: with all her continual No,
I'd only need a kiss to cool
50   my hot heart down,
for no other balsam can do it.

If she helps me,
whose man I am,
gives shelter,
55   citadel of virtue,[1]
to the mute
prayers
I hold drawn up in ranks within,
my thought will come
60   clear   IV
before her:
by now I'd be dead,
but learn patience
from one hope
65   that I beg her cut short with fulfillment,
that keeps me going gay and proud:

---

[1] "Citadel of virtue": phrase stolen from André Berry.

que d'als iauzir
no·m val jois una poma.

Doussa car', a
70   totz aips volgutz,
sofrir
m'er per vos mainz orguoills,
car etz
decs
75   de totz mos fadencs,
don ai mains brutz

pars,[2]   V
e gabars
de vos no·m tortz
80   ni·m fai partir
avers,
c'anc non amei
ren tan ab meins d'ufaut,
anz vos desir
85   plus que Dieu cill de Doma.
Era·t para,
chans e condutz,
formir
al rei qui t'er escuoills;
90   car Pretz,
secs
sai, lai es doblencs
e mantengutz
dars   VI
95   e maniars:
de ioi la·t portz,
son anel mir
si·l ders:
c'anc non estei
100   iorn d'Aragon q'el saut

_____
[2] They make fun of him for his love.

for the joy of enjoying
another isn't worth an apple.

Sweet face,
70 with every trait desired,
to suffer
the arrogance of many will be mine for you,
for you are
the bourne
75 of all my follies;
that gets me many crude

friends; [2]   V
but no mockery
can twist me away from you,
80 nor would I go from here
for riches,
for I never loved
anything so much, with less display,
no, I desire you
85 more than the monks of Doma God.

Get ready now,
my song and melody,
to bring
your meaning to the king, who will receive you well;
90 for Glory,
dry
here, there has double foliage,
where repasts and the act of
giving   VI
95 survive.
Go there for joy,
venerate his ring
if he raises it:
for I have never been
100 a day from Aragón without desiring

no·i volgues ir,
mas sai m'a'n clamat Roma.[3]

Faitz es l'acortz,
q'el cor remir
105 totz sers
lieis cui dompnei   VII
ses parsonier, Arnaut,
q'en autr' albir
n'es fort m'entent' a soma.

39

En cest sonet coind'e leri
fauc motz e capuig e doli,
que serant verai e cert
qan n'aurai passat la lima;   I
5 q'Amors marves plan'e daura
mon chantar, que de liei mou
qui pretz manten e governa.

Tot iorn meillur et esmeri
car la gensor serv e coli
10 del mon, so·us dic en apert.
Sieus sui del pe tro q'en cima,   II
e si tot venta·ill freid'aura,
l'amors q'inz el cor mi plou
mi ten chaut on plus iverna.

15 Mil messas n'aug e·n proferi
e·n art lum de cer' e d'oli
que Dieus m'en don bon issert
de lieis on no·m val escrima;   III
e qan remir sa crin saura

[3] The reference to Rome is not understood. The word *roma* can also be taken as an imperative meaning: dwell here. See the discussion in the edition of Gianluigi Toja, *Canzoni* (Florence: Sansoni, 1961); cf. Hamlin, Ricketts,

to jump back to it,
but here Rome has summoned me away.[3]

It is agreed,

      for in my heart I gaze
105   each night
      on her I serve—I,   VII
      Arnaut, without a rival,
      and of every other thought
      my mind never reaches the end.

39

To this sweet and pretty air
I set words that I plane and finish;
and every word will fit well,
once I have passed the file there,   I
5 for at once Love polishes and aureates
my song, which proceeds from her,
ruler and guardian of merit.

Each day I am a better man and purer,
for I serve the noblest lady in the world,
10 and I worship her, I tell you this in the open.
I belong to her from my foot to the top of my head;   II
and let the cold wind blow,
love raining in my heart
keeps me warm when it winters most.

I hear a thousand masses and pay to have them said,
I burn lights of wax and oil,
so may God give me good luck with her,
for no defense against her does me any good.   III
When I look at her golden hair,

and Hathaway, p. 194. This line appears as follows in Toja: mas sai m'an
clamat: roma!

20 e·l cors q'es grailet e nou
   mais l'am que qi·m des Luserna.[1]

   Tant l'am de cor e la queri
   c'ab trop voler cug la·m toli
   s'om ren per ben amar pert.
25 Q'el sieus cors sobretracima   IV
   lo mieu tot e non s'eisaura;
   tant a de ver fait renou
   c'obrador n'a e taverna.

   No vuoill de Roma l'emperi
30 ni c'om m'en fassa apostoli,
   q'en lieis non aia revert
   per cui m'art lo cors e·m rima;   V
   e si·l maltraich no·m restaura
   ab un baisar anz d'annou
35 mi auci e si enferna.

   Ges pel maltraich q'ieu soferi
   de ben amar no·m destoli
   si tot me ten en desert,
   c'aissi·n fatz los motz en rima.   VI
40 Pieitz trac aman c'om que laura,
   c'anc plus non amet un ou
   cel de Moncli n'Audierna.[2]

   Ieu sui Arnautz q'amas l'aura,
   e chatz la lebre ab lo bou   VII
45 e nadi contra suberna.

[1] Possibly Lucena, in Aragón, in the province of Valencia; the scene of a
large part of the poem *Enfances Vivien*. He would love her more than he
would love the man who gave him this town.
[2] This allusion is not understood.

20 her soft young spirited body,
   if someone gave me Luserna, I'd still love her more.[1]

   I love her and seek her out with a heart so full,
   I think I am stealing her out of my own hands by too
                        much wanting,
   if a man can lose a thing by loving it well.
25 For the heart of her submerges   IV
   mine and does not abate.
   So usurious is her demand,
   she gets craftsman and workshop together.

   I do not want the empire of Rome,
30 do not make me pope of it
   so that I could not turn back to her
   for whom the heart in me burns and breaks apart.   V
   If she does not cure me of this torment
   with a kiss before new year's,
35 she murders me and sends herself to hell.

   But this torment I endure
   could not make me turn away from loving well,
   though it holds me fast in loneliness,
   for in this desert I cast my words in rhyme.   VI
40 I labor in loving more than a man who works the earth,
   for the Lord of Moncli did not love
   N'Audierna an egg's worth more.[2]

   I am Arnaut, who hoards the wind,
   and chases the hare on an ox,   VII
45 and swims against the tide.

40

Lo ferm voler q'el cor m'intra [1]
no·m pot ies becs escoissendre ni ongla
de lausengier, qui pert per mal dir s'arma;   I
e car non l'aus batr' ab ram ni ab verga,
5 sivals a frau, lai on non aurai oncle,[2]
iauzirai ioi, en vergier o dinz cambra.

Qan mi soven de la cambra
on a mon dan sai que nuills hom non intra
ans me son tuich plus que fraire ni oncle,   II
10 non ai membre no·m fremisca, neis l'ongla,
aissi cum fai l'enfas denant la verga:
tal paor ai no·l sia trop de l'arma.

Del cors li fos, non de l'arma,
e cossentis m'a celat dinz sa cambra!
15 Que plus mi nafra·l cor que colps de verga   III
car lo sieus sers lai on ill es non intra;
totz temps serai ab lieis cum carns et ongla,
e non creirai chastic d'amic ni d'oncle.

Anc la seror de mon oncle [3]
20 non amei plus ni tant, per aqest' arma!
C'aitant vezis cum es lo detz de l'ongla,   IV
s'a liei plagues, volgr' esser de sa cambra;
de mi pot far l'amors q'inz el cor m'intra
mieils a son vol c'om fortz de frevol verga.

---

[1] This is a sestina, a form that Arnaut seems to have invented. It consists of six strophes of six lines, the same rhymes appearing in a different order in each strophe. Lines that do not make too much sense in the translation are not clear in the original either.
[2] That is, to keep a watch on him; cf. ll. 9 and 18.
[3] That's his mother.

The firm desire that enters [1]
my heart no beak can tear out, no nail
of the slanderer, who speaks his dirt and loses his soul.   I
And since I dare not beat him with branch or rod,
5 then in some secret place, at least, where I'll have no
        uncle,[2]
I'll have my joy of joy, in a garden or a chamber.

When I am reminded of the chamber
where I know, and this hurts me, no man enters—
no, they're all more on guard than brother or uncle—   II
10 there's no part of my body that does not tremble, even
        my nail,
as the child shakes before the rod,
I am that afraid I won't be hers enough, with all my
        soul.

Let me be hers with my body, not my soul,
let her hide me in her chamber,
15 for it wounds my heart more than blows from a rod   III
that where she dwells her servant never enters;
I will always be as close to her as flesh and nail,
and never believe the reproaches of brother or uncle.

Not even the sister of my uncle [3]
20 did I love more, or as much, by my soul,
for as familiar as finger with nail   IV
I would, if it pleased her, be with her chamber.
It can do more as it wills with me, this love that enters
my heart, than a strong man with a tender rod.

25 Pois flori la seca verga [4]
   ni d'en Adam mogron nebot ni oncle,
   tant fin' amors cum cela q'el cor m'intra   V
   non cuig qu'anc fos en cors, ni eis en arma.
   On q'ill estei, fors en plaz', o dins cambra,
30 mos cors no·is part de lieis tant cum ten l'ongla.

   C'aissi s'enpren e s'enongla
   mos cors en lei cum l'escorss' en la verga;
   q'ill m'es de ioi tors e palaitz e cambra,   VI
   e non am tant fraire, paren ni oncle:
35 q'en paradis n'aura doble ioi m'arma,
   si ja nuills hom per ben amar lai intra.

   Arnautz tramet sa chansson d'ongl' e d'oncle,
   a grat de lieis que de sa verg' a l'arma,   VII
   son Desirat,[5] cui pretz en cambra intra.

---

[4] The dry branch that puts forth fruit is an image of the Virgin. Canello cites other instances of this image and observes that ll. 25–26 encompass the two epochs of the Old and New Testaments.
[5] *Senhal,* probably designating the lady.

25 Since the flower was brought forth on the dry rod,[4]
   and from En Adam descended nephews and uncles,
   a love so pure as that which enters   v
   my heart never dwelt in body, nor yet in soul.
   Wherever she stands, outside in the town or inside her
            chamber,
30 my heart is not further away than the length of a nail

   For my heart takes root in her and grips with its nail,
   holds on like bark on the rod,
   to me she is joy's tower and palace and chamber,   vi
   and I do not love brother as much, or father, or uncle;
35 and there'll be double joy in Paradise for my soul,
   if a man is blessed for loving well there and enters.

   Arnaut sends his song of the nail and the uncle,
   to please her who rules his soul with her rod,   vii
   to his Desired,[5] whose glory in every chamber enters.

BERTRAN DE BORN

(b. ca. 1140)

Bertran de Born was one of the minor noblemen whose fortunes
depended entirely on war, and his loyalty to this group never
wavered. He may have switched allegiances among the mighty
lords, but he was always the spokesman for the noble mercenaries
who saw their holdings, if they had any, confiscated if they
fought for the losing side, and who languished in poverty whenever there was a prolonged period of peace.

The life and the position of these petty nobles are lucidly
described by Marc Bloch in his classic work, *Feudal Society*.
Commenting on Bertran's *Be·m platz lo gais temps de Pascor*,
Bloch writes:

> The accurate observation and the fine verve, in contrast with the
> insipidity of what is usually a more conventional type of poetry,
> are the marks of an uncommon talent. The sentiment, on the
> other hand, is in no way extraordinary; as is shown in many
> another piece from the same social world . . . In war . . . the
> noble loved first and foremost the display of physical strength, the
> strength of a splendid animal, deliberately maintained by constant
> exercises, begun in childhood. "He who has stayed at school till
> the age of twelve," says a German poet [Hartmann von Aue], re-
> peating the old Carolingian proverb, "and never ridden a horse,
> is only fit to be a priest."
>   . . . Fighting was also, and perhaps above all, a source of profit
> —in fact, the nobleman's chief industry.
>   Bertran de Born made no secret of the less creditable reasons
> which above all disposed him "to find no pleasure in peace."
> "Why," he asks, "do I want rich men to hate each other?" "Because
> a rich man is much more noble, generous and affable in war than
> in peace." . . . The poet belonged to that class of petty holders of
> fiefs, the "vavasours"—he so described himself—for whom life in

the ancestral manor-house lacked both gaiety and comforts. War made up for these deficiencies by stimulating the liberality of the great and providing prizes worth having.

The baron, of course, out of regard for his prestige as well as his interest, could not afford to be niggardly in the matter of presents . . . Finally, in the face of the growing inadequacy of the vassal contingents, there was soon no army which could dispense with the assistance of that wandering body of warriors to whom adventure made so strong an appeal, provided that there was a prospect of gain as well as of mighty combats . . .

If the propensity to bloody deeds was prevalent everywhere— more than one abbot indeed met his death as the victim of a cloister feud—it was the conception of the necessity of war, as a source of honour and as a means of livelihood, that set apart the little group of "noble" folk from the rest of society.

(Translated by L. A. Manyon, University of Chicago Press, 1961, Vol. II, pp. 293–299.)

Bertran de Born thus expresses the viewpoint of the lower nobility, of the hired fighting hands whose gentle birth could not always be proved, and whose fortunes were uncertain; he speaks for those who had to look to the great ones higher up to sustain them and to make use of them. Bertran had his own castle, though he had earlier shared it with a brother whom he eventually managed to drive out. But the young men of this class who were in attendance in the courts of the mighty lords because they had no share in the ancestral fief owned nothing but a hereditary claim to nobility, and sometimes not even that. It was the interests and the aspirations of this inferior segment of courtly society, according to Erich Köhler, that formed the ethical and the sociological basis of the courtly love lyric. The relations in the love song reflect the social structure in which these aspiring young men wanted to find a dignified place. And the song, in representing true courtliness as an ethical condition that transcended all material distinctions, was thus intended to legitimize the position of these newcomers and to foster their integration into that privileged society.

Bertran joined a party of nobles in a revolt against Henry II and his son Richard Coeur de Lion. The revolt was led by the King's own eldest son, who was called "The Young King," and

[margin, handwritten:] portrays crusades, wars, frugal society

later generations believed that Bertran's songs were a major cause of this uprising of son against father, and brother against brother. In *Inferno* XXVIII, 113–142, Bertran appears with his head separated from his body, thus punished for pressing discord upon the members of the royal family. Whatever else it may signify, this grisly apparition is a great tribute to the power of Bertran's poetry. Dante's admiration is explicit in *De vulgari eloquentia*, II, 2, where he cites Bertran as the sole paragon of martial poetry.

The revolt failed. The Young King died in 1183, Bertran's castle of Hautefort was besieged and burned, and he became Richard's prisoner. Later, he managed to win Richard's pardon, and everything was restored to him; he always championed Richard's cause thereafter. The author of the *razo* has invented the following scene, erroneously substituting Henry II (who was not at the siege) for his son Richard:

And En Bertran, with all his people, was led to the pavilion of King Henry, and the King received him very badly, and King Henry said to him, "Bertran, Bertran, you have said that you never needed even half of your wit at any time, but know that today you truly need the whole of it." —"Lord," said En Bertran, "it is very true that I said it, and, indeed, I said the truth." And the King said, "I do believe that that wit of yours is failing you now." —"Lord," said En Bertran, "indeed, it is failing me." —"And how is that?" said the King. —"Lord," said En Bertran, "the day the valiant Young King, your son, died, I lost my wit, and my knowledge, and my understanding." And the King, when he heard what En Bertran said to him, weeping, about his son, great grief came to his heart, from pity, and to his eyes, and he could not keep from fainting with grief. And when he came out of the faint, he cried out and said, weeping: "En Bertran, En Bertran, you are right, and you have good cause, if you have lost your wit for my son, because he loved you more than any man in the world. And I, for love of him, set free your body, and your goods, and your castle, and I give you back my love and my grace, and I give you five hundred marks of silver for the losses you have suffered." And En Bertran fell at his feet, thanking him. And the King, with all his host, went away.

Bertran was one of the most exciting and original poets of the Middle Ages. The conventional troubadour themes are rethought in his poetry—note, for example, what happens to the *Natureingang* in no. 45. He celebrated the ritual beauty and horror of medieval warfare, with none of the vicious and sentimental archaism that now distinguishes the language of hawks; for war made a man and made money.

Text: *Die Lieder Bertrans von Born,* ed. Carl Appel. Halle: Max Niemeyer, 1932.

Lo plaintz qu'en Bertrans de Born fetz de·l rei jove no porta
autra razo si no que·l reis joves era lo melher om de·l mon, e'n
Bertrans li volia mielhs qu'ad ome de·l mon, e lo reis joves ad el
mielhs qu'ad ome de·l mon e plus lo crezia que home de·l mon;
per que lo reis Henrics, sos paire, e·l coms Richartz, sos fraire,
volian mal a'n Bertran. E per la valor que·l reis joves avia e per
lo gran dol qu'en fo a tota la gen el fetz lo plaint de lui que
dis . . .

    Mon chan fenisc ab dol et ab maltraire
    per totz temps mais e·l tenh per remasut,
    quar ma razo e mon gauch ai perdut
    e·l melhor rei que anc nasques de maire:
5   larc e gen parlan
    e be chavalgan,
    de bela faisso   I
    e d'umil semblan
    per far grans honors;
10 tan crei que·m destrenha
    lo dols, que m'estenha,
    quar en vau parlan.
    A dieu lo coman,
    que·l meta en luoc Saint Johan.

15 Reis de·ls cortes e de·ls pros emperaire
    foratz, senher, si acsetz mais viscut,
    quar "reis joves" aviatz nom agut
    e de joven eratz vos guitz e paire,
    et ausberc e bran
20 e bel bocharan,
    elm e gonfano   II
    e perponh e pan
    e jois et amors
    non an qui·ls mantenha

41

The planh that En Bertran de Born made for the Young King
bears no other explanation but that the Young King was the best
man in the world, and En Bertran loved him more than any
man in the world, and the Young King loved and trusted him
more than any man in the world, wherefore King Henry, his
father, and Count Richard, his brother, bore ill will against En
Bertran. And for the Young King's excellence and the great
grief over him among all the people, he made the planh for him
which says . . .

    I end my song in grief and misery,
    I hold it ended forever,
    for I have lost my cause and my pleasure,
    losing the greatest king ever born of woman,
5 large-handed, nobly spoken,
    well riding,
    graceful in his form   I
    and meek in his manner
    of giving great honors.
10 I feel the grief drawing tight
    around me, putting out my life
    even as I speak of it.
    I give him in trust to God,
    may He put him in the dwelling of Saint John.

15 King of the courtly and emperor of the valiant
    you would have been, Lord, if you had lived,
    for you came to be called the Young King,
    you were the guide and the father of all who are young.
    Hauberks and swords,
20 and handsome fabrics,
    helms and gonfalons,   II
    quilted doublets, rich garments,
    and joy, and love,
    these things have no one to preserve them,

25 ni qui los retenha,
    mas lai vos segran,
    qu'ab vos s'en iran
    e tuit ric fach ben estan.

    Gen acolhir e donar ses cor vaire
30 e bel respos e "be-siatz-vengut"
    e gran ostal paiat e gen tengut,
    dos e garnirs et estar ses tort faire,
    manjar ab mazan
    de viula e de chan
35 ab pro companho,   III
    ardit e poissan
    de totz los melhors:
    tot vuolh qu'ab vos tenha,
    qu'om re no·n retenha
40 a·l segle truan
    pe·l malastruc an,
    que nos mostret bel semblan.

    Senher, en vos non era res a faire,
    que totz lo mons vos avia elescut
45 pe·l melhor rei que anc portes escut
    e·l plus ardit e·l melhor torneiaire;
    des lo temps Rotlan
    ni de lai denan
    no vi hom tan pro   IV
50 ni tan guerreian
    ni don sa lauzors
    tan pe·l mon s'empenha
    ni si lo revenha
    . . . . an cerchan
55 per tot a garan
    de·l Nil tro·l solelh coljan.

    Senher, per vos mi vuolh de joi estraire,
    e tuit aquilh que·us avian vegut
    devon estar per vos irat e mut

25 no one to keep them here—
   no, they will follow you there,
   they will go away with you,
   with every right and noble act.

   Gentle receptions, giving without a changing heart,
30 handsome replies, and "Be Welcome,"
   grand lodgings accorded and nobly kept,
   gifts, bestowals of garments, abiding without doing
                wrong,
   repasts to the noise
   of viol and song
35 with a brave companion   III
   valiant and strong,
   among all the best—
   I want all these things to stay with you,
   let nothing remain
40 in this rabble world
   in this forsaken year,
   that once made us think it was beautiful.

   Lord, in you not one thing was missing,
   for all the world had chosen you
45 the greatest king that ever carried shield,
   the best, the bravest fighter in tournaments,
   from the time of Roland,
   and before that time,
   I never saw a man so brave,   IV
50 so warlike,
   nor whose renown
   so presses through the world
   and restores it,
   seeking it forth
55 in every corner, keeping vigil,
   from the Nile to the sunset.

   Lord, for you I want to wrest myself away from joy,
   and everyone who saw you
   now must stand mad with grief for you, and mute,

60 e ja mais jois la ira no m'esclaire;
   Engles e Norman,
   Breto et Yrlan,
   Guia et Guasco;   V
   et Anjaus pren dan
65 e Maines e Tors,
   Franza tro Compenha
   de plorar no·s tenha,
   e Flandres de Gan
   tro·l port de Guisan
70 ploren, neis li Alaman!

   Loirenc e Braiman,
   quan torneiaran,   VI
   auran dol, quan no·us veiran.

   No pretz un bezan
75 ni·l cop d'un aglan   VII
   lo mon ni cels que·i estan,

   per la mort pesan
   de·l bo rei prezan,   VIII
   on tuit devem aver dan.

42

   Miei sirventes vuolh far de·ls reis amdos,[1]
   qu'en brieu veirem qu'aura mais chavaliers:
   de·l valen rei de Castela, n'Anfos,
   qu'auch dir que ve e volra soudadiers;   I
 5 Richartz metra a muois et a sestiers
   aur et argen e te·s a benananza
   metr' e donar e no vol s'afianza,
   anz vol guerra mais que qualha esparviers.

[1] Alfonso VIII of Castile (1158–1214), son-in-law of Henry II of England; and Richard I (Coeur de Lion).

60 and never again will joy light up my gloom.
   Men of England and Normandy,
   Brittany and Ireland,
   Gascony and Aquitaine,   V
   and Anjou suffer this loss.
65 And Maine and Tours,
   all France to Compiègne
   cannot keep from weeping,
   and Flanders from Ghent
   to the port of Wissant,
70 and the Germans, too, let them weep.

   The men of Lorraine and Brabant
   when they are in the jousts   VI
   will have grief when they do not see you.

   It is not worth a cent,
75 not the cup of an acorn,   VII
   the world of those here who remain,

   now, after the sad death
   of the glorious Young King,   VIII
   for whom we suffer loss and pain.

   I shall make a half *sirventes* about both kings,[1]
   for soon we shall see who will have more riders:
   the valiant king of Castile, En Alfons,
   who is coming, I hear, and will want soldiers for pay;   I
5 Richard will pay by the bushel and the pail
   gold and silver, and he thinks he is lucky
   to pay out and give, and he wants no treaties,
   no, he wants war more than a hawk wants quail.

S'amdui li rei son pro ni coratjos,
10 en brieu veirem champs jonchatz de quartiers,
d'elms e d'escutz e de brans e d'arzos
e de fendutz per bustz tro a·ls braiers;   II
et arratge veirem anar destriers
e per costatz e per pechs mainta lanza
15 e gauch e plor e dol et alegranza:
lo perdr' er grans e·l guazanhs er sobriers.

Trompas, tabors, senheras e penos
et entresenhs e chavals blancs e niers
veirem en brieu, que·l segles sera bos,
20 que hom tolra l'aver a·ls usuriers,   III
e per chamis non anara saumiers

jorn afiatz ni borges ses doptanza
ni merchadiers qui venha de ves Franza,
anz sera rics qui tolra volontiers.

25 Mas si·l reis ve, ieu ai en dieu fianza,   IV
qu'ieu serai vius o serai per quartiers;

e si sui vius, er mi grans benananza,   V
e si ieu muoir, er mi grans deliuriers.

43

Domna, puois de me no·us chal
e partit m'avetz de vos
senes totas ochaisos,
no sai on m'enquieira;
5 que ja mais   I
non er per me tan rics jais
cobratz; e, si del semblan
no trop domna a mon talan

If both of the kings are brave and spirited,
10 soon we shall see the fields bestrewn with fragments,
helms and shields and swords and saddlebows,
and corpses cloven through the trunk to the cinctures,   II
and the coursers we shall see running wild,
and in sides and breasts many lances,
15 and joy and weeping and grief and celebration:
the loss will be great, but the winnings will be greater.

Trumpets and tabors, ensigns and pennons,
banners and horses white and black
we shall soon see, and life will be good,
20 we shall pillage the stores of the usurers,   III
and on the roads the sumpters will not go

safely in the light, nor the burgher without wondering,
nor any merchant traveling from France,
no, but he will be rich who will gladly take.

25 If the King comes, I put my faith in God   IV
I shall be alive or in pieces.

And if I am alive, it will be great luck,   V
and if I am dead, a great deliverance.

Lady, since you do not care for me
and have sent me away
without any cause,
I do not know where to give my love,
5 for never   I
will I find such noble joy
again. And if in the look of her
I do not find a lady I desire,

que valha vos qu'ai perduda,
10 ja mais no vuolh aver druda.

Puois no·us puosc trobar engal,
que fos tan bela ni pros,
ni sos rics cors tan joios,
de tan bela tieira
15 ni tan gais   II
ni sos rics pretz tan verais,
irai per tot achaptan
de chascuna un bel semblan
per far domna soisseubuda,
20 tro vos mi siatz renduda.

Frescha color natural
pren, bels Cembelis, de vos
e·l doutz esgart amoros;
e fatz gran sobrieira
25 quar re·i lais,   III
qu'anc res de be no·us sofrais.
Midons n'Aelis deman
son adrech parlar gaban,
que·m don a midons aiuda;
30 puois non er fada ni muda.

De Chales la vescomtal
vuolh que·m done ad estros
la gola e·ls mas amdos.
Puois tenh ma charrieira,
35 no·m biais,   IV
ves Rochachoart m'eslais
als pels n'Anhes que·m dara·n;
qu' Iseutz, la domna Tristan,
qu'en fo per totz mentauguda,
40 no·ls ac tan bels a saubuda.

N'Audiartz, si be·m vol mal,
vuolh que·m do de sas faissos,

the equal of you, whom I have lost,
10 I do not want to love anyone again.

And since I can find no one as good as you,
none so beautiful and spirited,
or her noble body so full of rejoicing,
so graceful,
15 or so courtly,   II
or her proud fame so true,
I shall go everywhere collecting
from each lady one beautiful image,
and so make one assembled lady
20 until you are restored to me.

The pristine, natural color,
fair Cembelis, I take from you,
and the soft look full of love;
and I am guilty of extravagance,
25 leaving anything untaken,   III
for no good thing was ever missing in you.
Of my lady Aelis de Montfort I ask
her adroit and frolicsome speech,
let her help me with my lady,
30 who will not then be foolish and mute.

I ask the Vicomtesse of Chalais
to donate at once
the throat and both hands.
Then I hold my course,
35 I do not digress   IV
I rush to the hair of the lady Agnes
de Rochechouard, she will give me some.
For though Iseult, the lady of Tristan,
was celebrated for it everywhere,
40 we know even she did not have such beautiful hair.
Audiart of Malamort, though she wishes me ill,
I want her to give me something of her whole de-
            meanor.

que·lh estai gen liazos,
e quar es entieira,
45 qu'anc no·s frais   V
s'amors ni·s vols en biais.
A mo Mielhs-de-be deman
son adrech, nuou cors prezan,
de que par a la veguda,
50 la fassa bo tener nuda.

De na Faidid' autretal
vuolh sas belas dens en dos,
l'acolhir e·l gen respos
don es presentieira
55 dintz son ais.   VI
Mos Bels Miralhs vuolh que·m lais
sa gaieza e son bel gran,
e quar sap son benestan
far, don es reconoguda,
60 e no s'en chamja ni·s muda.

Bels Senher, ieu no·us quier al
Mas que fos tan cobeitos
d'aquesta com sui de vos;
qu'una lechadieira
65 amors nais,   VII
don mos cors es tan lechais:
mais vuolh de vos lo deman
que autra tener baisan.
Doncs midons per que·m refuda,
70 puois sap que tan l'ai volguda?

Papiols, mon Aziman [1]
m'anaras dir en chantan   VIII
qu'amors es desconoguda
sai e d'aut bas chazeguda.

[1] Folquet de Marseille (Appel).

for it sits like a noble garment on her,
it is perfect,
45   her love never decays   V
or twists in crooked ways.
Of my Mielhs-de-be I request
her adroit and glorious young body,
for the eyes can see, beholding my Better-than-Good,
50   what pleasure it would be to hold her nude.

Of Na Faidida, item,
I want her beautiful teeth in gift,
the reception and the soft response,
of which she is so bountiful
55   in her residence.   VI
I ask my Fair Mirror to give
her gladness and her perfect size;
she knows and does what most befits her,
and so her good fame widely ranges,
60   and she never fails in this, or changes.

Bel-Senher, I ask nothing else of you
except that I long
for this assembled lady as I long for you;
let one sensual
65   love be born,   VII
and my body as full of lust,
for I want the longing for you more
than kissing someone else in my arms.
Why then does my lady, as she knows
70   how I have wanted her, refuse?

Papiols, you will go for me
to tell my Magnet,[1] singing,   VIII
that love is unrecognized
here and fallen from high to low

44

Bel m'es, quan vei chamjar lo senhoratge,
que·lh vielh laissan a·ls joves lor maisos,
e chascus pot laissar en son linhatge
tans filhs que l'us puoscha esser pros:
5 adoncs m'es vis que·l segles renovel
mielhs que per flor ni per chantar d'auzel;
e qui senhor ni domna pot chamjar,
vielh per jove, be·s deu renovelar.

Per vielha tenh domna, [puois qu'a pelatge,]
10 et es vielha, quan chavalier non a;
vielha la tenh, [si de dos drutz s'apatge]
et es vielha, quant avols hom lo·lh fa;   II
vielha la tenh, si ama dintz son chastel,
et es vielha, quan l'a ops de fachel;
15 vielha la tenh, puois l'enoian joglar,
et es vielha, quan trop vuolha parlar.

Joves es domna que sap honrar paratge
et es joves per bos fachs, quan los fa,
joves si te, quan a adrech coratge
20 et ves bo pretz avol mestier non a;   III
joves si te, quan guarda son cors bel,
et es joves domna, quan be·s chapdel;
joves si te, quan no·i chal divinar,
qu'ab bel joven si guart de mal estar.

25 Joves es hom que lo sieu ben engatge,
et es joves, quan es be sofrachos;
per jove·l tenh, quan pro·lh costan ostatge,
et es joves, quan fai estragatz dos;   IV
joves, quan art s'archa ni son vaissel,
30 joves quan vol bastir cort e cembel;

It pleases me to see the lordship change
and the old relinquishing their mansions to the young;
every man can leave in his lineage
enough sons so that one, at least, is brave: I
5   it is this, and not some flower or the twittering of birds,
makes me feel the earth is new again.
And if a man wants to change his old lord or lady
for a young one, he will be in his best days again.

I say a lady is old when her hair falls out,
10   and she is old when no knight attends her;
old if she is pleasured by more than one lover,
old if some common brute does it to her,   II
old if she only grants her favors at home,
old if she must use witchcraft and little tricks,
15   and I consider her old when singers vex her,
and she is old when she likes to talk too much.

A lady is young when she honors her class,
and she is young in her good deeds, when she does them,
and stays young by her honest heart,
20   when she does not abuse good merit and fame,   III
young when she cares for her beauty,
and a lady is young when she bears herself well,
stays young when she isn't just dying to find something
          out,
and when she holds back, with some handsome youth,
          from doing wrong.

25   A man is young when he stakes everything he has,
and young when he has nothing left,
young when his hospitality costs him a fortune,
young when he makes reckless gifts,   IV
young when his money burns a whole in his pocket,[1]
30   and he wants to hold court and tournaments:

[1] Literally, "'when he burns up the chest and container."

per jove·l tenh, quan ben vuolha jogar,
et es joves, quan sap ben domneiar.

Vielhs es rics hom, quan re no met en gatge
e li sobra blatz e vis e bacos;
35 per vielh lo tenh, quan liura uous e fromatge
a jorn charnal (si non:) sos companhos;   v
per vielh, quan vest chapa sobre mantel,
per vielh, quan a chaval qu'om sieu apel;
vielhs es, quan vol un jorn en patz estar,
40 e vielhs, si pot guandir ses baratar.

Mo sirventesc port' e vielh e novel,   vi
Arnautz joglars, a Richart, que·l chapdel,
e ja tesaur vielh no vuolh' amassar,
qu'ab tesaur jove pot pretz guazanhar.

45

Be·m platz lo gais temps de pascor,
que fai fuolhas e flors venir;
e platz mi, quan auch la baudor
dels auzels, que fan retentir
5 lor chan per lo boschatge;   i
e platz mi, quan vei sobre·ls pratz
tendas e pavilhos fermatz;
et ai gran alegratge,
quan vei per champanha renjatz
10 chavaliers e chavals armatz.

E platz mi, quan li corredor
fan las gens e l'aver fugir;
e platz mi, quan vei apres lor
gran re d'armatz ensems venir;
15 e platz mi en mon coratge,   ii
quan vei fortz chastels assetjatz

and he stays young when he loves to sit down to a game,
and he is young when he knows how to serve a lady well.

A man of means is old when he won't risk a thing,
and he hoards up grain and wine and bacon;
35 and I consider him old when he puts eggs and cheese on
      the table
for himself and his friends on meat-eating days,   v
old when he has to wear a hood on top of his cloak,
old when he owns a horse another man has trained;
he is old when he wants to sit one day in peace,
40 and old when he can pull out before he squanders every-
      thing.

Arnaut jongleur, take my *sirventes* about young
and old to Richard, let it guide him,   VI
may he never want to pile up old-man's treasure
when he can win glory with the riches of the young.

45

I love the joyful time of Easter,
that makes the leaves and flowers come forth,
and it pleases me to hear the mirth
of the birds, who make their song
5 resound through the woods,   I
and it pleases me to see upon the meadows
tents and pavilions planted,
and I feel a great joy
when I see ranged along the field
10 knights and horses armed for war.

And it pleases me when the skirmishers
make the people and their baggage run away,
and it pleases me when I see behind them coming
a great mass of armed men together,
15 and I have pleasure in my heart   II
when I see strong castles besieged,

e·ls barris rotz et esfondratz
e vei l'ost el ribatge,
qu'es tot entorn claus de fossatz
20 ab lissas de fortz pals serratz.

Ee autresi·m platz de senhor,
quan es primiers a l'envazir
en chaval, armatz, ses temor,
qu'aissi fai los sieus enardir
25 ab valen vassalatge.   III

e puois que l'estorns es mesclatz,
chascus deu esser acesmatz
e segre·l d'agradatge,
que nuls om non es re prezatz,
30 tro qu'a maintz colps pres e donatz.

Massas e brans, elms de color,
Escutz trauchar e desguarnir
veirem a l'entrar de l'estor
e maintz vassals ensems ferir,
35 don anaran arratge   IV
chaval dels mortz e dels nafratz.
E quan er en l'estorn entratz,
chascus om de paratge
no pens mas d'asclar chaps e bratz,
40 que mais val mortz que vius sobratz.

Ie·us dic que tan no m'a sabor
manjar ni beure ni dormir
com a, quan auch cridar: "A lor!"
d'ambas las partz et auch ennir
45 chavals vochs per l'ombratge,   V
et auch cridar: "Aidatz! Aidatz!"
E vei chazer per los fossatz
paucs e grans per l'erbatge,
e vei los mortz que pels costatz
50 an los tronzos ab los cendatz.

the broken ramparts caving in,
and I see the host on the water's edge,
closed in all around by ditches,
20 with palisades, strong stakes close together.

And I am as well pleased by a lord
when he is first in the attack,
armed, upon his horse, unafraid,
so he makes his men take heart
25 by his own brave lordliness.   III

And when the armies mix in battle,
each man should be poised
to follow him, smiling,
for no man is worth a thing
30 till he has given and gotten blow on blow.

Maces and swords and painted helms,
the useless shields cut through,
we shall see as the fighting starts,
and many vassals together striking,
35 and wandering wildly,   IV
the unreined horses of the wounded and dead.
And once entered into battle
let every man proud of his birth
think only of breaking arms and heads,
40 for a man is worth more dead than alive and beaten.

I tell you there is not so much savor
in eating or drinking or sleeping,
as when I hear them scream, "There they are! Let's get
            them!"
on both sides, and I hear riderless
45 horses in the shadows, neighing,   V
and I hear them scream, "Help! Help!"
and I see them fall among the ditches,
little men and great men on the grass,
and I see fixed in the flanks of the corpses
50 stumps of lances with silken streamers.

Baro, metetz en gatge
chastels e vilas e ciutatz   VI
enanz qu'usquecs no·us guerreiatz!

Papiols, d'agradatge
55 a'n Oc-e-No t'en vai viatz [1]   VII
e dijas li que trop estai en patz.

[1] Richard Lion-Heart. The attribution of this song is not certain.

Barons, pawn your castles,
and your villages, and your cities   VI
before you stop making war on one another.

Papiols, gladly go
55 fast to my Lord Yes-and-No [1]   VII
and tell him he has lived in peace too long.

PEIRE VIDAL

(*fl. 1180–1205*)

As one can tell from the numerous personal references in his songs, Peire Vidal spent time in many places—including France, Italy, Spain, Palestine, and Hungary—and served many patrons, of whom the most important were Count Ramon V of Toulouse (the poet's native city), King Alfonso II of Aragón, and Vicomte Barral of Marseille.

As Ernest Hoepffner has pointed out, many of Peire Vidal's songs are in a "hybrid genre," combining the conventions of the love song (*canso*) and the political song (*sirventes*). The singer denounces the enemies (or, in one striking case, the ally) of his patron with the fierceness of a warrior, and praises the white skin and the gentleness of his lady with the longing of a lover— all in the same song, ringing with the names of cities and great personages and the *senhal* of his beloved. These songs, in which the courtly lover expresses his political passion and the partisan longs for joy, are unprecedented. It is the triumph of a performer who takes the stance of one character and speaks the words of another—in other words, of a performer who does not limit himself to the traditional rôles but mixes them up and so surprises his audience.

This same sense of the immediate personal presence of a named indivdual who speaks directly and not in rôles is conveyed by his boasts—the most wonderful boasts since Guillaume IX— which also rely for their effect on an audience that knows this man through and through. This intimacy with the audience and his performer's attitude of self-esteem and self-mockery are characteristic of his songs. His *vida* has made up some amazing adventures for him by taking his figurative expressions literally.

Peire Vidal was from Toulouse, the son of a furrier. And he

sang better than any man in the world. And he was one of the maddest men who ever were, for he believed to be true whatever pleased him and whatever he wanted. And making songs came to him more easily than to any other man in the world; and it was he who made the loveliest melodies and said the craziest things concerning arms and love and slandering another. And it was true that a knight of Saint Gilles had his tongue cut out, because he (Peire Vidal) gave him to understand that he (Peire Vidal) was the lover of his wife. And En Hugues of Les Baux had him taken care of and treated. And when he was cured, he went away across the sea. From there he led forth a Greek woman who had been given him as wife in Cyprus. And he was given to understand that she was the niece of the Emperor of Constantinople and that through her he ought, by right, to get the empire. And so he put all that he could earn into building a vessel, for he thought he was going to conquer the empire. And he bore imperial arms and had himself called emperor, and his wife empress. And he courted all the noble ladies he saw and asked them all for their love, and they all told him to do and say whatever he wished; and because of that he thought he was the lover of them all and that each one was dying for him. And he always led noble steeds and bore noble arms and the imperial seat. And he thought he was the best knight in the world and the one most loved by ladies.

Text: *Poesie,* ed. D'arco Silvio Avalle. 2 vols. Milan and Naples: Riccardo Ricciardi, 1960.

46

Drogoman senher, s'ieu agues bon destrier,[1]
en fol plag foran intrat tuich mei guerrier:
qu'aqui mezeis quant hom lor mi mentau   I
mi temon plus que cailla esparvier,
5 e no prezon lur vida un denier,
tan mi sabon fer e salvatg' e brau.

Quant ai vestit mon fort ausberc doblier
e seint lo bran que·m det En Gui l'autrier,
la terra crolla per aqui on ieu vau;   II
10 e non ai enemic tan sobrancier
que tost no·m lais las vias e·l sentier,
tan mi dupton quan senton mon esclau.

D'ardimen vaill Rotlan et Olivier
e de domnei Berart de Mondesdier; [2]
15 car soi tan pros, per aquo n'ai bon lau,   III
que sovendet m'en venon messatgier
ab anels d'aur, ab cordon blanc e nier,
ab tals salutz don totz mos cors s'esjau.

En totas res sembli ben cavallier;
20 si·m sui, e sai d'amor tot son mestier
e tot aisso qu'a drudairi' abau;   IV
anc en cambra non ac tan plazentier
ni ab armas tan mal ni tan sobrier,
don m'am' e·m tem tals que no·m ve ni m'au.

25 E s'ieu agues caval adreg corsier
suau s'estes lo reis part Balaguier

---

[1] "Drogoman" is a *senhal*, probably designating, according to Ernest Hoepffner, Guillaume VIII of Montpellier, who was an ally of Alfonso II of Aragón ("the King"—l. 31) in his war against Raimon V of Toulouse ("the
Count"—l. 32). The Count was one of the earliest of Peire Vidal's patrons,
and Peire seems to have broken with him around 1186. Balaguer (l. 26), a

46

My Lord Go-Between, if only I had a good horse,[1]
my enemies would be in one hell of a fix,
for as soon as they hear my name   I
they're more afraid of me than a quail is of a hawk
5 and do not think their life is worth a cent,
that's how cruel they know I am, and wild, and terrible.

When I have put on my great double hauberk
and girded on the sword En Guy gave me the other day,
the earth trembles where I set my foot.   II
10 And I have no enemy so proud
he does not leave the roads and paths for me, and fast,
that's how much they fear me when they hear my step.

For warrior's nerve I am worth Roland and Olivier,
and for making love to these ladies Bérard de Mont-
didier,[2]
15 and I am such a man—I am famous for this—   III
messengers keep coming to me
with golden rings and a silken ribbon in black and
white,
and love letters that fill me with joy.

No matter what I do, I look like a knight,
20 for I am a knight, and in love I am a master of the craft,
and of everything that fits when a man is with a woman;   IV
there never was a man so pleasing in a chamber
or so savage and excellent in armor,
and so I am loved and dreaded by such as do not even
see me or hear my words.

25 And if only I had a good running horse
the King would be serene outside of Balaguer,

city in the kingdom of Aragón.
[2] An epic hero (Hoepffner).

e dormis si planamen e suau;   V
que·il tengr'en patz Proens' e Monpeslier,
que raubador ni malvatz rocinier
30 no rauberon ni Autaves ni Crau.[3]

E si·l reis torn' a Tholos' el gravier,
e n'eis lo coms e siei caitiu dardier,
que tot jorn cridon: "Aspa et Orsau!" [4]   VI
de tan mi van qu'ieu n'aurai·l colp premier,
35 e ferrai tan que n'intraran doblier,
et ieu ab lor, qui la porta no·m clau.

E si'ieu cossec gilos ni lauzengier
qu'ap fals cosselh gastan l'autrui sabrier
e baisson joi a presen et a frau,   VII
40 per ver sabra qual son li colp qu'ieu fier:
que s'avia cors de fer o d'acier
no lur valra una pluma de pau.

Na Vierna, merce de Monpeslier [5]
en raina sai amaretz cavailler;   VIII
45 don jois m'es mais cregutz per vos, Dieu lau.

47

Ab l'alen tir vas me l'aire
qu'eu sen venir de Proensa;
tot quant es de lai m'agensa,
si que, quan n'aug ben retraire,   I
5 ieu m'o escout en rizen
e·n deman per un mot cen:
tan m'es bel quan n'aug ben dire.

---

[3] "If Peire thus defended these rocky regions, it is all the more certain that he would not let anyone enter the regions more hospitable to culture and habitation." (Hamlin, Ricketts, and Hathaway)

and sleep so softly and so quietly,   V
for I would keep his peace in Provence and Montpellier,
and no robbers, no miserable bandits on their nags
30 would even rob La Crau or Le Tavez.[3]   .

And if the King turns toward Toulouse, along the stony
          banks,
and the Count comes out with those broken-down arch-
          ers of his
forever shouting "Aspa!" and Orsau!" [4]   VI
the first blow will be mine, now this much I boast,
35 and I will strike so that they will run back in twos, one
          on top of the other,
and I with them, unless they shut the gate on me.

And if ever I catch up with those jealous cuckolds and
          those lisping spies
who ruin a man's pleasure with their lies
and bring down joy, openly, or in secret,   VII
40 I swear they'll know what blows I strike:
because if they had bodies of iron and steel,
it won't help them worth a feather from a peacock's tail.

Na Vierna, thanks to Montpellier,[5]
now you will love a warrior in this battle;   VIII
45 and as you have made my joy increase, I praise God.

47

With my breath I draw toward me the air
that I feel coming from Provence;
everything that comes from there rejoices me,
so that when I hear good of it   I
5 I listen smiling,
and for every word demand a hundred:
so much it pleases me when I hear good of it.

[4] Two valleys in the Pyrénées, hence the war cry of the Basque mercenaries
in the Count's army.
[5] Na Vierna, one of the ladies frequently celebrated in P. V.'s songs.

Qu'om no sap tan dous repaire
com de Rozer tro qu'a Vensa,
10 si cum clau mars e Durensa,
ni on tant fins jois s'esclaire.   II
Per qu'entre la franca gen
ai laissat mon cor jauzen
ab lieis que fa·ls iratz rire.

15 Qu'om no pot lo jorn mal traire
qu'aja de lieis sovinensa,
qu'en liei nais jois e comensa.
E qui qu'en sia lauzaire,   III
de ben qu'en diga no·i men;
20 que·l mielher es ses conten
e·l genser qu'el mon se mire.

E s'ieu sai ren dir ni faire,
ilh n'aia·l grat, que sciensa
m'a donat e conoissensa,
25 per qu'ieu sui gais e chantaire.   IV
E tot quan fauc d'avinen
ai del sieu bell cors plazen,
neis quan de bon cor consire.

48

Ajostar   e lassar
sai tan gent motz e so,
que del car   ric trobar
no·m ven hom al talo,
5 quant n'ai bona razo.
Mas auci   me aissi
la bella de cui so,
cum s'ieu fes mespreizo   I
vas lieis o tracio.
10 Quant la vi   si·m feri

For no one knows so sweet a country
as from the Rhône to Vence,
10 enclosed between the sea and the Durance,
and nowhere knows a joy so pure that shines.   II
And so among those noble people
I have left my rejoicing heart
with her who brings laughter back to the afflicted.

15 For a man cannot draw bad luck
the day he thinks of her,
for joy is born in her and comes forth to us.
And whoever praises her   III
and whatever he says, he tells no lie:
20 for there's no arguing: she's the best
and the gentlest beheld in this world.

And if I can do or say a thing or two,
let the thanks be hers, for she
gave me the understanding and the craft,
25 because of her I am courtly, and a poet.   IV
And everything I do that is fitting
I infer from her beautiful body,
and even these words of longing, rising from my heart.

48

I can put together and inter-
lace words and music with such skill,
in the noble art of song
no man comes near my heel,
5 when I have a good subject.
And yet, behold, she kills me,
the beautiful one I belong to:
as though I had done some wrong,   I
some treachery, against her.
10 When I first saw her, she struck

mon coratge gloto,
qu'ades poinh el sieu pro,
e no·m fai si mal no.
Mal mi vol e no sai per que,
15 mas sol quar am lieis mais que me.

Assatz par que lonhar
me volc de sa reio,
quan passar mi fes mar,
per qu'ieu la·n ochaizo.
20 Mas no·i ai sospeisso,[1]
qu'ieu·l servi ab cor fi,
tan quan puec a bando,
e no·n aic guizardo,   II
mas sol d'un pauc cordo.

25 Si agui, qu'un mati
intrei dins sa maizo
e·lh baiziei a lairo
la boca e·l mento.
So n'ai agut e no mais re
30 e sui totz mortz, si·l plus rete.

Sospirar e plorar
mi fai manta sazo,
qu'alegrar e chantar
volgra mais, si·l fos bo;
35 mas cor a de drago,
qu'a me di mal e ri
als autres deviro,
e·m fai huelhs de leo: III
per aital faillizo
40 fes de mi pelegri,
qu'anc romieus d'orazo
mais ta forsatz no fo.
E qui·l ver en despo,

---

[1] *Sospeisso* means both "hope" and "fear."

my ravening heart so
that always I take pains for her good,
and she takes no pains for me, except for ill.
She wishes me ill, and I don't know why,
15 except that I love her more than myself.

It's clear enough, she wanted
to get me far away from her own land
when she made me cross the sea,
and I reproach her for that.
20 But I don't look ahead in love,[1]
and I served her with a faithful heart,
with all my strength, without holding back,
and I had no requital,   II
except for a bit of ribbon once.

25 Well, yes, I had this one morning:
I entered her chamber
and kissed her like a thief
on the mouth and the chin.
That's what I've had of her, and not another thing,
30 and I am dead if she holds back the rest.

She makes me weep
and sigh many times,
when I would prefer to rejoice
and to sing, if that pleased her.
35 But she has the heart of a dragon,
because to me she says cruel things and smiles
to the others around, and smiling   III
makes lion's eyes to me.
Now through such unkindness
40 she's made a pilgrim out of me,
and no man bound on a holy voyage
was ever more miserable.
And to lay bare the truth,

totz hom deu percassar son be,
45 ans que mals seinhers lo malme.

Abrazar   e cremar
mi fai cum fuecs carbo.
Quan l'esgar,   tan vei clar
sos heulhs e sa faisso,
50 que non sai guerizo,
si·m cambi   ni·m desvi
d'amar liei. Hai baro!
Co·m te en sa preizo   IV
Amors, que Salamo,
55 e Davi   atressi
venquet e·l fort Samso,
e·ls tenc en son grillo,
qu'anc non ac rezemso
tro a la mort; e pus mi te,
60 ad estar m'er a sa merce.

Esperar   e muzar
mi fai coma Breto,[2]
qu'anc l'amar   ni l'honrar
no·lh mis en contenso.
65 Ans, si Dieus mi perdo,
m'en parti   de tal qui
m'agra dat tan ric do,
que·l bos reis d'Arago   V
for' honratz; e doncs co

70 me faidi? Qu'ie·us afi,
quan n'aug dir bon resso,
gaugz entiers mi somo
qu'en deia far chanso.
E doncs pus tan l'am e la cre,
75 ja no·i dei trobar mala fe.

---

[2] That is, like one who waits for King Arthur's return.

a man had better ferret out what he wants
45 before a bad lord starts mistreating him.

She kindles me and sets me
aflame like fire on coal.
When I gaze on her I see such light
in her eyes and her face,
50 I cannot be restored
if I change or turn away
from loving her—o, lords,
how Love holds me in his prison,   IV
Love, who conquered Solomon,
55 yes, and conquered David,
and the mighty Samson,
held them in his chains,
and there was no deliverance
till death, and now since he holds me,
60 I will have to be at his mercy.

She makes me hope and wait
around like a Breton,[2]
and yet loving and honoring her
was never a thing I debated about.
65 Rather, God forgive me,
I parted from one such
as would have given me so rich a gift
the good king of Aragón himself   V
would have been honored by it; then how

70 did I go into exile? Because I swear to you,
when I hear her good fame spread
one simple joy summons me
to make a song of it.
Well then, since I love her so and follow her command,
75 I should not find bad faith in her.

Pus pauzar ni finar
no puesc nulha sazo,
retornar et anar
m'en vuelh ad espero
80 entr' Arle e Tolo
a tapi, quar aqui
am mais un pauc cambo,
qu'aver sai Lo Daro,   VI
ni aver Lo Toro
85 n'Ibeli: [3] mas frairi
fals lauzengier gloto
m'an moguda tenso
e lunhat del Peiro,[4]
e'N Drogomans no m'au ni·m ve,
90 quar mon car Amic part de se.[5]

A mon amic Folco [6]
tramet lai ma chanso   VII
que la chant en bon loc per me,
al tenen on joi vai e ve.

95 Mal astre Dieus li do,
qui·l comte d'Avinho [7]   VIII
mesclet tan malament ab me,
per que Na Vierna no·m ve.

Mas a Tripol [8] m'ado,
100 que quan l'autre baro   IX
caço prez, et el lo rete
e no·l laissa partir de se.

[3] All localities in Palestine.
[4] In Toulouse.
[5] According to Avalle, *Amic* is Eudoxia of Constantinople, repudiated by her
husband, Guillaume VIII of Montpellier ("Drogoman"), in 1187, a wrong
that Peire Vidal has not forgiven.
[6] Folquet de Marseille (q.v.), who sang of the same woman called Vierna.
[7] Raimon V, Count of Toulouse, one of Peire Vidal's protectors. A quarrel
between them may have been caused by one of Vidal's lyrics, *Son ben apode-
ratz*, in which he attacks Raimon.
[8] Raimon II, cousin of the Count of Toulouse, d. 1187.

Since I cannot come to rest
or find the end in any season,
I want to come back
on the spur and walk around
80 between Arles and Toulon,
secretly, unseen, for there
I love one little field more
than getting fortresses and cities here,   VI
Le Daron, or Le Toron,
85 or Ibelin; [3] but those slimy
grubbing slanderers with their lies
have launched a campaign against me
and kept me far from Lo Peiro, [4]
and En Drogoman does not hear me or see me any
                    more,
90 for he casts my dear Friend away. [5]

To my friend Folco, [6]
there, I send my song,   VII
let him sing it for me in a good place,
where joy comes and goes.

95 God give them an unlucky star
who stirred up the Count   VIII
of Avignon [7] against me and did me harm,
so that Na Vierna does not see me now.

But I give myself to the Lord
100 of Tripoli, [8] who, when other lords   IX
chase out worth, he retains it
and never lets it part from him.

49

Bon' aventura don Dieus als Pizas,[1]
quar son ardit e d'armas ben apres,
e an baissat l'erguelh des Genoes,
que·ls fan estar aunitz e soteiras: I
5   per qu'ieu volrai tostemps l'onor de Piza,
quar an baissatz los perfietz ergulhos;
que sol l'enueis dels vilas borbonos
me trenca·l cor e·l me franh e·l me briza.

Alamans trop descauzitz e vilas,
10 e quan negus si fenh d'esser cortes,
ira mortals cozens et enueitz es:
e lor parlars sembla lairar de cas;   II
per qu'ieu no vuelh esser senher de Friza,
qu'auzis soven lo glat dels enuios:
15 ans vuelh estar entre·ls Lombartz joyos,
pres de midons, qu'es blanqu' e gras' e liza.

E pus mieus es Monferratz e Milas,[2]
a mon dan giet Alamans e Ties;
e si·m creira Richartz, reis dels Engles,
20 em breu d'ora tornara per sas mas   III
lo regisme de Palerm' e de Riza,
quar lo conquis la soa rezemsos.
De mi dic ben: si pel Marques no fos,

---

[1] In 1194–1195, Henry VI, the German Emperor, launched a campaign against Sicily and Apulia. Peire Vidal in this song exhorts the cities of Lombardy, which were divided into two antagonistic groups headed, respectively, by Milan and Pavia, to unite against the Emperor. Richard Coeur de Lion was a captive of the Emperor, who, in Vidal's eyes, treated Richard badly, exacting an enormous ransom for his release (l. 22), which helped him launch his campaign. This violent attack against the Germans is a little surprising,

49

God give good luck to the men of Pisa [1]
because they are brave and expert in arms,
and they have brought down the pride of the Genoans
and made them stand shamed and degraded.   I
5 Therefore, I will always want Pisa to be on top,
for they have humbled men of perfect insolence.
One thing alone, the mischief of those lowborn lisping
                liars
tears my heart, cracks my heart, breaks my heart.

The Germans, I find, are gross and vulgar,
10 and when one of them gets it into his head he's a courtly
                man,
it is a burning mortal agony, an insult,
and that language of theirs sounds like the barking of
                dogs.   II
Therefore, I do not want to be the lord of Frisia
and have to hear the yapping of those pests all day.
15 Rather, I want to be among these joyous Lombards,
near my lady, she is gay, white-skinned, and gentle.

And since Montferrat and Milan are mine,[2]
I despise all Germans;
and if Richard, King of the English, believes me,
20 in a short time the power of Palermo   III
and Reggio will come into his hands,
because he paid for it with that ransom of his.
But speaking for myself: if it weren't for the Marquis

because the Marquis of Montferrat, Boniface I, Vidal's patron at this time
(ll. 17 and 26—Canavès was to become a part of the Marquisate of Mont.-
ferrat), was an ally of the Emperor. All of the anti-German remarks in this
song—Frisia (13) stands in general for the Emperor's German realm—are
part of the anti-Imperial polemic (Avalle). Alaçaïs (41) is Adelaide of
Saluzzo, sister of the Marquis.
[2] They are "his" becaues they have given him hospitality.

no pretz cinc marcs una rota camiza.[3]

25 Ara m'alberc Dieus e Sains Julias
   e la doussa terra de Canaves;
   qu'en Proensa no tornarai ieu ges,
   pus sai m'acuelh Laneris et Aillans.   IV
   E s'aver puesc selha qu'ai tant enquiza,
30 de lai s'estei lo valens reis N'Amfos,[4]
   qu'ieu farai sai mos vers e mas chansos
   per la gensor qu'anc fos d'amor enquiza.

   E pus Milas es autz e sobeiras,
   ben volgra patz de lor e dels Paves,
35 e que estes Lombardi' en defes
   de crois ribautz e de mals escaras.   V
   Lombartz, membre·us cum Polla fo conquiza,
   de las dompnas e dels valens baros,
   cum las mes hom en poder de garsos:
40 e de vos lai faran peior deviza.

   E! N'Alaçais, tant vos ai ades quiza,
   qu'ar l'uns en ten l'autre per enoios;   VI
   eu remandrai tant quan er fait lo dos,
   quar genser es qu'anc fos d'amor enquiza.

[3] "I think that the key to these verses is in the *tornada*, where the poet, turn-ing to the sister of the Marquis, Adelaide, the wife of another marquis, Manfred II of Saluzzo, frankly acknowledges that he has been importunate (*enoios*), but adds that he will remain near her till he is given the 'gift.' Here the poet borders on impudence in revealing in plain words the price of his praises; is it not therefore possible that in this strophe . . . he affirms —putting it in such a way that to the praise of the Marquis is added a good dose of impertinence—that if those five marks had not come from the Mar-quis, if it were not for the fact that they were given to him by the Marquis, they would have no value for him? in other words, that they would not be

I would not think five marks is worth a torn shirt.[3]

25 God and Saint Julian shelter me now
    in this sweet land of Canavès;
    for I shall never go back to Provence,
    Lanerio and Agliano make me welcome here.   IV
    And if I could have her, whom I have so long entreated,
30 let the valiant King En Alfons remain up there,[4]
    and I would make my poetry and songs right here,
    for the gentlest lady ever begged for love.

    And since Milan is at the crest,
    I wish it were at peace with Pavia,
35 and Lombardy defending itself
    from vicious brutes and murderous bandits.   V
    Lombards, remember how Apulia was defeated,
    remember the ladies and the brave barons,
    how they were put into the hands of common soldiers.
40 You are divided now: the Germans will divide you worse.

    And N'Alaçaïs, I have desired you so much,
    now one finds the other wearisome.   VI
    I will stay until the gift is given
    with you, the gentlest ever begged for love.

sufficient to buy his praises, while on the other hand the money of the un-
deserved ransom was sufficient for the conquest of [Palermo and Reggio]?
This *sirventes* has perhaps been a bit too idealized: Vidal takes the part of
the 'Lombards' against the Emperor, but he was not for that reason to sell
his wares for free. A clever man like him could even permit himself some
impertinences, which, spoken gracefully, would not only get him off a whip-
ping . . . but would thus confirm that reputation for 'mad things' that had
undoubtedly preceded him into Italy." (D'arco Silvio Avalle)
[4] Alfonso II, King of Aragón, lord of Provence.

RAIMBAUT DE VAQUEIRAS

(b. 1155–1160; fl. 1180's–1205)

The poet was born in the region of Vaucluse and was of poor and lowly origin. His lifelong patron and friend was Boniface I of Montferrat (in northern Italy), to whose court he came as a very young man and by whose side he probably perished in 1207, during the Fourth Crusade. From Boniface's earliest expeditions, to his service in the Sicilian campaign of the Emperor Henry VI, to the siege of Constantinople, to his battles in Greece, Raimbaut fought in his ranks; and Boniface rewarded the poet at the end of the Sicilian campaign by knighting him—an unprecedented honor for a troubadour, though bestowed in recognition of his service as a soldier. Though Raimbaut also visited the court of Hugues I des Baux (in the region of his birth) on different occasions and was also present in the court of the Malaspinas, his life was tied to the life of Boniface, who became Marquis of Montferrat in 1192 and maintained a court of high culture, welcoming many notable poets. Among these were Peire Vidal and, possibly, Conon de Béthune, with whom, years later, Raimbaut exchanged a *partimen* in Constantinople.

Raimbaut was a poet of considerable merit. Furthermore, as Joseph Linskill, the editor of his songs, observes, his "true significance and place in the history of troubadour poetry can only be fully appreciated if account is taken of . . . the poet's great impact on the development of Italian cultural and literary life. Here Raimbaut's role was unique . . . The first real impetus towards the diffusion of the Provençal lyric in the peninsula was given by our troubador, whose poetic activity revolved almost entirely around the court of Montferrat, where he stayed longer than any other poet. From this court, Raimbaut's influence radiated first into the neighbouring courts of Malaspina, Este,

and Savoy, and then into the towns . . . Of the many troubadours who crossed the Alps in the wake of our poet, none can
claim to have influenced to such an extent the future course of
Italian literary development."

Text: *The Poems of the Troubadour Raimbaut de Vaqueiras,*
ed. Joseph Linskill. The Hague: Mouton, 1964.

No m'agrad' iverns ni pascors
ni clars temps ni fuoills de garrics,
car mos enans mi par destrics
e totz mos majer gaugz dolors,
5 e son maltrag tuit miei lezer
e desesperat miei esper;   I
e si·m sol amors e dompneis
tener gai plus que l'aiga·l peis!
E pois d'amor me sui partitz
10 cum hom issillatz e faiditz,
tot' autra vida·m sembla mortz
e totz autre jois desconortz.

Pois d'amor m'es faillida·il flors
e·l dolz fruitz e·l grans e l'espics,
15 don gauzi' ab plazens prezics
e pretz m'en sobrav' et honors
e·n sabi' entre·ls pros caber,
era·m fai d'aut en bas cazer;   II
e si no·m sembles fols esfreis,
20 anc flama plus tost non s'esteis
q'ieu for' esteins e relinquitz
e perdutz en faitz et en digz
lo jorn qe·m venc lo desconortz
que non merma, cum qe·m refortz.

25 Bels armatz e bos feridors,
setges e calabres e pics,
e traucar murs nous et antics,
e vensser bataillas e tors
vei et aug; e non puosc aver
30 ren qe·m puosc' ad amor valer!   III
E vauc cercan ab rics arneis
gerras e coitas e torneis,

I have no pleasure in winter or spring,
the season of brightness, the oak leaf,
my advancement seems like my undoing,
and my greatest joy my grief.
5 My diversions all are torments,
and my hopes have lost hope: I
once, love and serving my lady
kept me in greater joy than water keeps a fish;
but since I have parted from love
10 like a broken man, in exile,
for me any other life is death,
and any other joy desolation.

Since love puts forth no flower for me,
no sweet fruit, grain, or ear,
15 though I used to know its joy in gentle conversation,
and its honor and renown overflowed in me,
and I could take my place among the valiant,
now from that high eminence I have fallen down;   II
and if it did not seem like mad despair,
20 no flame was ever snuffed out as fast
as I would have been, all effaced,
my noble gestes and words erased,
the day this desolation first came on,
that will not lessen, though I resist.

25 Handsome arms, good fighters,
sieges and catapults and pikes,
piercing ancient walls and new,
vanquishing battalions and their towers,
I see all this, I hear all this, and cannot win
30 a single thing to help me in love.   III
I go seeking, with rich accouterments,
wars and skirmishes and tournaments,

don sui conqueren enriquitz;
e pois jois d'amor m'es faillitz,
35 totz lo mons no·m parri' us ortz,
ni mos chans no m'es mais confortz.

Doncs, qe·m val conquistz ni ricors?
qu'eu ja·m tenia per plus rics
qand er' amatz e fis amics,
40 e·m paissi' ab n'Engles [1] amors;
n'amava mais un sol plazer
que sai gran terr' e gran aver,   IV
c'ades on plus mos poders creis
ai major ir' ab mi mezeis,
45 pois mos Bels Cavalliers [2] grazitz
e jois m'es loignatz e fugitz,
don mais no·m naissera conortz,
per q'es majer l'ir' e plus fortz.

Pero no·m comanda valors,
50 se be·m sui iratz ni enics,
q'ieu don gaug a mos enemics
tan q'en perda pretz ni lauzors,
q'ancar puosc dan e pro tener,
e sai d'irat joios parer   V
55 sai entre·ls Latins e·ls Grezeis;
e·l marques, que l'espaza·m seis,
gerreia Blacs e Drogoiz, [3]
et anc pois lo mons fon bastitz
nuilla gens non fetz tant d'esfortz
60 cum nos, cui Dieus a gent estortz.

Lo marques n'es honratz e sors

---

[1] *Senhal* designating the Marquis Boniface of Montferrat, whom Raimbaut
joined on the Fourth Crusade. At the time this lyric was written (dated
1205 by Linskill), things were going badly. Salonica and Constantinople
were threatened by the Bulgarians, who had just captured the Latin Emperor, Baldwin, at Adrianople. Boniface had been given the Kingdom of
Salonica, and it was from there that Raimbaut wrote this last of his extant
lyrics.
[2] *Senhal* designating his lady.

and, always conquering, I grow rich;
but since I never won the joy of love,
35 the whole world would seem less than a little garden,
and my song no longer comforts me.

And so, what's all this wealth and conquest worth to me?
I thought I was far wealthier
when I was loved and a faithful lover
40 and love fostered me by the side of En Engles: [1]
I love one little pleasure of that time more
than all the great land and great possessions here,   IV
for now the more my power increases,
the more regret I have within,
45 since my much praised Fair Courtier [2]
and joy have gone far from me, fled from me,
and so no comfort will be born in me again,
and my regret is greater and more bitter.

But my manliness does not command me—
50 though I am bitter and full of unease—
to give pleasure to my enemies
by losing all my fame and praise.
For I can still do damage and do good,
and I know how to give the look of joy to my regret,   V
55 here, among these Latins and these Greeks.
And the Marquis, who tied the sword around me,
fights against Wallachians and Drogobites,[3]
and since this world was made
no people ever did such things
60 as we have done, and God has mercifully delivered us.

The Marquis is honored by it and upraised,

[3] "The allusion in this line, important for the dating of the poem, is to the
invasion of the Latin Empire (Romania) by Johannitza, Tsar of the Wal-
lacho-Bulgarians, following the defeat of the Emperor Baldwin at Adrianople
on April 14, 1205 . . . The Drogobites, a people inhabiting Macedonia to
the west of Salonika . . . have been recently identified as Romanian" (Linskill) .

e·l Campanes e·l coms Enricx,[4]
Sicar, Montos e Salanicx
e Costantinople socors,
65 quar gent sabon camp retener,
e pot hom ben proar en ver: VI
qu'anc mais nulha gent non ateis
aitan gran honor, apareys.
Per bos vassals, valens, arditz,
70 es nostr' emperis conqueritz,
e Dieus trameta nos esfortz
cossi·s tray' a cap nostra sortz!

Anc Alixandres non fetz cors
ni Carles ni·l reis Lodoics
75 tan honrat, ni·l pros n'Aimerics [5]
ni Rotlans ab sos poignadors
non saubron tan gen conquerer
tan ric emperi per poder   VII
cum nos, don poja nostra leis;
80 q'emperadors e ducs e reis
avem faitz, e chastels garnitz
prop dels Turcs e dels Arabitz,
et ubertz los camins e·ls portz
de Brandiz tro al Bratz Sain Jorz.[6]

85 Per nos er Domas envazitz
e Jerusalem conquertiz   VIII
e·l regnes de Suri' estortz,
que·ls Turcx o trobon en lur sortz.

Los pellegris perjurs, fraiditz,[7]
90 qi nos an sai en camp geqitz,   IX

<hr>

[4] *Campanes*, identified by Linskill as a councillor of Boniface, Guillaume of
Champlitte, who "had conquered the Peloponnese in the winter of 1205."
Henry of Flanders was the brother of Baldwin.
[5] Aimeri de Narbonne, like the others mentioned in this passage, was an
epic hero.
[6] The Bosporus.

and the man of Champagne, and Count Henry; [4]
Sicar, Montos, Salonica,
Constantinople, all are saved,
65 for these men can hold the field,
anyone can tell that: VI
for never did any people win
such great honor, this is known.
Through these good vassals, brave and courageous,
70 our empire is regained.
and may God send us armies,
that what has been ordained for us may come to pass.

Alexander never mounted a campaign,
no, nor King Louis, nor Charlemagne,
75 so honored. And the brave Lord Aimeri [5]
and Roland, with all their warriors,
could not conquer with such nobility
and with all their might an empire so rich and strong   VII
as we have conquered; and now our holy law is soaring.
80 We have made emperors, dukes, and kings,
we have fortified castles
close to the Turks and the Arabs,
and opened up the roads and ports
from Brindisi to the Straits of St. George.[6]

85 Because of us Damascus will be attacked,
and Jerusalem won,   VIII
and the kingdom of Syria delivered,
for the Turks find all this in their prophecies.

Those pilgrims who broke their word, those deserters [7]
90 who left us alone on the field,   IX

[7] This *tornada* "is directed against the body of armed men (seven thousand, according to Villehardouin) lying in the harbour of Constantinople who, panic-stricken by the news of the Adrianople disaster, abandoned the almost defenceless capital, and despite the entreaties of the military and religious leaders, sailed for home on April 17th" (Linskill).

qi los manten e cortz es tortz,
que chascuns val mens vius que mortz.

Belhs dous Engles, francx et arditz,
cortes, essenhatz, essernitz,   x
95 vos etz de totz mos gaugz conortz,
e quar viu ses vos, fatz esfortz.

it is wrong for any lord to give them bread,
for they aren't worth as much alive as dead.

My fine sweet Englishman, brave and kind,
  courtly, well-bred, chosen out,   X
95 you give all my joys their strength,
  and in living without you I perform a feat.[8]

[8] This last line is taken from Linskill's translation.

FOLQUET DE MARSEILLE
(*d. December 25, 1231*)

Born in Marseille, the son of a Genoese merchant, Folquet became prosperous as a merchant himself. He began composing around 1180 and was in several courts in Southern France and in the Kingdom of Aragón; in his songs he praises Alfonso II, Raimon Bérenger, and Richard Lion-Heart, among others. Sometime around the turn of the century he entered a monastery. He became the Bishop of Toulouse in 1205, in which office he was very cruel during the Albigensian Crusade, sending hundreds of persons to their deaths, according to a contemporary poem, which calls him Antichrist.

Text: *Le troubadour Folquet de Marseille,* ed. S. Stronski. Cracow, 1910.

Vers Dieus, el vostre nom et de sancta Maria
m'esvelharai hueimais, pus l'estela del dia
ven daus Jerusalem, que m'ensenha qu'ieu dia:
estatz sus e levatz,
5 senhor que Dieu amatz!
   Que·l jorns es aprosmatz
e la nuech ten sa via;
e sia·n Dieus lauzatz   I
per nos et adoratz;
10 e·l preguem que·ns don patz
a tota nostra via.
   La nuech vai e·l jorns ve
ab clar cel e sere
e l'alba no·s rete,
15 ans ven bel' e complia.

   Senher Dieus que nasquetz de la Verge Maria
per nos guerir de mort e per restaurar via,
e per destruir' Enfern que·l diables tenia,
e fotz en crotz levatz
20 d'espinas coronatz,
   e de fel abeuratz,
Senher, merce vos cria
aquest pobles onratz;   II
que·lh vostra pietatz
25 lor perdon lor peccatz.
Amen, Dieus, aissi sia.
   La nuech vai e·l jorns ve
ab clar cel e sere
e l'alba no·s rete,
30 ans ven bel' e complia.

   Qui no sap Dieu pregar obs es que o aprenda
et auja qu'ieu dirai et escout et entenda:

True God, in your name and Saint Mary's
I shall be wakeful from this day forth, for the morning
           star
rises toward Jerusalem and teaches me to say:
Arise, stand,
5 you lords who love God,
day has come,
night passes on:
now let us praise   I
God and adore him;
10 and pray Him give us peace
all our days.
Night passes, day comes,
the heaven is calm and bright,
the dawn does not hold back,
15 it rises fair and full.

Lord God, born of the Virgin Mary
to heal us of death and restore our life,
and destroy Hell, which was in the Devil's power,
you who were hung on the cross
20 and crowned with thorns
and given gall to drink,
Lord, these good people
cry to you for mercy;   II
may your pity
25 forgive them their sins.
Amen, God, so be it.
Night passes, day comes,
the heaven is calm and bright,
the dawn does not hold back,
30 it rises fair and full.

Whoever does not know how to pray to God let him learn
and listen to what I say, hear me now, understand:

Dieus, que comensamens etz de tota fazenda,
laus vos ren e merce
35 del amor e del be
que m'avetz fach ancse;
e prec, Senher, que·us prenda
grans pietatz de me   III
que no·m truep ni·m malme,
40 ni m'engane de re
Diables ni·m surprenda.
La nuech vai e·l jorns ve
ab clar cel e sere
e l'alba no·s rete,
45 ans ven bel' e complia.

Dieus, dontaz mi saber e sen ab qu'ieu aprenda
vostres sanhs mandamens e·ls auja e·ls entenda
e vostra pietatz que·m gueris que·m defenda,
d'aquest segle terre
50 que no·m trabuc ab se;
quar ie·us ador e·us cre,
Senher, e·us fauc ufrenda
de me e de ma fe,   IV
qu'aissi·s tanh e·s cove;
55 per so vos crit merce
e de mos tortz esmenda.
La nuech vai e·l jorns ve
ab clar cel e sere,
e l'alba no·s rete,
60 ans ven bel' e complia.

Aquel glorios Dieus que son cors det a venda
per totz nos a salvar prec qu'entre nos estenda
lo sieu Sant Esperit que de mal nos defenda
e d'aitan nos estre
65 josta los sieus nos me
lai sus, on se capte   V
e·ns meta dins sa tenda.

God, you who are the beginning of all things,
I praise you and give thanks
35 for the love and the good
that you have always given me:
and I pray you, Lord, take
great pity on me,   III
that the Devil may not find me,
40 mislead me, deceive me,
overwhelm me.
Night passes, day comes,
the heaven is calm and bright,
the dawn does not hold back,
45 it rises fair and full.

God, give me the knowledge and wisdom to learn
your holy commandments, to hear them, to understand
                        them;
and may your pity save me, and protect me,
from this world of earth,
50 let it not destroy me with itself;
for I adore you, I believe in you,
Lord, and I make you the offering
of myself and my faith,   IV
for so it should be;
55 therefore I beg you for mercy
and correction for my wrongs.
Night passes, day comes,
the heaven is calm and bright,
the dawn does not hold back,
60 it rises fair and full.

That glorious God, who gave his body to pay
to save us all, I pray: may he pour out
the Holy Spirit upon us, to keep us from evil,
and give us the gift
65 of leading us among his own,
above, where he reigns,   V
and put us in his paradise.

La nuech vai e·l jorns ve
ab clar cel e sere
70 e l'alba no·s rete,
ans ven bel' e complia.

Night passes, day comes,
the heaven is calm and bright,
70 the dawn does not hold back,
it rises fair and full.

PEIRE CARDENAL

(c. 1180–c. 1278)

Peire Cardenal was born in Puy-en-Velay of a noble family. Although he was early trained for an ecclesiastical career, he became a troubadour and found his chief patrons in Raimon VI and Raimon VII, the counts of Toulouse. The cruelty and hypocrisy of the Albigensian Crusade, which had caused great destruction in his region, was the impetus for many of his bitterest satires.

He was the greatest poet of the moral *sirventes*. The objects of his attacks were constant: the viciousness of the French, the venality of the clergy, the violence and corruption of the higher nobility. Ninety-six songs are extant.

Text: *Poésies complètes du troubadour Peire Cardenal*, ed. René Lavaud. Bibliothèque Méridinonale, 2d ser. vol. XXXIV. Toulouse: Privat, 1957.

A humanist
preached of love of God
wrote of hypocrisy

Ar me puesc ieu lauzar d'Amor,[1]
que no·m tol manjar ni dormir;
ni·n sent freidura ni calor
ni no·n badail ni no·n sospir
5 ni·n vauc de nueg arratge.   I
  Ni·n soi conquistz ni·n soi cochatz,
ni·n soi dolenz ni·n soi iratz
ni no·n logui messatge;
ni·n soi trazitz ni enganatz,
10 que partitz m'en soi ab mos datz.[2]

Autre plazer n'ai ieu maior,
que no·n traïsc ni fauc traïr,
ni·n tem tracheiris ni trachor
ni brau gilos que m'en azir;
15 ni·n fauc fol vassalatge,   II
ni·n soi feritz ni derocatz
ni no·n soi pres ni deraubatz;
ni no·n fauc lonc badatge,
ni dic qu'ieu soi d'amor forsatz
20 ni dic que mos cors m'es emblatz.

Ni dic qu'ieu mor per la gensor
ni dic que·l bella·m fai languir,
ni non la prec ni non l'azor
ni la deman ni la dezir.
25 Ni no·l fas homenatge   III
ni no·l m'autrei ni·l me soi datz;
ni non soi sieus endomenjatz

---

[1] "It is not love that is ridiculed here, nor the lady, nor even the lover, but the *canso*, with its clichés, its excesses, and the poets who repeat them endlessly" (Ernest Hoepffner). The catalogue of familiar topics is illustrated in the first three strophes, the casuistry in the fourth, the compulsive ornamentation in the fifth and the *tornada*. Peire's lyric reveals how far the

Now I can congratulate myself on love,[1]
for it does not snatch away my appetite or sleep,
nor do I feel its cold or heat,
nor do I stand openmouthed for it or sigh,
5 nor, for love, do I wander about in the night.   I
Nor am I vanquished or oppressed by it,
nor am I grieving or chagrined through it,
nor do I have to pay the messenger of it.
Nor am I betrayed or tricked because of it,
10 for I have walked away from it with my dice.[2]

I have a different pleasure now, and a greater:
I neither betray, nor cause to betray, for its sake,
nor do I fear any man's or woman's treachery through it,
nor some brute of a jealous husband who hates me for
      love,
15 nor must I do some stupid service for it.   II
Nor am I beaten or upended by it,
nor stolen from or despoiled because of it,
nor do I wait and wait in vain for it.
Nor do I say, I am oppressed by love, blah blah blah
20 nor do I say, The heart of me has been stolen away, blah
      blah

Nor do I say, Oh, I die for the noblest one,
nor do I say, The beautiful lady makes me languish,
nor do I entreat her, nor do I adore her,
nor do I demand her, nor do I desire her,
25 nor do I swear myself her man;   III
nor do I deliver, nor have I given, myself to her,
nor am I a servant inscribed in her charter,

whole genre was played out in his generation. Cf. Giraut de Bornelh, *Quan
lo freitz* (no. 32).
[2] That is, I do not play the game any more.

ni a mon cor en gatge,
ni soi sos pres ni sos liatz,
30 anz dic qu'ieu li soi escapatz.

Mais deu hom lauzar vensedor
non fai vencut, qui·l ver vol dir,
car lo vencens porta la flor
e·l vencut vai hom sebelir;
35 e qui venc son coratge   IV
de las desleials voluntatz
don ieis lo faitz desmezuratz
e li autre outratge,
d'aquel venser es plus onratz
40 que si vensia cent ciutatz.

Pauc pres prim prec de pregador,
can cre qu'il, cuy quer convertir,
vir vas vil voler sa valor,
don dreitz deu dar dan al partir;
45 si sec son sen salvatge,   V
leu l'er lo larcx laus lag loinhatz;
plus pres lauzables que lauzatz:
trop ten estreg ostatge
dreitz drutz del dart d'amor nafratz.
50 Pus pauc pres, pus pres es compratz.

Non voilh voler volatge
que·m volv e·m vir mas voluntatz   VI
mas lai on mos vols es volatz.[3]

[3] The lover who sets out to seduce a lady with his pretty speeches is con-
temptible; and if he does not observe due measure, his reputation will suffer.
The courtly lover hardly deserves respect, although his posturings are much
in vogue: he narrows his whole life to the pursuit of seduction and the culti-

nor does she have my heart in gage;
nor am I her thrall, no more her liege man,
30 rather, I say I have escaped from her clutches.

One should praise the conqueror more
than the conquered, to tell the truth,
for the conqueror bears the flower,
and the conquered they are going to bury.
35 And one who conquers his heart away   IV
from the lawless lusts
where that outrageous act is born,
and the other offenses,
he is more honored for this conquest
40 than if he had conquered a hundred cities.

I judge as jejune the cajoling of the cajoler,
when he surmises that she whom he seeks to seduce
will warp her worth for his wicked will,
wherefore propriety will pay the price at the parting;
45 if he does not restrain his prurient rage,   V
he will find the fullness of good fame shamefully far off.
I prize the respectable more than the respected:
he clings to his close captivity,
the courtly lover injured by the arrow of love.
50 The greater the cost of requital, the less I consider it
       grace.

I do not want a volatile will
which whirls and revolves my volitions   VI
everywhere, but where my own free will has flown.[3]

vation of his lechery; and when he does win the lady's favor, it is hardly a
great boon, since he has invested so much time and effort and probably
money. *Tornada:* I do not want an uncontrollable will that makes me the
victim of my own desires and never leads where reason points.

53

Clergue si fan pastor
e son aucizedor;
e par de gran sanctor
qui los vei revestir,
5   e·m pren a sovenir
    que n'Ezengris,[1] un dia,   I
volc ad un parc venir:
mas pels cans que temia
pel de mouton vestic
10   ab que los escarnic,
puois manget e traïc
tot so que li·abelic.

Rei e emperador,
duc, comte e comtor [2]
15   e cavalier ab lor
solon lo mon regir;
ara vei possezir
    a clers la seinhoria   II
ab tolre e ab traïr
20   e ab ypocrezia,
ab forsa e ab prezic;
e tenon s'a fastic
qui tot non lor o gic,
e sera, quan que tric.

25   Aissi can son major
son ab mens de valor
et ab mais de follor,
et ab meins de ver dir
et ab mais de mentir,

---

[1] The wolf of the beast epic.
[2] More accurately, the *comtor* is of a lower rank than viscount.

*Cuts down
church
p. 301*

Clerics pretend to be shepherds,
but they are the killers;
the likeness of sanctity is on them
when you see them in their habit,
5   and it puts me in mind
that Master Ysengrim,[1] one day,   I
wanted to get into a sheepfold,
and because he feared the dogs
he put on the skin of a sheep
10   with which he tricked them all.
Then he gobbled and glutted
as much as he liked.

Kings, emperors,
dukes, counts, viscounts,[2]
15   and knights, together,
used to rule the world.
Now I see the power
in the hands of clerics   II
with stealing, betrayal,
20   hypocrisy,
violence, and sermons.
And they are highly offended
if you don't hand it all over to them,
and so it shall be, though it may take a while.
25   The greater they are
the less they are worth
and the greater their folly,
the less their truthtelling
and the greater their lying,

30 et ab meins de paria   III
    et ab mais de faillir,
    et ab meins de clerzia.
    Dels fals clergues o dic:
    que anc hom non auzic
35 a Dieu tant enemic
    de sai lo tems antic.

    Can son en refreitor
    no m'o tenc ad honor,
    c'a la taula aussor
40 vei los cussons assir
    e premiers s'escaussir.
    Aujas gran vilania: IV
    car i auzon venir
    et hom no los en tria.
45 Pero anc non lai vic
    paubre cusson mendic
    sezen laz cusson ric:
    d'aitan los vos esdic.

    Ja non aion paor
50 Alcais ni Almansor
    que abat ni prior
    los anon envazir
    ni lor terras sazir,
    que afans lor seria;   V
55 mas sai son en cossir
    del mon consi lor sia
    e com en Frederic
    gitesson de l'abric:
    pero tals l'aramic
60 qui fort no s'en jauzic.[3]

[3] Probable reference to Frederick II of Sicily, whose lands were often under papal attack. One such attack, in 1229, was led by his own father-in-law and was repulsed.

30   the less their friendship   III
      and the greater their dereliction,
      and the less they keep faith with their calling.
      Of false clerics I say this:
      I have never heard of any man
35   so great an enemy to God
      since the ancient of days.

      When I am in a refectory
      it's no great honor to me,
      because up at the high table
40   I see those shysters sitting
      and the first to serve themselves the soup.
      Listen to this great villainy: IV
      that such truck dare to come there
      and no one picks them out.
45   On the other hand, I never saw
      one poor begging shyster there
      sitting next to any well-established shyster:
      of that much, anyway, I exonerate them.

      Let the Arab chiefs
50   and sultans never fear
      that abbots or priors
      might ever attack them
      and take their lands,
      for that would be hard work.   V
55   No, they stay home rapt in thought,
      how the whole world might be theirs
      and how they might have cast
      En Frederick from his sanctuary.
      But there was one who attacked him
60   and did not rejoice in it much.[3]

Clergue, qui vos chauzic
ses fellon cor enic   VI
en son comte faillic,
c'anc peior gent non vic.

54

Un sirventes novel vueill comensar,
que retrairai al jor del jujamen
a sel que·m fes e·m formet de nien.
S'el me cuja de ren arazonar   I
5 e s'el me vol metre en la diablia
ieu li dirai: "Seinher, merce, non sia!
Qu'el mal segle tormentiei totz mos ans.
E guardas mi, si·us plas, dels tormentans."

Tota sa cort farai meravillar
10 cant auziran lo mieu plaideiamen;
qu'eu dic qu'el fa ves los sieus faillimen
si los cuja delir ni enfernar.   II
Car qui pert so que gazanhar poiria,
per bon dreg a de viutat carestia,
15 qu'el deu esser dous e multiplicans
de retener las armas trespassans.

Los diables degra dezeretar
et agra mais d'armas e plus soven
e·l dezeretz plagra a tota gen
20 et el mezeis pogra s'o perdonar,   III
car per mon grat trastotz los destruiria,
pos tut sabem c'absolver s'en poiria:
"Bels seinhers Dieus! sias dezeretans
dels enemix enuios e pezans!
25 Vostra porta non degras ja vedar,
que sans Peires i pren trop d'aunimen

Clerics, whoever depicted you
without a cruel and vicious heart   VI
erred in his account,
for a worse breed I never saw.

54

I wish to begin a new *sirventes*,
which I shall deliver on Judgment Day
to Him who created me, Who formed me out
                of nothing.
If He has it in His eternal Mind to call me to account   I
5 for anything, and He wants to stick me with the devils,
I shall tell Him: "Lord, for pity's sake, stop it,
I suffered all my life in that damned world,
now if you don't mind, keep me from those fellows with
                their forks."

I shall make His whole court wonder
10 when they hear my defense;
for I say He wrongs His own
if He figures on destroying them or putting them in Hell.   II
Anyone who loses things he could possess
doesn't deserve much, he deserves to be hard up,
15 for He should be tender and put himself everywhere to hold on to the souls that transgress.

Let Him rob the devils of their share,
then He will get more souls, and more often,
and that expropriation will make everyone glad,
20 and He could pardon Himself for it,   III
because if I had my way He'd exterminate every last one
                of those mothers,
since we all know He could give Himself absolution for
                it afterwards:
"Sweet Lord God, dispossess
our enemies grievous and hateful.

25 You must never forbid your door,
for that would bring shame to Peter, a saint,

que n'es portiers: mas que intres rizen
tota arma que lai volgues intrar. IV
Car nuilla cortz non er ja ben complia
30 que l'uns en plor e que l'autre en ria;
e sitot ses sobeirans reis poissans,
si no m'ubres, er vos en fatz demans.

Ieu no me vueill de vos dezesperar:
anz ai en vos mon bon esperamen,
35 que me vaillas a mon trespassamen:
per que deves m'arma e mon cors salvar. V
E farai vos una bella partia:
que·m tornetz lai don moc lo premier dia
o que·m siatz de mos tortz perdonans.
40 Qu'ieu no·ls fora si non fos natz enans.

S'ieu ai sai mal et en enfern l'avia,
segon ma fe tortz e peccatz seria, VI
qu'ieu vos puesc ben esser recastenans
que per un ben ai de mal mil aitans.

45 Per merce·us prec, donna sancta Maria
c'al vostre fill mi fassas garentia, VII
si qu'el prenda lo paire e·ls enfans
e·ls meta lay on esta sans Johans."

55

Vera vergena, Maria,
vera vida, vera fes,
vera vertatz, vera via,
vera vertutz, vera res,
5 vera maire, ver' amia, I
ver' amors, vera merces:
per ta vera merce sia
qu'eret en me tos heres!

the keeper of your gate: instead, give orders that every
    soul
who desires to enter should enter and exult,   IV
for no court is ever well assembled,
30 when one man cries and another smiles as a result;
and though You are the supreme and omnipotent King,
open up, or You'll be served up there with a complaint

I do not want to despair of You;
on the contrary, I have my good hope in You,
35 that you will help me when I trespass;
therefore you ought to save my soul and my body.   V
And I shall make you a fair proposal in this circum-
    stance:
either send me back where I came from when my life
    began,
or pardon all my wrongs,
40 for I couldn't have done them if I hadn't been born in
    advance.

If I suffer here and suffer more in Hell,
I say that would be an injustice and a sin,   VI
because I can easily reproach You
that for one good I get a thousand times more of the bad.

45 For pity, I pray you, Saint Mary, my Lady,
be my witness with your Son,   VII
may He receive both father and children,
and put them in the dwelling of Saint John."

55

True virgin, Mary,
true life, true belief,
true truth, true way,
true power, true reality,
5   true mother, true friend,   I
true love, true pity:
by your true pity let it be
that your heir inherits me.

De patz, si·t plai, dona, traita,
10 qu'ab to filh me sia faita!

Tu restauriest la follia
don Adams fon sobrepres,
tu iest l'estela que guia
los passans el san paes,
15 e tu iest l'alba del dia   II
don lo tieus filhs solelhs es,
que·l calfa e clarifia,
verais, de dreitura ples.
De patz, si·t plai, dona traita,
20 qu'ab to filh me sia faita!

Tu fust nada de Suria,
gentils e paura d'arnes,
umils e pura e pia
en fatz, en ditz, et en pes;
25 faita per tal maïstria: III
sos totz mals, mas ab totz bes.
Tan fust de doussa paria
per que Dieus en tu se mes.
De patz, si·t plai, dona, traita,
30 qu'ab to filh me sia faita!

Aquel que en te se fia,
ja no·l cal autre defes,
que sitot lo mons peria
aquel non perria ges;
35 quar als tieus precx s'umilía   IV
l'auzismes, a cui que pes,
e·l tieus filhs non contraria
ton voler neguna ves.
De patz, si·t plai, dona, traita,
40 qu'ab to filh me sia faita!

Treat of peace, if it please you, Lady,
10 let it be made with your Son, for me.

You repaired the madness
in which Adam was seized,
you are the star that guides
travelers to the Holy Land,
15 you are the dawn of the day   II
and your Son is its sun,
who brings it warmth and clarity,
righteous, full of justice.
Treat of peace, if it please you, Lady,
20 let it be made with your Son, for me.

You were born in Syria,
of great nobility and poor in things,
humble, and pure, and filial,
in deeds, in words, in thoughts,
25 made with such mastery,   III
free of all evil, abounding in good.
You waited with such sweet welcoming,
God put Himself in you.
Treat of peace, if it please you, Lady,
30 let it be made with your Son, for me.

He who trusts in you
needs no other to defend him,
for if all the world should perish,
he would not perish.
35 Before your prayers the Most High in heaven   IV
humbles Himself—that weighs heavily on someone—
and your Son does not oppose
your sweet will, ever.
Treat of peace, if it please you, Lady,
40 let it be made with your Son, for me.

David, en la prophetia
dis, en un salme que fes,[1]
qu'al destre de Dieu sezia,
del rey en la ley promes,
45   una reÿna qu'avia   V
vestirs de var e d'aurfres:
tu iest elha, ses falhia;
non o pot vedar plaides.
De patz, si·t plai, dona, traita,
50   qu'ab to filh me sia faita!

Quar al latz Dieu estas, traita,   VI
que·m sia patz de luy faita.

56

Tartarassa ni voutor
no sent tan leu carn puden
quom clerc e prezicador
senton ont es lo manen.   I
5   Mantenen son sei privat,
e quant malautia·l bat,
fan li far donassïo
tel que·l paren no·i an pro.

Franses e clerc an lauzor
10 de mal, quar ben lur en pren;
e renovier e trachor
an tot lo segl' eissamen,   II
c'ab mentir et ab barat
an si tot lo mon torbat
15 que no·i a religïo
que no'n sapcha sa leisso.

[1] Psalm 45 (Vulgate 44).

David, in his prophecy,
says, in a psalm that he made,[1]
beside the right hand of God,
beside the King we are promised in the Law,
45   there sat a Queen   V
in rich raiments of gold:
you are that Queen, o immaculate,
no lawyer can contest it.
Treat of peace, if it please you, Lady,
50   let it be made with your Son, for me.

Because you are beside the hand of God, treat,   VI
that peace with Him be made for me.

56

Buzzards and vultures
do not smell out stinking flesh
as fast as clerics and preachers
smell out the rich.   I
5   They circle around him, at once, like friends,
and as soon as sickness strikes him down they get him
to make a little donation,
and his own family gets nothing.

Frenchmen and clerics win praise
10   for their felonies, because they succeed;
usurers and traitors
take the whole world that way,   II
for by falsehood and fraud
they have so confounded the earth,
15   there is not one religious order
which does not know their "rule."

Saps qu'endeven la ricor
de sels que l'an malamen?
Venra un fort raubador
20 que non lur laissara ren: III
so es la mortz, que·ls abat,
c'ab catr' aunas de filat
los tramet en tal maizo
ont atrobon de mal pro.

25 Hom, per que fas tal follor
que passes lo mandamen
de Dieu, quez es ton senhor
e t'a format de nien?   IV
La trueia ten al mercat [1]
30 sel que ab Dieu si combat:
que·l n'aura tal guizardo
com ac Judas lo fello.

Dieus verais, plens de doussor,
Senher, sias nos guiren!
35 Gardas d'enfernal dolor
peccadors e de turmen,   V
e solves los del peccat
en que son pres e liat,
e faitz lur veray perdo,
40 ab vera confessio!

57

Una ciutatz fo, no sai cals,
on cazet una plueia tals   I
que tug l'ome de la ciutat
que toquet foron dessenat.

---

[1] As Lavaud explains, this is a foolish thing to do: one should keep the sow
as long as she is fruitful, one sells the porkers. "For an immediate profit he
sacrifices the future."

Do you know what happens to the wealth
of those who get it badly?
A mighty robber will come
20 who will not let them keep one thing—   III
Death, who strikes them down,
who sends them across in four ells of linen,
in a strange mansion,
where they find a great hoard of affliction.

25 O Man, why commit such madness,
transgressing the commandment
of God, who is your Lord,
who formed you out of nothing?   IV
He sells his sow in the market place [1]
30 who fights with God,
he shall get the wages
Judas traitor got.

O true God, full of sweetness,
Lord, be our protector,
35 keep all sinners from the suffering
of Hell, and from the torture,   V
and untie them from the sin
in which they are caught and bound up,
and give them faithful pardon
40 when they keep faith in their confession.

57

There was a city, I do not know which,
where a certain rain fell   I
such that all the men in the city
it touched became mad.

5   Tug desseneron mas sol us;
       aquel ne escapet, ses plus: II
       que era dins una maizo
       on dormia, quant aiso fo.

       Aquel levet cant ac dormit
10   e fo se de ploure gequit,   III
       e venc foras entre las gens.
       E tug feron dessenamens:

       L'uns ac roquet, l'autre fon nus
       e l'autre escupi ves sus;   IV
15   l'uns traïs peira, l'autre astella,
       l'autre esquintet sa gonella.

       E l'uns ferit e l'autre enpeis,
       e l'autre cuget esser reis   V
       e tenc se ricamen pels flancx,
20   e l'autre sautet per los bancx.

       L'uns menasset, l'autre maldis,
       l'autre juret e l'autre ris,   VI
       l'autre parlet e non saup que,
       l'autre fes metolas dese.

25   E aquel qu'avia son sen
       meravillet se mot fortmen   VII
       e vi ben que dessenat son.
       E garda aval et amon

       s'i negun savi n'i veira,
30   e negun savi non i ha.   VIII
       Granz meravillas ac de lor,
       mas mot l'an il de lui major

       que·l vezon estar suaumen.
       Cuidon c'aia perdut son sen   IX

5   They all became mad, except one alone,
       he escaped, no others: II
       he was in a house
       asleep, when this thing happened.

       He got up when he finished sleeping
10   and it had stopped raining,   III
       and he went outside, among his fellow citizens.
       And they were all committing madness.

       One of them wore a little shirt, another was naked,
       and another spit upward;   IV
15   one was throwing a stone, another a stick,
       another was tearing his tunic.

       One punched, another pushed,
       another thought he was king   V
       and stood royally, hands on hips,
20   and another jumped over the benches.

       One made threats, another cursed,
       another swore, another laughed,   VI
       another spoke and did not know what,
       another made terrible faces the whole time.

25   And this man who had kept his senses
       wondered greatly,   VII
       and he saw clearly they were mad.
       He looks down, and up,

       whether he might not see one reasonable man,
30   and one reasonable man is not there.   VIII
       He was greatly astonished at them,
       but they are more so at him,

       when they see him standing there in peace.
       They think he has lost his sanity.   IX

35   car so qu'il fan no·l vezon faire,
          A cascun de lor es veiaire

          qu'il son savi e ben senat,
          mas lui tenon per dessenat.   X
          Qui·l fer en gauta, qui en col.
40   El no pot mudar no·s degol.

          L'uns l'empenh e l'autre lo bota.
          El cuia eusir de la rota;   XI
          l'uns esquinta, l'autre l'atrai,
          el pren colps e leva e quai.

45   Cazen levan, a grans scambautz,
          s'en fug a sa maizo de sautz,   XII
          fangos e batutz e mieg mortz,
          et ac gaug can lor fon estortz.

          Aquist faula es per lo mon:
50   semblanz es als homes que i son.   XIII
          Aquest segles es la ciutatz,
          quez es totz plens de dessenatz.

          Que·l majer sens c'om pot aver
          si es amar Dieu e temer   XIV
55   e gardar sos comandamens;
          mas ar es perdutz aquel sens.

          Li plueia sai es cazeguda:
          Cobeitatz, e si es venguda   XV
          un' erguelhoz' e granz maleza
60   que tota la gen a perpreza.

          E si Dieus n'a alcun gardat,
          l'autre·l tenon per dessenat   XVI
          e menon lo de tomp en bilh
          car non es del sen que son ilh.

35   for what they are doing they do not see him do.
To each of them it is clear

they are reasonable and full of good sense,
but him they hold for mad.   X
Some strike him on the cheek, some on the neck.
40   He cannot help falling down.

One pushes, another shoves.
He thinks of getting away from this mob,   XI
one tears his clothes, another drags him around,
he feels the punches, and gets up, and falls.

45   Falling, getting up, in big strides,
skipping, he runs away to his house,   XII
muddy, beaten, half-dead,
but glad he got away from them.

This fable is an image of the world,
50   a semblance of the people in it.   XIII
This world is the city,
because this world is full of madmen.

For the greatest sanity a man can have
is to love God, yes, and to fear him,   XIV
55   and to keep his commandments;
but this sanity is lost in our time.

The rain of Covetousness has fallen
here, and thus upon us   XV
comes a tremendous proud maliciousness
60   that has laid hold of all the people.

And if God has preserved one man,
the others hold him for mad,   XVI
and they make him do tricks in the air,
because he is not of their mind.

65   Que·l sens de Dieu lor par folia,
     e l'amix de Dieu, on que sia,   XVII
     conois que dessenat son tut,
     car lo sen de Dieu an perdut.

     E ilh, an lui per dessenat,   XVIII
70   car lo sen del mon a laissat.

65 For the wisdom of God is madness to them,
 and the friend of God, wherever he is,   XVII
 knows they are mad, the pack of them,
 for they have lost the sense of God.

 And they, they hold him for mad,   XVIII
70 for he has renounced the mad sanity of this world.

SORDEL

(c. 1200–c. 1270)

Sordel, a minor nobleman, came from Goito, near Mantua.
It was probably in 1228 that Sordel left Italy, but he was in
Spain for some time before arriving in Provence, where he found
a number of patrons, including Blacatz and Raimon Bérenger
IV, the Count of Provence. In 1265 he returned to Italy after
nearly forty years, and four years later he was granted certain
lands and castles in Abruzzi by Charles d'Anjou. He probably
died soon afterwards.

Sordel was certainly a gifted poet. Like most of the later
troubadours, he was less interested in the *canso* (of which there
are only twelve among the forty extant pieces) than in the other
forms, particularly the *sirventes* and the *partimen*. But his fame
has reached a level far beyond that which his poetry might have
attained because of what Dante made of him. Sordel appears in
Purgatorio VI and VII as a majestically righteous and prophetic
figure—"o anima lombarda,/come ti stavi altera e disdegnosa/
e nel mover delli occhi onesta e tarda!" (VI, 61–63) —and he and
Vergil embrace each other as fellow poets and fellow Mantuans.
At this point Dante castigates the rulers of Europe. Thus Sordello's appearance and rôle in *Purgatorio*—he leads Vergil and
Dante to the Valley of the Princes—are clearly inspired by his
planh for Blacatz.

Text: Cesare de Lollis, *Vita e poesie di Sordello di Goito,* in
Romanische Bibliotek, XI (Halle, Max Niemeyer, 1896). A crit-
ical edition of Sordel's poetry was published by Marco Boni in
1954 (Bologna).

Planher vuelh en Blacatz [1] en aquest leugier so
ab cor trist e marrit, et ai en be razo,
qu'en luy ai mescabat senhor et amic bo,
e quar tug l'ayp valent en sa mort perdut so: I
5 tant es mortals lo dans, qu'ieu noy ai sospeisso
que jamais si revenha, s'en aital guiza no,
qu'om li traga lo cor, e qu'en manjo·l baro
que vivon descorat, pueys auran de cor pro.

Premiers manje del cor, per so que grans ops l'es,
10 l'emperaire de Roma,[2] s'elh vol los Milanes
per forsa conquistar, quar luy tenon conques,
e viu deseretatz, malgrat de sos Ties;   II
e deseguentre lui manj' en lo reys frances,[3]
pueys cobrara Castella, que pert per nescies;
15 mas, si pez' a sa maire, elh no 'n manjara ges,
quar ben par a son pretz qu'elh non fai ren que·l pes.

Del rey engles [4] me platz, quar es pauc coratjos,
que manje pro del cor, pueys er valens e bos,
e cobrara la terra, per que viu de pretz blos,
20 que·l tol lo reys de Fransa quar lo sap nualhos;   III
e lo reys castelas [5] tanh qu'en manje per dos,
quar dos regismes ten, e per l'un non es pros;
mas, s'elh en vol manjar, tanh qu'en manj' a rescos,
que, si·l mair' o sabia, batria·l ab bastos.

[1] A nobleman of Provence, and a patron of many troubadours; died between
1235 and 1239.
[2] Frederick II. See note to Peire Cardenal's *Clergue si fan pastor*, no. 53; and
Walther von der Vogelweide, *Ich saz ûf eime steine*. Frederick fought all his
life against the Pope and the second Lombard League (led by Milan), winning a great victory in 1237. Thus, as Sordel's most recent editor, Marco
Boni, points out, this song cannot have been written after that year (*Sordello, Le Poesie*, ed. Marco Boni. Bologna: Libreria Antiquaria Palmaverde,
1954).
[3] Louis IX (Saint Louis), whose mother, Queen Blanche, gave him the right
to claim Castile.

I want to mourn for En Blacatz [1] in this simple song
with a sad and desolate heart, and I have cause,
for in him I have given up my dear friend and lord,
and in his death every dignifying quality is lost.   I
5 I have no hope this loss will ever be restored,
it is so terrible, unless they draw
his great heart out of him and give the barons, who have
        no heart,
to eat of it. Then they will have heart once more.

Let the Emperor of Rome, [2] for his need is great,
10 be first to eat of this heart, if he wants to break
the Milanese by force, for now they have him beaten,
and, despite his Germans, he lives robbed of his inheri-
        tance.   II
And after him let the French king [3] eat, then he will
        retake
Castile, which he loses through incompetence.
15 But should it displease his mother, he will not partake,
for he, to his credit, does nothing to make her irate.

I would like the English king, [4] since he has little courage,
to eat plenty of this heart, then he will be brave
and regain the land, for having lost it he lives without
        merit—
20 the King of France took it away from him, knowing he
        does nothing.   III
And the King of Castile, [5] let him eat enough for two,
since he has two kingdoms and isn't man enough for one:
but if he wants to eat of this heart, he must do it under
        cover,
if his mother found out, she would beat him with a club.

[4] Henry III, the son of John Lackland. The King of France (20): Philippe
Auguste. The two kings fought over several realms in France.
[5] Ferdinand III of Castile and León.

25 Del rey d'Arago[6] vuel del cor deja manjar,
   que aisso lo fara de l'anta descarguar
   que pren sai de Marcella e d'Amilau, qu'onrar
   no·s pot estiers per ren que puesca dir ni far;   IV
   et apres vuelh del cor don hom al rey navar,[7]
30 que valia mais coms que reys, so aug comtar:
   tortz es quan Dieus fai home en gran ricor pojar,
   pus sofracha de cor lo fai de pretz bayssar.

   Al comte de Toloza[8] a ops qu'en manje be,
   si·l membra so que sol tener ni so que te,
35 quar, si ab autre cor sa perda non reve,
   no·m par que la revenha ab aquel qu'a en se.   V
   E·l coms proensals[9] tanh qu'en manje, si·l sove
   c'oms que deseretatz viu guaire non val re,
   e, sitot ab esfors si defen ni·s chapte,
40 ops l'es mange del cor pel greu fais qu'el soste.

   Li baro·m volran mal de so que ieu dic be,
   mas ben sapchan qu'ie·ls pretz aitan pauc quon ylh me.   VI

   Belh Restaur,[10] sol qu'ab vos puesca trobar merce,   VII
   a mon dan met quascun que per amic no·m te.

[6] James I, cousin of Raimon Bérenger IV; he tried to bring Marseille back into the power of the Count of Provence (Boni). He also had a claim to the viscounty of Milhau.

[7] Thibaut de Champagne. See introduction to Thibaut in Section II.

[8] Raimon VII, who had lost a great part of his possessions to the Crown of France in 1229 (Boni).

[9] Raimon Bérenger IV, who had lost Marseille and other territories through revolt and the depredations of his enemy.

[10] Boni suggests this senhal designates Guida, the Countess of Rodez, where Sordel may have been a guest.

25 The King of Aragón,⁶ I want him to eat of this heart,
    then it will relieve him of the burden of shame
    he bears now for Marseille and Milhau; whatever he may
            say
    or do, he will not find his honor in any other way.   IV
    And next, I want them to give of this heart to the King
            of Navarre,⁷
30 he was worth more as count than king, I hear them say.
    It is wrong, when God raises a man to a noble state,
    that lack of heart should make him fall from fame.

    For the Count of Toulouse ⁸ there is great need that he
            eat well,
    if he thinks of what he used to possess and what he pos-
            sesses,
35 for if he does not recoup his loss with the heart of some-
            one else,
    I doubt he will do it with the heart he has in himself.   V
    And the Count of Provence,⁹ it is well that he eats if he
            remembers
    a man's worth nothing living robbed of his inheritance,
    and for all his effort to hold his ground and defend
            himself,
40 he must eat of this heart for the heavy burden he bears.

    The barons will wish me ill for the things that I speak
            well,   VI
    but they know I think as little of them as they of me.

    Sweet Relief,¹⁰ if only I could find some pity by your
            side,   VII
    I scorn every man who does not take me for his friend.

GUIRAUT RIQUIER

(*c. 1230–1292*)

"The last of the troubadours" was born at Narbonne, where he stayed for the greater part of his life, under the patronage of the Vicomte Amalric IV; then, after the death of Amalric in 1270, he spent the next ten years in the court of Alfonso X of Castile. In France again he found various patrons, including the "count of Astarac," whom he praises at the end of the *pastorela*.

Throughout the whole variety of Guiraut's work sounds the discontent of a man aware that he has arrived on a scene when the best part of it is over. He continually complains that few are left who can appreciate the old poetry—a venerable troubadour theme, but now suddenly a statement of the actual truth. In the latter part of his life, his songs were centered on religious themes, and Bel Deport, the *senhal* of the lady in his love lyrics, came to designate the Virgin Mary. *Be·m degra de chantar tener* (no. 60), dated 1292, is his last song, and it typifies his later work.

Perhaps his most original innovation was in the *pastorela*. The essential element in this genre had always been the transcience and isolation of the experience—it told of an encounter off the road, a moment set apart while the knight was passing by; and the outcome was either some stolen brutal pleasure, or, more usually among the troubadours, the embarrassment of the knight's lust and a reaffirmation of social order, all through the common sense of the peasant girl (see Marcabru, *L'autrier*, no. 14). At any rate, it is the sense both of the transient and the timeless that produces the chief effect—it is a moment out of context; the knight is free of the influence and surveillance of the court, and in the woods, alone, far from all restraint and the recognition of his peers, he can enjoy the prospect of some natural pleasure, or test the strength of his *mezura* and the qualities that identify him as a knight; because it is a moment guaranteed without consequences, and there are no restraints on the knight's behavior apart from his own ethical sense, which is revealed almost always as inadequate.

Guiraut made something new of this moment by returning it to the flow of time. Over a period of twenty years he wrote six *pastorelas* about the same knight and woman. In the first she is a young girl with a fiancé, later she is a young mother, finally a widow no longer young. The dialogue is always gay and witty, he is always full of importunate flattery, she levelheaded and in complete command. The stability of their characters contrasts with the proofs of the passing of time: her great joy has become her married daughter, and he, beneath his gay amorousness, senses the emptiness of his life and his calling. The effect of these *pastorelas* is something altogether new: the movement of time, and the human response to time, the cyclings of nature and the finality of human character, are all revealed in the pattern of these isolated moments.

Guiraut was a prolific poet, and much of his work is extant: beside fifteen rhymed epistles, eighty-nine lyrics of considerable variety, for Guiraut cultivated many of the genres that the earlier poets neglected, e.g., *descort, alba, retroencha.*

A Sant Pos de Tomeiras [1]
vengui l'autre dia,
de plueja totz mullatz,
en poder d'ostaleyras
5   qu'ieu no conoyssia;
ans fuy meravelhatz,
per que·l viella rizia,
qu'a la jove dizia   I
suau calque solatz;
10   mas quasquna·m fazia
los plazers que sabia
tro fuy gen albergatz;
que agui sovinensa
del temps que n'es passatz,
15   e cobrey conoyssensa
de·l vielha, de que·m platz.

E dissi·l: "Vos etz selha
que ja fos bergeira
e m'avetz tant trufat."
20   Elha·m dis, non pas felha:
"Senher, mais guerreira
no·us serai per mon grat."
"Pro femna, de maneira
tal vos vey segon teyra   II
25   qu'esser deu chastïat."

"Senher, s'ieu fos leugeira
non a trop qu'en carreira
fuy de trobar mercat."
"Pro femna, per aizina

---

[1] Text: *La Pastourelle dans la poésie occitane du moyen âge,* ed. Jean Audiau (Paris: de Boccard, 1923), pp. 73–79.

At Saint-Pons-de-Thomières [1]
the other day, soaked
from the rain, I came
to a place two landladies owned,

5   whom I didn't recognize.
But I was puzzled
because the old one laughed
and whispered something   I
that amused her to the girl.

10   But each one made me
comfortable, as she knew how,
so I had quite good lodgings.
Then I began to remember
back to an earlier time,

15   and I recollected that
old lady, with pleasure.

And I said to her, "You're the one
that used to be a shepherdess
and made fun of me all the time."

20   And she said, without spite,
—"Lord, I won't be your enemy
anymore, not willingly."
—"My good woman, the way
you always are when I see you,

25   you deserve to be told a thing or two."   II

—"Lord, I may have been carefree once,
but it's not been long since
I was on the point of making a deal."
—"Good woman, you said that to comfort

30   fon dich d'ome cohat."
         "Senher, ans suy vezina
         d'est amic non amat."

         "Pros femna, d'aital toza
         cum vos deu amaire
35   fort esser dezirans."
         "Senher Dieus! Per espoza
         mi vol; mas del faire
         no suy ges acordans."
         "Pros femna, de maltraire
40   vos es ben temps d'estraire,   III
         si es hom benanans."
         "Senher, assatz ad aire
         pogram viure; mas paire
         lo sai de ·vii· efans."
45   "Pros femna, gent servida
         seretz per sos filhs grans."
         "Senher, ja·n suy marida
         q'un no n'a de ·x· ans."

         "Na Femna descenada,
50   de mal etz estorta,
         e peitz anatz sercan."
         "Senher, ans suy membrada,
         que·l cor no m'i porta
         si que·n fassa mon dan."
55   "Pros femna, via torta
         queretz, don seretz morta,   IV
         so·m pes, enans d'un an."
         "Senher, ve·us qui·m coforta,
         quar de mon gaug es porta,
60   selha que·ns es denan."
         "Pros femna, vostra filha
         es, segon mon semblan."
         "Senher, pres de la Ilha,
         nos trobes vos antan." [2]

───────────────

[2] In the fourth *pastorela* the daughter is an infant; in the fifth, a little girl.

30   some tormented man."
    —"Lord, I'm his neighbor,
    the neighbor of this friend I don't love."

    —"Good woman, for a young girl
    like you a lover
35   must be full of desire."
    —"Lord God, he wants me
    for his wife. But for that marriage
    business, my heart isn't in it."
    —"Good woman, you've had a hard life,
40   this is your chance to get out of it,   III
    if he's well-to-do."
    —"Lord, we could live quite
    comfortably. But the fact is,
    he's got ·VII· kids."
45   —"Good woman, the older ones
    will help you."
    —"Lord, I'm sorry to say,
    he doesn't even have one ten years old."

    —"My mad woman,
50   you get pulled out of one mess,
    and you go looking for a worse."
    —"Lord, no, I'm just using my head
    so that I don't get carried
    away by my feelings and get hurt."
55   —"Good woman, you're taking
    the wrong road, it'll kill you   IV
    in a year, and that makes me sad."
    —"Well, my lord, here is my comfort,
    the gate to my joy,
60   this girl before you."
    —"Good woman, your daughter,
    I presume."
    —"Lord, you found us, once,
    near l'Isle Jourdain." [2]

65   "Pros femna, doncx emenda
convenra que·m fassa
per vos de motz pezars."
"Senher, tant o atenda
qu'a sso marit plassa,
70   pueys faitz vostres afars."
"Pros femna, no·us espassa,
enquers, e dura·us massa   V
maishuey vostre trufars."
"En Guiraut Riquier, lassa
75   suy quar tant seguetz trassa
d'aquestz leugiers chantars."
"Pros femna, quar vilheza
vos a faitz chans amars."
"Senher, de vos se deza
80   tant qu'als vielhs non etz pars!"

    "Pros femna, de mal dire
no·m feratz temensa,
mas aisso solatz par."
"Senher, ges no m'albire
85   que ma malsabensa
vos saubessetz pessar."
"Pus e vostra tenensa
suy, ben devetz sufrensa   VI
de tot ab mi trobar."
90   "Senher, ges no m'agensa
qu'ie·us diga ren per tensa,
ni·us fassa malestar."
"Dona, ja no poiriatz,
quar no us puesc desamar."
95   "Senher, quant o fariatz,
ye·us vuelh totz temps honrar."

    "Al pro Comte agensa
d'Astarac nostra tensa,
Dona, qu'om deu lauzar."

65 —"My good woman, in that case
it is only right that *she* make
amends for many griefs you've given me."
—"Lord, let her just wait
till her husband consents,
70 then go right ahead."
—"Good woman, you haven't stopped it
yet, you go right on   v
laughing at me."
—"En Guiraut Riquier, I'm sad
75 because you follow the path
of those foolish songs."
—"Good woman, you say that because old age
has sung some bitter songs to you."
—"Lord, it keeps away from you so well,
80 you don't look at all like the other old men."

—"Good woman, none of your harsh words
could make me afraid,
but now you are jesting."
—"Lord, I really don't think
85 you could have the slightest
idea how displeased I am."
—"I'm a guest in your
house, you have to take   vi
whatever I say."
90 —"Lord, I don't get any pleasure
out of picking a quarrel with you,
or making you uncomfortable."
—"Madame, you couldn't do either,
because I cannot fall out of love with you."
95 —"Lord, when you do just that,
I want to honor you always."

—"The noble count of Astarac,
whom everyone should praise,
Madame, will be amused by our little quarrel."

100   "Senher, sa grans valensa
       lo fai ab bevolensa   VII
       a totas gens nomnar."
       "Dona, si·l sa veziatz,
       saubessetz l'amparar?"
105   "Senher, ben auziriatz
       que n'ay en cor a far."

                          60

       Be·m degra de chantar tener,[1]
       quar a chan coven alegriers;
       e mi destrenh tant cossiriers
       que·m fa de totas partz doler   I
5   remembran mon greu temps passat,
       esgardan lo prezent forsat
       e cossiran l'avenidor
       que per totz ai razon que plor.

       Per que no·m deu aver sabor
10   mos chans, qu'es ses alegretat;
       mas Dieus m'a tal saber donat
       qu'en chantan retrac ma folhor,   II
       mo sen, mon gauch, mon desplazer,
       e mon dan et mon pro per ver,
15   qu'a penas dic ren ben estiers;
       mas trop suy vengutz als derriers.

       Qu'er non es grazitz lunhs mestiers
       menhs en cort que de belh saber
       de trobar; qu'auzir e vezer
20   hi vol hom mais captenhs leugiers   III
       e critz mesclatz ab dezonor;
       quar tot, quan sol donar lauzor

[1] Text: J. Anglade, *Anthologie des troubadours*. Paris: de Boccard, 1927;
2d ed., 1953.

100   —"Lord, because of his great worth
       people say his name   VII
       with much love."
       —"Madame, if you saw him right here,
       would you know how to welcome him?"
105   —"Lord, you'd find out
       what it's in my heart to do for him."

60

       I should abstain from singing,[1]
       for the lightness of joy alone befits the song,
       and I am weighed down by thoughts
       on every side that make me grave,   I
5   thinking back upon my heavy past,
       and my present, seeing how it is oppressed,
       pondering the future,
       I have cause for tears and deep unrest.

       My song would not have its savor for me,
10   because it does not have that lightness;
       except that God has given me the skill
       such that singing I must retrace my foolishness,   II
       my sense, my rejoicing, my chagrin,
       the truth of my loss and gain,
15   for otherwise there is no good to what I say.
       But I have come too late.

       For now no craft is less esteemed
       at court than the beautiful mastery
       of song, because they notice nothing
20   there but their ridiculous manners   III
       and their shrieks of dishonor.
       The things the court would once applaud

es al pus del tot oblidat,
que·l mons es guays totz en barat.

25 Per erguelh e per malvestat
dels Christias ditz, luenh d'amor
e dels mans de Nostre Senhor,
em del sieu Sant Loc discipat   IV
ab massa d'autres encombriers;
30 don par qu'elh nos es aversiers
per desadordenat voler
e per outracujat poder.

Lo greu perilh devem temer
de dobla mort, qu'es prezentiers,
35 que·ns sentam Sarrazis sobriers,
e Dieus que·ns giet a non chaler;   V
et entre nos, qu'em azirat,
tost serem de tot aterrat;
e no·s cossiran la part lor,
40 segon que·m par, nostre rector.

Silh que crezem en unitat,
poder, savieza, bontat,
done a sas obras lugor,
don sian mundat peccador.   VI
45 Dona, Maires de caritat,
acapta nos per pietat
de ton filh, nostre redemtor,
gracia, perdon et amor.

are all forgotten now,
for the world exults in fraud.

25   Through the malice and the pride
of so-called Christians far from the love
of our God and His law,
we have been thrown out of His Holy Place,   IV
with a great mass of vexations.
30   Now it seems He has turned against us,
for our disordered will
and outrageous power.

We should fear the grave peril
of the double death upon us,
35   let us feel the Saracens overrunning us,
and God casting us away in His indifference.   V
And we who rage at one another,
we shall be driven into the ground,
and those who govern us renounce
40   their part, I see this now.

May He, in whom our faith reveals
oneness, wisdom, power, goodness,
bring light upon His works,
that sinners may be purified.   VI
45   Mary, Mother of Charity,
for pity call down upon us from above,
from our Savior, your Son,
grace, forgiveness, love.

PART II

---

*Lyrics of the
Trouvères*

Guide to the Pronunciation
of Old French

All of the letters are pronounced, except for *s* in certain conditions: *s* is not pronounced in the middle of a word before a consonant (*isle* was pronounced as in modern French *île*). Otherwise, the safest rule is to pronounce *s* and every other letter as well.

For the dipthongs the rules are the same as in Old Provençal, with each letter retaining its value. Thus *aumosne* ("charity") should be pronounced *áoomone*. The diphthong *oi* or *oy* was pronounced as in English "boy" throughout the twelfth century. In the course of the following century it came to be pronounced *wé*. The triphthongs, again like Old Provençal, stressed the middle element: eáu.

The pronunciation of palatalized *l* (usually spelled *ill*) and *n* (*ign*) is like that in modern Spanish or Italian (see the rules for Old Provençal).

In the twelfth century *ch* and *j* were pronounced as in "catch" and "judge." *C* and *g* before a front vowel (i or e) were pronounced *ts* and *dj*, respectively. In the thirteenth century they evolved into their modern French sounds.

The *r* was rolled, as in modern Spanish or Italian.

X represents *us. Dex-Deus.*

Z at the end of a word was pronounced *ts* in the twelfth century. Afterwards it was reduced to a simple *s* sound.

Remember that unstressed final *e* was pronounced, even when it followed another *e: nee* ("born," past participle) has two syllables.

The long close *o* (as in modern French *rôle*) had an even closer sound in Old French, approximately like the *u* in "full": *chanson-tshansun.*

Otherwise, be guided by modern French—the *u*, for example, already had its modern French sound.

Contents

CONON DE BÉTHUNE

(c. 1150–December 17, 1219 or 1220)

The poet belonged to a great and noble family in Artois and was related to the first French emperor of Constantinople, Baudouin IX. He was in the Third Crusade (1189–1193) and was a principal figure in the Fourth Crusade beginning in 1200, from which time he was called on repeatedly to conduct important political and military negotiations. He was Seneschal and then Regent of Constantinople, where he died.

He was one of the first trouvères to compose in the style of the troubadours. Only ten of his lyrics are extant, but their variety is striking. He was widely renowned as a poet in his day and continues to be regarded as one of the best of the northern French poets.

Text: *Chansons,* ed. Axel Wallensköld. Helsingfors: Imprimerie Centrale, 1891.

1

Si voirement com chele dont je cant
vaut mius ke toutes les bones ki sont,
et je l'aim plus ke rien ki soit ou mont,
si me doint Deus s'amour sans dechevoir; I
5 ke tel desir en ai et tel voloir,
o tant o plus, Deus en set le vreté.
Si com malades desire santé,
desir jou li et s'amour a avoir.

Or sai jou bien ke riens ne puet valoir
10 tant com cheli de cui j'ai tant canté,
c'ore ai vëu et li et se biauté,
et si sai bien ke tant a de valour II
ke je doi faire et outrage et folour
d'amer si haut—ke ne m'avroit mestier—;
15 et non por cant maint povre chevalier
fait riches cuers venir a haute honour.

Ains ke fusse sorpris de cheste amour,
savoie jou autre gent conseillier,
et or sai bien d'autrui jeu enseignier
20 et si ne sai mie le mien juer; III
si sui com chil ke as escas voit cler
et ki tres bien ensaigne autres gens,
et cant il jue, si pert si sen sens
k'il ne se set escoure de mater.

25 Hé, las! dolens je ne sai tant canter
ke me dame perchoive mes tormens,
n'encor n'est pas si grans mes hardemens
ke je li os dire les maus ke trai, IV
ne devant li n'en os parler ne sai,
30 et cant je sui aillours, devant autrui,

1

As truly as she of whom I sing
is worth more than all the good women there are,
and I love her more than anything in the world,
so God give me her love without failing me,   I
5 for my desire is so great, and my longing—
how great God knows.
As a sick man longs for health,
I long to have her and her love.

I know now, no being can be worth
10 as much as this lady I have so often sung about,
for now I have seen her and her beauty
and know she is so great   II
I must be outrageous and crazy
to love so high—higher than I need to.
15 And yet many a poor knight
is borne to great honor by a noble heart.

Before this love surprised me
I knew how to give counsel to others.
And even now I am good for advice in another's game
20 and do not know how to play my own.   III
I am like one who sees all the moves in chess
and teaches others very well,
and when he sits down to play loses all his skill
and cannot save himself from mate.

25 Alas, full of grief I cannot manage by singing
to make my lady see my torment,
nor am I bold enough
to dare tell her what I suffer face to face: IV
nor do I dare speak in her presence, I can't.
30 When I am elsewhere, with someone else,

lors i parol, mais si peu m'i dedui
c'un anui vaut li deduis ke j'en ai.

Encor devis coment je li dirai
le grant dolour ke j'en trai sans anui,
35 ke tant l'aour et desir, cant j'i sui,
ke ne li os descovrir me raison;   V
si vait de moi com fait dou campïon
ke de lonc tens aprent a escremir,
et cant il vient ou camp as cous ferir,
40 si ne set rien d'escu ne de baston.

2

Mout me semont Amours ke je m'envoise,
cant je plus doi de canter estre cois;
mais j'ai plus grant talent ke je me coise,
por chou s'ai mis men canter en defois;   I
5 ke men langage ont blasmé li Franchois
et mes canchons, oiant les Campenois,
et le Contesse encor, dont plus me poise.[1]

Le Roïne n'a pas fait ke cortoise,
ki me reprist, ele et ses fius, li Rois.[2]
10 Encor ne soit me parole franchoise,
si le puet on bien entendre en franchois;   II
ne chil ne sont bien apris ne cortois,
s'il m'ont repris, se j'ai dis mos d'Artois,
car je ne fui pas noris a Pontoise.[3]

---

[1] The Countess of Champagne, Marie de France, daughter of Eleanor of
Aquitaine. Axel Wallensköld, Conon's editor, writes as follows about this
lyric: "Strophes 1 and 2 are of a certain importance for the history of the
French language, because we find there explicit mention of dialectal differences in the French-speaking area toward the year 1181. One can also see
there the first signs of the absorbing influence that the dialect of the Île de
France was going to exert over other dialects." It should be noted that the
original text does not contain as many dialectal forms as the translation.

then I speak, but delight in it so little
the pleasure I get amounts to vexation.

Still I think up ways to tell her,
without offense, of the great pain I suffer,
35 for I adore her and want her so much, when I am with
       her
   I don't have the nerve to tell her what I have in mind.   v
   It goes with me as with a champion
   who has long practiced fighting in arms,
   and when he comes, to strike some blows, into the field,
40 can't remember what you do with lance or shield.

2

Love summons me now to dispawt
when maw than evah I should silence my sawng;
what is maw, I have a greatah desiah to keep still,
wheafaw I have put an end to my singing;   I
5 faw the French have criticeoized my language
   and my sawngs in the presence of the Champenois,
   and the Countess too, which heuits me even maw.[1]

The Queen did not act cueuiteously
to reproach me, she and huh son, the King.[2]
10 Even though my weuids ahw not exactly French,
   they can undastand them in French.   II
   They ahw not well leuined or cueuiteous
   who reproved me faw speaking Ahtesian dialect,
   because I was not, aftuhawl, brawt up in Pontoise.[3]

Medieval courtly poets adhered to a basic literary language, though they
sometimes peppered their songs with forms borrowed from their dialects,
largely for the sake of rhyme. The translation reflects what we imagine as
the performance situation.
[2] The Queen: Adèle de Champagne, widow of Louis VII. The King: Philippe-
Auguste.
[3] Often cited as the place where the best French was spoken.

15   Deus! ke ferai? Dirai li men corage?
      Li irai jou dont s'amour demander?
      Oïl, par Deu! car tel sont li usage
      c'on n'i puet mais sans demant rien trover;   III
      et se je sui outrajous dou trover,
20   si n'en doit pas me dame a moi irer,
      mais vers Amour, ki me fait dire outrage.

3

      Ahi! Amours! com dure departie
      me covenra faire de le meillour
      ki onkes fust amee ne servie!
      Deus me ramaint a li, par se douchour,   I
5   si voirement ke m'en part a dolour!
      Las! c'ai jou dit? Ja ne m'en part jou mie!
      Se li cors vait servir nostre Seignour,
      li cuers remaint dou tout en se baillie.

      Por li m'en vois sospirant en Surie,
10   car je ne doi faillir men creatour.
      Ki li faura a chest besoing d'aïe,
      sachiés ke il li faura a graignour;   II
      et sachent bien li grant et li menour
      ke la doit on faire chevalerie
15   ou on conkiert Paradis et honour
      et los et pris et l'amour de s'amie.

      Deus! tant avons esté prou par oiseuse,
      ore i parra ki a chertes iert preus;
      s'irons vengier le honte doloreuse,
20   dont cascuns doit estre iriés et honteus;   III
      car a no tens est perdus li sains leus
      ou Deus sofri por nous mort angoisseuse;
      s'ore i laissons nos anemis morteus,
      a tous jours mais iert no vie honteuse.

15 God, what shall I do? Shall I speak my haht to huh?
Shall I go to huh to ask faw huh love?
Yes, by God, faw the way things get done,
if you don't speak up, then you have nothing to expect.   III
And if I am outlandish in my sawng,
20 my lady should get angry not at me
but at Love, who makes me say wild things in dialect.

3

Alas, Love, what hard leave
I must take from the best lady
a man ever loved and served.
May God in his goodness lead me back to her   I
5 as surely as I part from her in grief.
Alas, what have I said? I do not part from her at all.
If my body goes to serve our Lord,
my heart remains all in her power.

For Him I go sighing into Syria,
10 for I must not fail my Creator.
Whoever fails Him in this need for help—
do not doubt he shall fail in a greater need.   II
Let the great ones and the little ones know
that *there* is the place for the great chivalric deed,
15 where one wins Paradise and honor
and praise and the love of his beloved.

God! we have long been brave in idleness,
now we shall see who is brave in deed;
we shall go to avenge the burning shame
20 which ought to make us all angry and ashamed;   III
for in our time the Holy Place is lost
where God suffered death in agony for us;
if now we let our enemies remain,
our life will be forever more a life of shame.

25 Ki chi ne veut avoir vie anoieuse,
   si voist por Deu morir liés et joieus,
   ke chele mors est douche et savoreuse
   dont on conkiert le regne prechïeus,   IV
   ne ja de mort n'en i morra uns seus,
30 ains naisteront en vie glorïeuse.
   Ki revenra mout sera ëureus;
   a tous jours mais en iert honours s'espeuse.

   Tuit li clergié et li home d'eage
   ki en aumosne et en bien fait manront,
35 partiront tuit a chest pelerinage,
   et les dames ki castement vivront   V
   et loiauté feront a chiaus ki vont;
   et s'eles font par mal conseil folage,
   a lasches gens et mauvais le feront,
40 car tuit li bon iront en chest voiage.

   Deus est assis en sen saint iretage;
   ore i parra com chil le secorront
   cui il jeta de le prison ombrage,
   cant il fu mors en le crois ke Turc ont.   VI
45 Sachiés: chil sont trop honi ki n'iront,
   s'il n'ont poverte o vieilleche o malage;
   et chil ki sain et juene et riche sont,
   ne puent pas demorer sans hontage.

   Las! je m'en vois plorant des eus dou front
50 la ou Deus veut amender men corage,   VII
   et sachiés bien c'a le meillour dou mont
   penserai plus ke ne fas a voiage.

25 Whoever does not want a life of misery here,
   let him go die joyfully for God,
   for the taste of such a death is sweet and good,
   for which one wins the precious kingdom.   IV
   No, not a single one of them will die into death,
30 but all will be born into glorious life.
   Whoever comes back will be full of happiness;
   honor to the end of his days will be his wife.

   All clergy and aged men
   who shall remain behind for charity
35 will take part, all, in this pilgrimage,
   and the ladies who will live in chastity   V
   and keep faith with those who go.
   And if through evil counsel they do foolishness,
   they will do it with cowards, with scum,
40 for all good men will be gone on this voyage.

   God is besieged in his holy heritage;
   now we shall see how they come to his aid
   whom he let loose from the dark prison
   when he died on the Cross the Turks possess.   VI
45 Be sure of this: those who will not go bring dishonor on
                        their name,
   unless they are poor, or old, or sick.
   Those who are healthy, young, and rich
   cannot stay home without shame.

   Alas! I go away weeping from my eyes,
50 I go where God wants to amend my heart,   VII
   and I say I shall think of the best in this world
   more than the voyage on which I part.

4

Se rage et derverie
et destreche d'amer
m'a fait dire folie
et d'amour mesparler,   I
5   nus ne m'en doit blasmer.
S'ele a tort m'i fausnie,
Amours, cui j'ai servie,
ne me sai ou fier.

Amours, de felonie
10   vos vourai esprover;
tolu m'avés le vie
et mort sans desfïer.   II
La m'avés fait penser
ou me joie est perie;
15   chele cui jou en prie
me fait d'autre esperer.

Plus bele k'image
chele ke je vos di,
mais tant a vil corage,
20   anoious et failli,   III
k'ele fait tout aussi
com le louve sauvage,
ki des lous d'un boscage
trait le poiour a li.

25   N'a pas grant vasselage
fait, s'ele m'a traï;
nus ne l'en tient por sage,
ki sen estre ait oï;   IV
mais puis k'il est ensi

4

If rage and madness
and the violence of loving
have made me speak crazily
and say bad things of love,   I
5   no one must blame me.
If Love, whom I have served,
wrongly plays me false,
I do not know what to rely on.

Love, I would like
10   to convince you of your crime;
you have destroyed my life,
killed me without a challenge;   II
you made me turn my mind
to where my joy is damned.
15   She whom I beg for love
has something different planned.

More beautiful than a statue,
this one I tell you of,
but the heart of her is something vile,
20   mean and vicious,   III
and she acts
like a wild bitch
that gets the worst dogs
in the bushes to come to her.[1]

25   It took no great act of prowess
for her to betray me;
no one who hears what she's done
will think she is wise;   IV
but since that's how it is

[1] Literally, she is like a vixen that gets the worst wolves.

30   k'ele a tort m'i desgage,
je li rent sen homage
et si me part de li.

Mout est le tere dure,
sans eue et sans humour,
35   ou j'ai mise me cure,
mais n'i keurai nul jour   v
fruit ne fueille ne flour,
s'est bien tens et mesure
et raisons et droiture
40   ke li rende s'amour.

5

L'autrier avint en chel autre païs   2
c'uns chevaliers ot une dame amée.
Tant com le dame fu en son bon pris,
li a s'amour escondite et veée.   I
5   Puis fu uns jours k'ele li dist: "Amis,
mené vos ai par parole mains dis;
ore est l'amours conëue et mostrée;
d'ore en avant serai a vo devis."

Li chevaliers le resgarda ou vis,
10 si le vit mout pale et descolorée.
"Dame," fait il, "chertes mal sui baillis,
ke n'ëustes piecha cheste pensée.   II
Vostre clers vis, ki sanloit flours de lis,
est si alés, dame, de mal en pis
15 k'il m'est avis ke me soiés emblée.
A tart avés, dame, chest conseil pris!"

Cant le dame s'oï si ramponer,
grant honte en ot, si dist par se folie:
"Par Deu, vassaus, jel dis por vous gaber.

30   and she wrongfully dismisses me,
        I now renounce my service as her man,
        and I quit her.

        The ground is very hard,
        dry, without water,
35   where I have spent much labor;
        I shall never gather   V
        fruit or flower or leaf.
        It is now the time,
        and it is just and right,
40   that I renounce her love.

                        5

        The other day it happened in another land
        there was a knight who loved a lady.
        All the while she was at her best
        she refused his love and said no.   I
5   Then there came a day when she told him, "Friend,
        I have led you along from day to day with talk;
        now your love is proved,
        from now on I shall do what you like."

        The knight looked at her face,
10   saw it very pale, its color gone.
        "Lady," he said, "it's my bad luck
        you didn't decide this long ago.   II
        Your bright face, that once looked like a lily,
        has gone, lady, from bad to worse,
15   so that now I feel I have been robbed of you.
        Lady, you made up your mind too late."

        When the lady heard herself mocked like that,
        she was greatly ashamed and said, in her foolishness,
        "By God, vassal, I only said it to make fun of you.

20 Cuidiés vos dont c'a chertes le vos die?   III
    Onkes nul jour ne me vint en penser.
    Savriés vos dont dame de pris amer?
    Nenil, par Deu! ains vos prendroit envie
    d'un bel varlet baisier et acoler."

25 "Dame," fait il, "j'ai bien oï parler
    de vostre pris, mais che n'est ore mie;
    et de Troie rai jou oï conter
    k'ele fu ja de mout grant seignorie;   IV
    or n'i puet on fors les plaches trover,
30 et si vos lo ensi a escuser
    ke chil soient reté de l'iresie
    ke des or mais ne vos vouront amer."

    "Par Deu, vassaus, mout avés fol pensé,
    cant vos m'avés reprové men eage.
35 Se j'avoie men jovent tout usé,
    si sui jou riche et de si grant parage   V
    c'on m'ameroit a petit de biauté.
    Encor n'a pas un mois entier passé
    ke li Marchis m'envoia sen message,
40 et li Barrois a por m'amour josté." [1]

    "Dame," fait il, "che vos a mout grevé,
    ke vos fiés en vostre seignorage;
    mais tel set ont ja por vous sopiré,
    se vos estiés fille au roi de Cartage,   VI
45 ki ja mais jour n'en avront volenté.
    On n'aime pas dame por parenté,
    mais cant ele est bele et cortoise et sage.
    Vos en savrés par tens le verité!"

---

[1] Identified by Wallensköld respectively as Boniface II of Montferrat (1192–1207), one of the heroes of the Fourth Crusade; and Guillaume de Barrès, who defeated Richard Coeur de Lion in single combat.

20 Do you really think I'm speaking seriously?   III
    It never once entered my head.
    Besides, would you be able to love a great lady?
    No, by God, I think you'd much prefer
    to kiss and hug a pretty boy instead."

25 "Lady," says he, "I have indeed heard talk
    of your greatness, but there is nothing left of it.
    I have also heard talk of Troy,
    how it was once a great power;   IV
    nowadays they can just barely find the site.
30 And therefore I advise you to acquit
    all those from the charge of unorthodox sex
    who won't be wanting to love you any more."

    "By God, vassal, you figured foolishly
    when you reproached me for my age.
35 Even if I have used up all my youth,
    I am still so rich and of such high degree   V
    I could be loved with little beauty.
    Not one month has passed
    since the Marquis sent me his message
40 and de Barrès jousted for my love." [1]

    "Lady," he says, "it has bothered you very much
    that you have to rely on your high birth;
    but those seven who sighed for you in your youth,
    now, if you were the daughter of the king of Carthage,   VI
45 will not want to any more.
    One doesn't love a lady for her family,
    but when she is beautiful and courteous and wise.
    It won't be long before you learn the truth."

LE CHÂTELAIN DE COUCI

(d. 1203)

The poet has been identified with Guy, the châtelain of Coucy, who died at sea during the Fourth Crusade. As his title indicates, he was important: a châtelain was high up in the feudal hierarchy, being a vassal of the king or of a duke or a count, the governor of a castle, and the justice of the region; and Coucy (in Vermandois, in southern Picardy) was a powerful and well-known castellany—one of the most powerful in the twelfth century, according to the poet's editor, Alain Lerond. The poet became even more famous as the hero of a thirteenth-century romance; he dies at sea in that, too, and his heart is sent to his beloved, the lady of Fayel, and fed to her by her jealous husband.

His lyrics are clearly modeled on troubadour themes and forms, but he innovates also, quite in the spirit of their pride in technique (*Li nouviauz tanz*, no. 8, for example, which, as published by Lerond, has an unprecedented strophic order, with identical rhymes in i, ii, and iv, and in iii, v, and vi; note that these strophes can be rearranged into *coblas ternas*, three successive strophes with identical rhymes). The mournful lover's tone of his lyrics hardly varies, but within that range he is unsurpassed.

Text: *Chansons attribuées au Chastelain de Couci*, ed. Alain Lerond. Publications de la Faculté des lettres et sciences humaines de Rennes, vol. 7. Paris: Presses Universitaires de France, 1964.

6

A vous, amant, plus k'a nulle autre gent,
est bien raisons que ma doleur conplaigne,
quar il m'estuet partir outreement
et dessevrer de ma loial conpaigne;   I
5 et quant l'i pert, n'est rienz qui me remaigne;
et sachiez bien, amours, seürement,
s'ainc nuls morut pour avoir cuer dolent,
donc n'iert par moi maiz meüs vers ne laiz.

Biauz sire Diex, qu'iert il dont, et conment?
10 Convenra m'il qu'en la fin congié praigne?
Oïl, par Dieu, ne puet estre autrement:
sanz li m'estuet aler en terre estraigne;   II
or ne cuit maiz que granz mauz me soufraigne,
quant de li n'ai confort n'alegement,
15 ne de nule autre amour joie n'atent,
fors que de li—ne sai se c'iert jamaiz.

Biauz sire Diex, qu'iert il du consirrer
du grant soulaz et da la conpaignie
et des douz moz dont seut a moi parler
20 cele qui m'ert dame, conpaigne, amie?   III
Et quant recort sa douce conpaignie
et les soulaz qu'el me soloit moustrer,
conment me puet li cuers u cors durer
qu'il ne s'en part? Certes il est mauvaiz.

25 Ne me vout pas Diex pour neiant doner
touz les soulaz qu'ai eüs en ma vie,
ainz les me fet chierement conparer;
s'ai grant poour cist loiers ne m'ocie.   IV
Merci, amours! S'ainc Diex fist vilenie,
30 con vilainz fait bone amour dessevrer:
ne je ne puiz l'amour de moi oster,
et si m'estuet que je ma dame lais.

6

To you, lovers, more than all the others,
it is right that I lament my grief,
for I must, absolutely, go away
and part from my true love;   I
5 and when I lose her, I have nothing left.
Now, Love, take note of this and do not doubt it:
if a man ever died from a grieving heart—
there will not be another song from me, not one strophe.

Dear Lord God, what will happen, and how?
10 Shall I have to take my leave at last?
Yes, by God, it can't be otherwise:
I must go, without her, into a strange land;   II
Now I do not think I shall lack big sorrows,
for I shall not have her comfort or her words,
15 and I look for my joy to no other love
but the love of her and do not know if that shall ever be.

Dear Lord God, must I do without
that great delight and company
and those always gentle words of her
20 who was my lady, my friend, my love?   III
When I remember her gentle presence
and the pleasures she revealed to me,
how can the heart in my body keep
from breaking out? It must be a poor thing.

25 God does not want to give me free
all the pleasures I have had in my life,
but makes me pay dear;
now I fear this toll will destroy me.   IV
Love, pity! If ever God did something base,
30 he has, like a brute, broken true love in two:
I cannot put this love away from me,
and yet I must leave my lady.

Or seront lié li faus losengeour,
qui tant pesoit des biens qu'avoir soloie;
35 maiz ja de ce n'iere pelerins jour
que ja vers iauz bone volenté aie;   V
pour tant porrai perdre toute ma voie,
quar tant m'ont fait de mal li trahitour,
se Diex voloit qu'il eüssent m'amour,
40 ne me porroit chargier pluz pesant faiz.

Je m'en voiz, dame! A Dieu le Creatour
conmant vo cors, en quel lieu que je soie;
ne sai se ja verroiz maiz mon retour:
aventure est que jamaiz vous revoie.   VI
45 Pour Dieu vos pri, en quel lieu que je soie,
que nos convens tenez, vieigne u demour,
et je pri Dieu qu'ensi me doint honour
con je vous ai esté amis verais.

7

L'an que rose ne fueille
ne flour ne puet paroir,
que n'oi chanter par brueille
oisel n'au main n'au soir,
5 adonc flourist mes cuers en un voloir   I
di fine amour ki m'a en son pooir,
dont ja ne quier issir;
et s'il est nus ki m'en voelle partir,
je nel quier ja savoir, ne Diex nel voelle!

10 Bien est droiz que m'en dueille,
quant ma doleur desir,
et mieuz aim que ne sueille
ce dont je ne puis joïr,
et bien connoiz que n'i doi avenir;   II
15 s'amours ne vaint raison, g'i doi faillir,

Now the slanderers will celebrate
who used to groan under the weight of my joys;
35 I will never be pilgrim enough
to wish them well;   V
and so I may waste this voyage,
for those traitors have done me so much harm,
if God commanded me to love *them*
40 He couldn't weigh me down with a heavier burden.

I go, Lady. To God the Creator
I commend you, wherever I find myself.
I do not know whether you will ever see my return:
perhaps I shall never see you again.   VI
45 In God's name I ask you, wherever I may be,
keep our promises, whether I return or stay,
and I pray God give me honor as surely
as I have loved you faithfully.

7

The season when no rose or leaf
or flower can come forth,
when I hear no bird chanting
in the woods in the morning or night—
5 that is when my heart flowers in one desire   I
for perfect love, which has me in its power,
which I do not want to be free of;
and if there is anyone who wants to get me out of it,
I do not want to know him, and may God not want it!

10 I am right when I grieve,
because I want my suffering,
and I love more than ever
what I cannot have
and know I shall never reach;   II
15 if Love does not overcome Reason, I have to fail,

ce di je tout de voir.
Pour Dieu, amours, vueilliez en nonchaloir
metre raison, tant qu'ele m'i acueille!

Dame, nus maus que j'aie
20 ne m'est fors alegier,
quar sanz vous ne porroie
vivre, ne je nel quier.
Sanz vous amer ne m'a vie mestier,   III
se je ne vueill tout le monde anoier
25 ou aler m'ent morant.
Ja Damedieuz ne m'i doint vivre tant
qu'al siecle anuie et perde amour veraie!

Par maintes foiz m'esfroie
Amours et fait pensant,
30 et souvent me rapaie
et done cuer joiant;
einsi me fait vivre melleement   IV
d'ire et de bien; ne sai s'ele a talent
que me vueille assaier,
35 u s'el le fait de gré pour moi irrier,
pour esprouver se pour mal requerroie.

Mainte longue semainne
trai, quant sui loig de li,
et passant a grant painne,
40 souvent les en maudi.
Je n'en puiz rienz, las, quar je desir si   V
a recevoir cele donc pas n'oubli
les mos ne les samblanz,
ainz m'i recort et m'i sui remembranz,
45 si m'i confort quant ele m'est lontainne.

I speak the truth.
For God's sake, Love, let Reason lose
its influence till she accepts me.

Lady, I have no torment
20 that is not my joy,
for without you I could not
live and do not want to.
Without loving you my life has no use—   III
unless I want to get on everyone's nerves
25 or walk around dying.
Mother of God, let me not live long enough
to annoy the world and lose true love.

Many times Love
scares me and fills me with thoughts,
30 yet often she restores my peace
and gives me a heart full of joy;
thus she makes me live in a wild disorder   IV
of grief and happiness, and I don't know whether
she does this to try me,
35 whether she does it for pleasure, to torture me,
to see if the pain makes me give up.

Many a long week
I drag out far from her,
and in my suffering
40 I curse and curse the days away from her.   V
There is nothing I can do, alas, for I want
to win her, whose words and ways
I do not forget,
no, I think of her and behold her in my mind,
45 and that is my comfort when she is far away.

8

Li nouviauz tanz et mais et violete
et lousseignolz me semont de chanter,
et mes fins cuers me fait d'une amourete
si douz present que ne l'os refuser.   I
5 Or me lait Diex en tele honeur monter
que cele u j'ai mon cuer et mon penser
tieigne une foiz entre mes braz nuete
ançoiz qu'aille outremer!

Au conmencier la trouvai si doucete,
10 ja ne quidai pour li mal endurer,
mes ses douz vis et sa bele bouchete
et si vair oeill, bel et riant et cler,   II
m'orent ainz pris que m'osaisse doner;
se ne me veut retenir ou cuiter,
15 mieuz aim a li faillir, si me pramete,
qu'a une autre achiever.

Las! pour coi l'ai de mes ieuz reguardee,
la douce rienz qui fausse amie a non,
quant de moi rit et je l'ai tant amee?
20 Si doucement ne fu trahis nus hom.   III
Tant con fui mienz, ne me fist se bien non,
mes or sui suenz, si m'ocit sanz raison;
et c'est pour ce que de cuer l'ai amee!
N'i set autre ochoison.

25 De mil souspirs que je li doi par dete,
ne m'en veut pas un seul cuite clamer;
ne fausse amours ne lait que s'entremete,
ne ne me lait dormir ne reposer.   IV
S'ele m'ocit, mainz avra a guarder;[1]

---

[1] Because he is her "prisoner."

8

The new season, May, and violets
and the nightingale summon me to sing,
and my faithful heart makes me so sweet a present
of my love, I cannot refuse.   I
5 Now may God let me rise to the honor
of holding her, in whom I have set my heart
and mind, once, a little naked, in my arms—
before I cross the sea.

At the start I found her so gentle
10 I never thought I'd suffer pain because of her,
no, her sweet face and her pretty mouth
and vair eyes—beautiful, smiling, bright—   II
captured me before I even dared surrender;
if she will neither keep me nor let me go free,
15 I still prefer to fail with her, if she gives me a promise,
than succeed with any other.

Alas, why did my eyes behold her,
that gentle thing named False Love,
since she laughs at me, and I have loved her so?
20 No man was ever so pleasantly betrayed.   III
As long as I was my own man, she did nothing but make
                me happy;
Now I am hers, and for no reason she kills me.
It must be because I have loved her with a faithful heart.
She cannot have another cause.

25 Of the thousand sighs I owe her
she will not excuse me from a single one;
and False Love does not stop being busy,
she will not let me rest or sleep.   IV
If she kills me, she'll have less to watch over,[1]

30 je ne m'en sai vengier fors au plourer;
quar qui amours destruit et desirete,
ne l'en doit on blasmer.

Sour toute joie est cele courounee
que j'aim d'amours. Diex, faudrai i je dont?
35 Nenil, par Dieu; teus est ma destinee,
et tel destin m'ont doné li felon;   V
si sevent bien qu'il font grant mesprison,
quar qui ce tolt dont ne puet faire don,
il en conquiert anemis et mellee,
40 n'i fait se perdre non.

Si coiement est ma doleurs celee
qu'a mon samblant ne la recounoist on;
se ne fussent la gent maleüree,
n'eüsse pas souspiré en pardon: VI
45 Amours m'eüst doné son guerredon.
Maiz en cel point que dui avoir mon don,
lor fu l'amour descouverte et moustree;
Ja n'aient il pardon!

9

Merci clamans de mon fol errement,
ferai la fin de mes chançons oïr,
quar trahi m'a et mort a escïent
mes jolis cuers que je doi tant haïr;   I
5 cest mal m'a fait pour le gré d'autre gent.
Tout sunt parti de moi joieuz talent,
et quant joie me faut, bien est raisons
qu'avec ma joie faillent mes chançons.

30 and I don't know what revenge to take except to weep.
When a man is destroyed and despoiled by Love,
he should not be blamed for it.

She is crowned above every joy,
this one I love with love. God, must I fail with her
then?
35 I won't get her, by God; it's my destiny,
a destiny I got from slanderers;   V
they know they're doing wrong,
and so a man who takes away and keeps what he cannot
make a gift of
wins enemies for that, and war,
40 and has to lose.

So silently is my pain hidden,
no one notices it in the way I look;
if it were not for those damned people,
I would not have sighed in vain;   VI
45 Love would have given me her reward.
But just at the moment when I was supposed to get my
gift
Love was discovered and denounced.
Let them never be forgiven.

9

Imploring mercy for the mad thing I have done,
I shall sound the last note of my songs,
for my loving heart has purposely betrayed
and slain me, and I ought to hate it—   I
5 it has made me suffer to give others pleasure.
Every happy mood of mine is gone,
and since I have no joy, it is right
that with my joy my songs should cease.

Bien sai qu'il est lieus et poins et saisons
10 qu'a touz les biens d'amours doive faillir,
quar pourquis l'ai, et moie est l'ochoisons,
et qui mal quiert, il doit bien mal soufrir.   II
Diex doinst que mors en soit mes guerredons,
ainz que de moi voie liez les felons!
15 Maiz pour mon pis vivrai et pour veoir
ma bele perte et pour pluz mal avoir.

As fins amans proi qu'il dient le voir:
li queuz doit mieuz par droit d'amours joïr,
cil qui aime de cuer sanz decevoir,
20 si ne s'en set mie tres bien couvrir,   III
ou qui prie sanz cuer pour decevoir
et bien s'en set guarder par son savior?
Dites, amant, qui vaut mieuz par raison:
loiauz folie u sage trahison?

25 S'ainc fins amans ot de mesfait pardon,
dont m'i devroit amour bon lieu tenir,
quar je fourfis en bone ententïon
et bien cuidai que me deüst merir;   IV
maiz ma dame ne quiert se mon mal non;
30 pour ce si has moi et ma guerison,
et quant mi mal li sunt bel et plesans,
pour ce me haz et me sui mal vueillans.

Hé, franche riens, por cui je mur amans,
faites en vos amors plux biaul fenir!
35 Sor toute riens est ceu la muels vaillans.
Et nonporcant se puis je bien mentir,   V
car fins d'amors ne puet estre avenans,
se mors nes pairt; por ceu morai souffrans
et chanterai sens joie et sens fineir,
40 ke nuls ne doit a fin d'amors penseir.

De pouc me sert ki me veult conforteir
d'autrui ameir; muelz l'en varoit taisir,

I know well it is the time, the moment, the season
10 when I should lack all the joys of love,
for I have deserved it, and I am to blame,
and if one wants suffering, he should suffer.   II
God grant that death be my reward
before I see those slanderers rejoicing over me.
15 But I shall live, for my greater pain, to see
my exquisite destruction and to suffer worse.

I beg true lovers for the answer to this:
who has a better right to be happy in love,
one who loves from the heart and does not deceive,
20 not understanding very well what he's supposed to hide,   III
or one who begs for love with an empty heart, to deceive,
and knows well from experience how to be a hypocrite?
Lovers, tell me, which is worth more, according to reason:
loyal artlessness or expert treason?

25 If ever a lover was pardoned for doing wrong,
then Love ought to hold a good place for me,
for I transgressed meaning well
and really thought I would deserve requital;   IV
but my lady only seeks my suffering,
30 and so she hates me, can't stand my being well.
And since my pains come sweet to her,
I hate myself and wish myself much pain.

You noble one, for whom I die of love,
make love come completely to an end in you.
35 That would be the best remedy of all.
And yet, maybe I am wrong,   V
for the end of love cannot be pleasant
unless it is death that ends it; so I shall suffer till I die
and sing without joy and without ending,
40 for no one should think about the end of love.

He serves me badly who wants to comfort me
with another woman's love, he'd do better to keep still,

car je ne puis pais en mon cuer troveir
ke jai de li tornaisse mon desir.

45 Siens seux, coment ke me doie greveir,
et se s'amor me fait plux conpaireir,
tout li perdoing en mon definement,
et quant mon cors li toil, mon cuer li rant.

LE CHÂTELAIN DE COUCI 363

for I cannot find it in my heart
to turn my love away from her.

45 I am hers, no matter how I must torment myself,
and if love of her makes me pay more and more,
I'll forgive her when I come to the end,
and when I take my body from her, I shall render her my
       heart.

BLONDEL DE NESLE

(*second half twelfth century*)

Nothing is known about this poet except what can be gleaned from his lyrics. One of his lyrics is addressed, in the envoi, to Gace Brulé, two others to Conon de Béthune; but he is not mentioned by other poets. Blondel is a family name; Nesle is his birthplace, probably in Picardy, judging by his language.

He is best known for the story that attached itself to his name and that of Richard Lion-Heart. This story has a kernel of historical truth: King Richard was taken prisoner on his return from the Third Crusade in December 1192, and handed over to Duke Leopold of Austria, to be kept at Dürrenstein fortress; he was finally freed in February 1194 upon payment of an enormous ransom (see Part I, no. 49). In the story, Blondel is a minstrel in Richard's retinue and wanders for a year and a half seeking his master; he finally arrives at a castle town where he learns of an illustrious prisoner. The next morning he offers himself to the castle lord as a minstrel and stays the whole winter, but without being able to learn anything about the prisoner. One day, at Easter, he passes by the dungeon as King Richard is looking out of the window. The King recognizes his minstrel, and to make himself known he sings the first strophe of a song that the two of them had composed together and that no one had ever heard. Blondel is overjoyed; he returns to England as soon as he is given leave and tells the Barons where their King languishes as a prisoner. They secure his ransom for a cool two hundred thousand marks of silver.

The story has a certain historical value for us, even though it is not historically true, based as it is on a folklore theme with worldwide analogues; but the fact that the poet's name attracted the story shows that he must have been highly esteemed in his

own and in succeeding generations. This conclusion is borne out
by the great number of manuscripts containing his songs.

Text: *Die Lieder des Blondel de Nesle,* ed. Leo Wiese. Gesellschaft für romanische Literatur, vol. 5. Dresden: Max Niemeyer, 1904.

Se savoient mon tourment   3
et auques de mon afaire
cil, qui demandent, conment
je puis tant de chançons faire,
5   il diroient vraiement,   I
que nus a chanter n'entent,
qui mieuz s'en deüst retraire.[1]
Maiz pour ce chant seulement,
que je muir pluz doucement.

10   Trop par me grieve forment,
que cele est si debonaire
qui tant de dolour me rent
ce, qu'a tout le mont doit plaire.
Maiz ne me grevast noient,   II
15   se la tresbele au cors gent
me feïst touz ces maus traire.
Maiz ce m'ocit voirement,
qu'el ne set que pour li sent.

Se seüst certeinnement
20   mon martire et mon contraire
cele, por cui je consent,
que Amours me tient et maire,   III
je croi bien, qu'alegement
m'envoiast procheinnement;
25   quar par droit le deüst faire,
se reguars a escïent
de ses biaux ieus ne me ment.

Chançons, va isnelement
a la bele au cler viaire,

[1] "Precisely because he has little success through his songs with his beloved, who grants him no favor." (L. Wiese)

10

If those who wonder
how I can make so many songs
knew my suffering,
knew anything about my state,
5   they would say—and they'd be right—   I
no man should force himself to sing
who would do better to give it up.[1]
But I sing only for one reason,
I die more pleasantly that way.

10   It makes me grieve
that she is so gentle
who turns into my agony
what is meant to be the whole world's pleasure.
And yet, it would not grieve me at all   II
15   that this beautiful and noble lady
makes me suffer all these pains.
The thing that truly kills me is this:
she does not know what I feel for her.

If she knew all about
20   my martyrdom and disease—
if she for whom I let Love
hold me and work me till I am weak, knew,
then I believe she would send   III
relief without delay;
25   for that's what she ought to do by right,
unless that deliberate look
in her beautiful eyes is a lie.

30 si li di tant seulement:
"Qui de bons est souef flaire." [2]
Ne l'os proier autrement,   IV
quar trop pensai hautement,
si n'en puis mon cuer retraire.
35 Et se pitiez ne l'en prent,
Blondiaus muert, que pluz n'atent.

11

Chanter m'estuet, quar joie ai recouvree,
qui me soloit foïr et esloignier;
ire et doleur ai maint jour comperee,
bien est maiz tans, que la doie laissier;
5 quar la bele, cui lonc tens ai amee,   I
qui de s'amour me soloit desfier,
nouvelement s'est a moi acordee.
Or me voudra douner et otroier
sa fine amour, que tant ai desirree,
10 qui me faisoit jour penser, nuit veillier.

He, Dieus d'amour! com as grant seignourie,
qui les amans pues ocirre et sauver!
L'un dounes mort, as autres dounes vie,
l'un fais languir, l'autre rire et joër.
15 Tu m'as ocis, or m'as rendu la vie,   II
seur toutes rienz te doi je aourer;
quar de cele, qui estoit m'anemie,
m'as fait ami, dont mout te doi amer.
Or chanterai de toi toute ma vie,
20 si te voudrai servir et honourer.

Ha, douce rienz, ou je ai ma fiance!
Pour Dieu vous pri, que ne m'entroubliez.

[2] "The image is taken from the flower: a noble flower radiates sweet fragrance, a good stock gives good fruit." (Wiese)

Song, go quickly
to my beautiful and bright-faced,
30   and tell her only this:
"Whatever comes from good stock smells sweet." [2]
I don't dare ask her in any other way,   IV
for my thought was always lofty,
and I cannot withdraw my heart.
35   If pity does not touch her,
Blondel dies, he has nothing left.

11

I must sing, for I have won joy again
that always fled from me and stayed far away;
I have paid with pain and sadness many a day—
now it is my time to be free of pain;
5 for the beautiful lady whom I have loved so long,   I
who used to war against me for her love,
has lately come to terms with me.
Now she will be willing to give me, to bestow on me
her noble love, that I have so desired,
10 that kept me full of thought all day and wakeful at night.

Ah, God of Love, how great is your lordship,
you can kill or save all those who love.
To one you give death, to others life,
one you let languish, another laugh and play.
15 You killed me, now you have given me back my life,   II
I ought to worship you above all things;
for the one who was my enemy
you made my friend, and I must love you for that.
Now I shall sing of you my whole life long,
20 and serve you willingly and honor you.

Oh, gentle one, in whom I have my trust!
In God's name I beg you, do not forget me with time.

Puiz qu'ensi est,   qu'Amours par sa puissance
amsdeus nos cuers   a ensamble liez,
25 pour Dieu, aiez   le mien en remembrance;   III
quar li vostres   est en mon cuer fichiez,
qui me donra   confort et soustenance.
Des ore maiz   iere joianz et liez
et prïerai,   que Dieus par sa puissance
30 nos guart touz jours   sains et saus et haitiez.

12

Mout se feïst   bon tenir de chanter,
quar en chantant   ne set l'on maiz que dire;
ne mot ne chant   ne puet l'on maiz trouver,
tant i sache hom   esguarder ne eslire,   I
5 que maintes foiz   ne soit estez redis;
s'en est chanters   pluz maz et desconfis,
ne ja pour ce   ne sera l'amours pire.

Endroit de moi   ne m'en puis consirrer;
qu'Amours m'ocit   d'un si plaisant martire,
10 qu'ele me fait   en aventure amer
cele, ou je puis   ma douce mort eslire.   II
Ne ja vers li   ne serai se hardis,
que mes tourmenz   li soit par moi gehis,
s'en chantant non,   pour tant me puet ocirre.[1]

15 Li tresgenz cors   ma dame et si oeill cler,
qui tant sevent   amourousement rire,
firent l'amour   dedenz mon cuer entrer,
que nule autre   ne li puet escondire;   III
qu'en ceste amour   m'est li tourmenz delis:
20 quant pluz ai mal,   lors cuit estre gueris.
Il n'aime pas,   qui contre Amour s'aïre.

[1] That is, by not listening and softening.

Since it is true now that Love with its power
has bound our two hearts together,
25 in God's name let my own be in your memory;   III
for your heart is set in mine,
it will give me comfort and sustenance.
I shall be joyful and happy from this day
and pray God with his power
30 keep us always safe and sound and full of joy.

12

It would be best to stop singing altogether,
for when one sings nowadays, one doesn't know what to
    say.
There's not a word or verse one can think up any more,
no matter how much one picks and chooses,   I
5 that hasn't been said and said again.
But though singing isn't good any more, though it's fin-
    ished,
Love will not suffer any loss, not for that reason.

As for me, I can't keep from singing,
for Love is killing me with a martyrdom so pleasant
10 it keeps me loving at my peril
her in whom I can make out my sweet death.   II
I shall never be brave enough in her presence
to tell her of my torments
except by singing; and that is how she can kill me.[1]

15 My lady's most noble figure and her shining eyes,
which know so well how to smile with love,
led love into my heart—
a heart no other lady can dispute her claim to;   III
for in this love, my torment comes as pleasure.
20 Just when I suffer most, I think I am all cured.
A man who gets angry at Love does not love.

Certes, dame, bien vous devez prisier,
qu'il est en vous   pluz biauté et vaillance,
qu'en nule autre, qu'Amours puist justisier;
25 en vous n'a rien, que ne vieigne en plaisance.   IV
Dame, en vous sont   tot li bien, que je di,
si m'a Amours   certes trop esbahi:
quant a vous pens, n'en fais nule samblance.

Mainz en i a, qui font au conmencier
30 samblant d'amour   et riche contenance,
puiz les en voi   partir si de legier,
que il n'en vont   querant fors la vantance.   V
Et cil, qui sont   fin et loial ami,
sont par tel gent   deceü et trahi,
35 s'en devroit bien   Amours prendre vengeance.

Maiz tant i a, que bien me puet aidier,
qu'en pou d'oure   doune Dieus grant cheance.
D'un dous reguart, d'un rire ou d'un baisier
m'avroit Amours   tourné a delivrance   VI
40 et de mes mauz   respassé et gueri.
Dame, aidiez moi, que je n'i muire einsi,
qu'onques vers vous   n'en oi fausse esperance.

Lady, to be sure, you have a right to boast,
for there is more beauty and worth in you
for Love to control than in any other woman.
25 There is nothing in you that does not bring pleasure. IV
Lady, every virtue is in you, so that I say,
Love has overwhelmed me with its shock:
when I think of you I am careful not to show it.

There are many who at first put on
30 a look of love and a noble attitude,
and then I see how they desert so easily—
they only want something to brag about.   V
And so, true and loyal lovers
are deceived and betrayed by such rabble.
35 Love ought to take revenge on them.

But there is one sufficient to help me,
and God would give me great luck in an instant.
With one kind look, with one smile or one kiss
Love would turn into my deliverance,   VI
40 and cure me of my pains.
Lady, help me, lest I die like this,
for when I long for you it is no pretense.

RICHARD COEUR DE LION

(*1157–1199*)

The following lyric was written during Richard's captivity (see the headnote to Blondel de Nesle). It is a *rotrouenge,* a chanson with a refrain, or refrain-like passage.

Text: Karl Bartsch, *Chrestomathie de l'ancien français,* 12th edition, ed. Leo Wiese. Leipzig, 1920.

13

Ja nus hons pris ne dira sa reson
adroitement, s'ensi com dolans non;
mes par confort puet il fere chançon.
Moult ai d'amis, mes povre sont li don;
5 hont en avront, se por ma reançon
sui ces deus yvers pris.

                                  I

Ce sevent bien mi honme et mi baron,
Englois, Normant, Poitevin et Gascon,
que je n'avoie si povre conpaignon
10 cui je laissasse por avoir en prixon.
Je nel di pas por nule retraçon,
mes encor sui ge pris.

                                  II

Or sai je bien de voir certainement
que mors ne pris n'a ami ne parent,
15 quant hon me lait por or ne por argent.
Moult m'est de moi, mès plus m'est de ma gent,
qu'après ma mort avront reprochier grant,
se longuement sui pris.

                                  III

N'est pas merveille, se j'ai le cuer dolent,
20 quant mes sires tient ma terre en torment.
S'or li menbroit de nostre serement,
que nos fëismes andui communaument,
bien sai de voir que ceans longuement
ne seroie pas pris.

                                  IV

25 Ce sevent bien Angevin et Torain,
cil bacheler qui or sont riche et sain,
qu'enconbrez sui loing d'aus en autrui main.
Forment m'amoient, mes or ne m'ainment grain.
De beles armes sont ores vuit li plain,
30 por tant que je sui pris.

                                  V

13

No prisoner will ever speak his mind
fittingly unless he speaks in grief.
But he can, for consolation, make a song.   I
I have many friends, but their gifts are poor.
5 It will be their shame if, for want of ransom,
I stay these two winters prisoner.

They know well, my men and my barons
of England, Normandy, Poitou, and Gascony,
I never had a poor companion   II
10 I would leave in prison for money.
I do not say this as a reproach,
but I am still a prisoner.

Now I know for sure,
a dead man or a prisoner has no friend or family,
15 because they leave me here for gold and silver.   III
That's my concern, but even more my people's,
for when I am dead they will be shamed,
if I die a prisoner.

It is no wonder I have a grieving heart,
20 for my lord keeps my land in torment.
Now if he remembered our vow   IV
that we both took together,
I know I would not long
be here a prisoner.

25 They know well, the men of Anjou and Touraine,
those bachelors, now so magnificent and safe,
that I am arrested, far from them, in another's hands.   V
They used to love me much, now they love me not at all.
There's no lordly fighting now on the barren plains,
30 because I am a prisoner.

Mes conpaignons, cui j'amoie et cui j'ain,
ceus de Cahen et ceus dou Percherain,
me di, chançon qu'il ne sont pas certain;   VI
qu'onques vers aus nen oi cuer faus ne vain.
35 S'il me guerroient, il font moult que vilain,
tant con je serai pris.

Contesse suer, vostre pris souverain
vos saut et gart cil a cui je me clain   VII
et par cui je sui pris.

40 Je ne di pas de celi de Chartain,   VIII
la mere Loöys.[1]

---

[1] The two ladies mentioned in this strophe are, first, Marie, Countess of Champagne, daughter of Eleanor of Aquitaine and Louis VII, thus half sister of Richard, son of Henry II of England and Eleanor; and Alis, Countess of Chartres, Richard's other half sister, with whom he was on bad terms.

Tell my companions whom 1 loved and love—
the men of Caen and Perche—
Song, tell them they are not men to rely on;   VI
the heart I had for them was never false or faltering.
35 If they turn against me now, they act like peasants,
as long as I remain a prisoner.

Countess, sister, may your sovereign worth
be watched and defended by Him I appeal to,   VII
for whose sake I am a prisoner.

40 I do not speak about the one in Chartres,   VIII
Louis's mother.[1]

GACE BRULÉ

(*fl. 1180–1213*)

The poet was a knight of Champagne (see no. 14). Brulé is derived from *burelé,* banded—barred in gules and silver, the design on his escutcheon. He had several patrons among the highest nobility, among them Marie de France. He probably took part in the Third Crusade and possibly in the Fourth. He is last attested in 1213.

He was venerated in his own time and long after his death. Dante cites *Ire d'amors* (no. 19) in DVE, II, 6, though he attributes this song to the King of Navarre, Thibaut de Champagne. Probably no other northern French poet adhered more closely to the themes and techniques of the troubadours. His resemblance to Bernart de Ventadorn is unmistakable, and it has been suggested that he was personally acquainted with Bertran de Born, Gaucelm Faidit, and Guiraut de Calanson. He also resembles Guillaume IX in explicitly distinguishing the songs addressed to a male audience from those intended for the full court: several of his lyrics begin with *Compaignons,* or *Seigners.*

Text: H. Peterson Dygve, *Gace Brulé, trouvère champenois.* Mémoires de la Société néophilologique de Helsinki, 16. Helsinki, 1951.

Les oiseillons de mon païs
ai oïs en Bretaigne.
A lor chant m'est il bien avis
q'en la douce Champaigne
5 les oï jadis,   I
se n'i ai mespris.
Il m'ont en si dolz panser mis
k'a chanson faire me sui pris
tant que je parataigne
10 ceu q'Amors m'a lonc tens promis.

De longe atente m'esbahis
senz ce que je m'en plaigne.
Ce me tout le jeu et le ris,
que nus q'Amors destrangne
15 n'est d'el ententis.   II
Mon cors et mon vis
truis si mainte foiz entrepris
qu'un fol samblant i ai apris.
Ki q'en Amors mespregne,
20 ainc, certes, plus ne li mesfis.

En baisant, mon cuer me ravi
ma dolce dame gente;
trop fu fols quant il me guerpi
por li qui me tormente.
25 Las! ainz nel senti,   III
qant de moi parti;
tant dolcement lo me toli
k'en sospirant lo traist a li;
mon fol cuer atalente,
30 mais ja n'avra de moi merci.

D'un baisier, dont me menbre si,
m'est avis, en m'entente,

14

The little birds of my country
I have heard in Brittany.
When their song rises up, I think
I used to hear them, once,
5 in sweet Champagne,   I
if I am not mistaken.
They have put me in such gentle thought,
I have set myself to sing
till I at last attain
10 what Love has long been promising.

I am troubled by long hope
and must not complain.
That takes away my joy and laughter,
for no one tormented by love
15 is mindful of anything else.   II
I find my body
and face poised on the thought of her so many times,
that now I have the look of a madman.
Others have done other wrongs in love,
20 but my great fault is to show my suffering.

My sweet gentle lady
kissing me stole away my heart;
it was crazy to quit me
for her who torments me.
25 Alas, I never felt it   III
leaving me;
she took it so gently,
she drew it to her as I sighed;
she covets my mad heart
30 but will never have pity for me.

That one kiss, which is always on my mind,
is over, I now realize—

k'il n'est hore, ce m'a trahi
q'a mes levres nel sente.
35 Quant ele soffri,　　　　　　　　　　　　　　　IV
Deus! ce que je di,
de ma mort que ne me garni!
Ele seit bien que je m'oci
en ceste longe atente,
40 dont j'ai lo vis taint et pali.

Por coi me tout rire et juer
et fait morir d'envie;
trop sovent me fait conparer
Amors sa conpaignie.
45 Las! n'i os aler,　　　　　　　　　　　　　　　V
que por fol sambler
me font cil fals proiant damer.
Morz sui quant jes i voi parler;
que point de trecherie
50 ne puet nus d'eus en li trover.[1]

15

Li pluseur ont d'Amours chanté
par esfors et desloiaument;
més de ce me doit savoir gré
c'onques ne chantai faintement.　　　　　　　　I
5 Ma bone fois m'en a guardé,
et l'amours, dont j'ai tel plenté
que merveille est se je rienz hé,
neïs cele anuieuse gent.

Certes, j'ai de fin cuer amé,
10 ne ja n'amerai autrement;
bien le puet avoir esprové

---

[1] In her sincerity she is likely to believe them.

it has betrayed me,
I do not feel it on my lips.
35 When she permitted,   IV
God! what I am telling of,
why didn't she furnish me against my death.
She knows I am killing myself
in this long expectation,
40 my face is pale and colorless.

And so she takes away my joy and laughter
and makes me die of longing;
Love makes me pay dearly
again and again for her obligingness.
45 Alas, I don't dare go to her,   V
because I have this crazy look
which these false lovers get me blamed for.
I am dead when I see them talking to her there,
because not one of them will find
50 any of their treachery in her.[1]

15

Most have sung of Love
as an exercise and insincerely;
so Love should give me thanks
because I never sang like a hypocrite.   I
5 My loyalty kept me from that,
and Love, which I have in such abundance
it is a miracle if I hate anything,
even that crowd of pests.

The truth is, I have loved with a loyal heart
10 and will never love another way;
my lady could have put this to the test

ma dame, se guarde s'en prent.   II
Je ne di pas que m'ait grevé
que ne soit a ma volenté,
15 car de li sunt tout mi pensé,
mout me plaist ce que me consent.

Se j'ai hors du païz esté
u mes bienz et ma joie atent,
pour ce n'ai je pas oublïé
20 coment on aimme loiaument;   III
se li merirs m'a demoré,
ce m'en a mout reconforté
qu'en pou d'eure a on recovré
ce c'on desirre longement.

25 Amours m'a par raison moustré
que fins amis sueffre et atent;
qui suens est, en sa poësté,
merci doit crïer franchement,   IV
ou c'est orgueuz: si l'ai prové.
30 Més cil faus amorous d'esté,
qui m'ont d'amors ochoisoné,
n'aiment fors quant talens lor prent.

S'enuieus l'avoient juré,
ne me vaudroient il noient
35 la dont il se sunt tant pené
de moi nuire a lor escïent.   V
Por ç'aient il renoié Dé;
tant ont mon anui pourparlé
qu'a painnes verrai achievé
40 la painne qui d'amours m'esprent.

Més en Bretaigne m'a loié
li cuens, cui j'aing tot mon aé,   VI
et s'il m'a bon conseill doné,
ce verrai je procheinnement.[1]

---

[1] The Count of Brittany, Geoffroi II, was one of the poet's patrons.

just by taking notice.   II
I do not say that I am irked
because she does not do as I wish:
15 all my thoughts are of her,
I am much pleased by whatever she permits.

If I have been outside the land
where I look for my pleasures and joy,
it has not made me forget
20 how one keeps faith in love;   III
if my requital has been slow in coming,
I have found much comfort in this thought:
in a little moment one has gotten
what one has wanted a long, long time.

25 Love has proved to me by reason
that a true lover suffers and waits;
whoever is hers and in her power
must beg for mercy openly,   IV
or it is pride: I have experienced this.
30 But these false summer lovers,
who have blamed me for my love—
they never love but when the lust comes on them.

Even if these slanderers had sworn to,
they would never be fine enough to be of any use
35 in this affair, where they have taken such great pains
to do me harm, with all their malice.   V
And they must have forsworn God himself.
They have conspired so busily for my unhappiness,
I shall scarcely see this suffering
40 end, that makes me burn with love.

But in Brittany the Count
has advised me, whom I have loved my whole life long,   VI
and if he has given me good counsel
I should know it very soon.[1]

16

De bone amour et de leaul amie
me vient sovant pitiez et remembrance,
si que ja mais a nul jor de ma vie
n'oblïerai son vis ne sa semblance;   I
5 pouroec, s'Amors ne s'en vuet plus sosfrir
qu'ele de touz ne face a son plaisir
et de toutes, mais ne puet avenir
que de la moie aie bone esperance.

Coment porroie avoir bone esperance
10 a bone amor ne a leal amie,
ne a vairs yeuz, n'a la douce semblance
que ne verrai ja més jor de ma vie?   II
Amer m'estuet, ne m'en puis plus sosfrir,
celi cui ja ne vanra a plaisir;
15 et si ne sai coment puist avenir,
qu'aie de li ne secours ne ahie.

Coment avrai ne secors ne ahie
vers fine Amour, la ou nus n'a puissance?
Amer me fait ce qui ne m'ainme mie,
20 dont ja n'avrai fors ennui et pesance;   III
ne ne li os mon corage gehir
celi qui tant m'a fait de max sentir,
que de tel mort sui jugiez a morir
dont ja ne quier veoir ma delivrance.

25 Je ne vois pas querant tel delivrance
par quoi amors soit de moi departie;
ne ja nul jor n'en quier avoir poissance,
ainz amerai ce qui ne m'ainme mie,   IV
n'il n'est pas droiz que li doie gehir
30 por nul destroit que me face sentir;

16

From good love and true beloved
pity and remembrance come to me so often
that never for a moment of my life
shall I forget her face or the way she looks.   I
5 And so, if Love will not be willing to refrain
from doing with all men as she pleases,
and all women, it can never come to pass
that my love will have good hope.

How could I have good hope
10 in good love or true beloved,
in vair eyes or gentle look
that I shall not see again in my life?   II
I must love—I cannot refrain—
one whom my love never pleases;
15 and I do not know how it could ever come to pass
that I get aid from her or succor.

How shall I get aid or succor
against True Love, where none has power?
Love makes me love one who loves me not at all,
20 and I will get nothing but pain and grief.   III
Nor do I dare tell what is in my heart
to the one who gives the pains I suffer,
for I am condemned to die a death
from which I do not want to see deliverance.

25 I do not want such deliverance
as would make me stop loving;
I do not ever want that power,
I will go on loving her who loves me not at all;   IV
nor is it right to tell her what is in my heart
30 no matter what torment she makes me suffer;

n'avrai confort, n'i voi que dou morir,
puis que je sai que ne m'ameroit mie.

Ne m'ameroit? Ice ne sai je mie;
que fins amis doit par bone atendance
35 et par soffrir conquerre haute amie.
Més je n'i puis avoir nulle fiance,   V
que cele est tex, por cui plaing et sopir,
que ma dolor ne doigneroit oïr;
si me vaut mieuz garder mon bon taisir,
40 que dire riens qui li tort a grevance.

Ne vos doit pas trop torner a grevance
se je vos aing, dame, plus que ma vie,
car c'est la riens ou j'ai greignor fiance
quant par moi seul vos os nonmer amie,   VI
45 et por ce fais maint dolorous sopir
que ne vos puis ne veoir ne oïr,
et quant vos voi, n'i a que dou taisir,
que si sui pris que ne sai que je die.

Mes biaus conforz ne l'en porra garir;
50 de vos amer ne me porrai partir,   VII
n'a vos parler, ne ne m'en puis taisir
que mon maltrait en chantant ne vos die.

Par Deu, Hüet, ne m'en puis plus soffrir,   VIII
qu'en Bertree est et ma morz et ma vie.

17

Pour verdure ne pour pree
ne pour fueille ne pour flour
nule chançons ne m'agree,
se ne muet de fine amour.   I

I will get no comfort, I see nothing but to die,
since I know she would love me not at all.

Would not love me? That I do not know at all,
for the true lover wins his gentle love
35 through patience and a willingness to wait.
But here I can have no trust,   v
for she is such—this one for whom I lament and sigh—
as would never consent to listen to my sorrow's voice.[1]
So it is better to keep my good silence
40 than say something she would take as an annoyance.

It should not cause you such annoyance
if I love you, Lady, more than my life,
because the dream in which I have most trust
is that I alone shall dare to call you my beloved,   vi
45 and for this I sigh many a painful sigh,
for I cannot see you, or hear your voice,
and when I see you I have no choice but silence,
for I am overwhelmed and do not know what I am tell-
      ing you.

My sweet dream can never cure my pain;
50 my loving you cannot cease,   vii
I cannot stop speaking to you, I cannot stay silent
about my pain; cannot keep, as I sing, from telling you.

By God, Huet, I can no longer refrain,   viii
for in Bertree I see my death and life.

17

No green thing, no meadow,
no leaf, no flower
could ever make me like a song
that did not start out from true love.   i

---

[1] Literally, "would never deign to hear about my pain."

5　　Maiz li faignant proieour
　　dont ja dame n'iert amee
　　ne chantent fors qu'en paschour;
　　lors se plaignent sanz dolour.

　　Dame tieg pour enganee
10　qui croit faus dru menteour,
　　quar honte a longe duree
　　qui avient par tel folour,　　　　　　　II
　　et joie a pou de savour
　　qui en tel lieu est gastee,
15　s'en li a tant de vigour
　　que hee sa deshounour.

　　Fausse drue abandounee
　　veut les nos et puis les lour,
　　ne ja s'amour n'iert emblee
20　que nel sachent li plusour.　　　　　　III
　　Maiz la dame de valour,
　　bele et bone et acesmee,
　　qui ne croit losengeour,
　　doit on prisier nuit et jour.

25　Mout m'a Amours atournee
　　douce painne et bel labour,
　　ne ja pour rienz qui soit nee
　　ne guerpirai ceste hounour　　　　　　IV
　　d'amer toute la meillour
30　qui soit par les bons loee.
　　Maiz de tant sui en errour
　　c'onques n'amai sanz freour.

　　Bien s'est amours afermee
　　en mon cuer a lonc sejour,
35　que j'ai pluz haute pensee
　　que tuit cist autre ameour;　　　　　　V
　　maiz li faus enquereour
　　font oevre maleüree,

5 But those whose prayers are lies
and who never loved a lady
always set their songs in spring;
then they complain, without suffering.

I think a lady has been badly fooled
10 when she believes these empty, lying lovers,
and the shame lasts long
that comes from such foolishness;   II
and joy has little savor
poured out in such a place—
15 if she has the life in her
to hate her dishonor.

A false mistress who falls to everyone
wants what we have, and then what they have,
and her love will never be kept secret,
20 everyone will know about it.   III
But a lady who has some worth,
who is beautiful, and good, and elegant,
who does not trust in flatterers—
let us praise her night and day.

25 Love has put upon me much
sweet pain and pleasant toil,
and I would not for anything born
give up this honor   IV
of loving the best of all women
30 ever praised by the good.
But I live in such uncertainty,
my love has never been without anxiety.

Love has settled down
in my heart for a long sojourn,
35 for I have a loftier intent
than all these other lovers;   V
but those slandering spies
do their wretched work,

engien de mainte coulour
40   jour tourner joie en tristour.

Dame, cele part ne tour
que m'amours ne soit doublee,   VI
et mi desirrier greignour,
dont je morrai sanz retour.

18

Li consirrers de mon païs
si longuement me trait a mort,
qu'en estranges terres languis,
las, sanz deduit et sanz confort,   I
5 et si dout mout mes anemis
qui de moi mesdient a tort,
maiz tant sent mon cuer vrai et fort
que, se Dieu plaist, ne m'en iert pis.

Ma douce dame, ne creez
10 touz ceus qui de moi mesdiront.
Quant vous veoir ne me poez
de vos biauz iex qui soupris m'ont,   II
de vostre franc cuer me veez.
Maiz ne sai s'il vous en semont,
15 quar tant ne dout rienz en cest mont
con ce que vous ne m'oublïez.

Par cuer legier de feme avient
que li amant doutent souvent,
maiz ma loiautez me soustient,
20 donce fusse je mors autrement!   III
Et sachiez de fine Amour vient
qu'il se doutent si durement,
quar nus n'aime seürement,
et false est amours qui ne crient.

      every kind of trick
40   to turn joy into sorrow.

      Lady, I do not go toward you,
      for then my love would double   VI
      and my desires increase,
      and I would die without a chance.

18

      Longing for my country
      has so long carried me toward death,
      I languish in foreign lands,
      weary, without delight, without comfort,   I
5   and I greatly fear my enemies
      who wrongly slander me;
      but I feel my heart so firm and true,
      God willing, it will not go ill with me.

      My sweet lady, do not believe
10   all those who will defame me.
      Though you cannot see me
      with your beautiful eyes, eyes that overwhelmed me,   II
      you see me with your free and noble heart.
      But I do not know whether it summons you to see me,
15   for I fear nothing in this world
      as much as your forgetting me.

      Because of woman's changing heart
      lovers are continually afraid.
      But my loyalty sustains me,
20   otherwise I would be dead.   III
      Do not doubt that true love is the cause
      why lovers fear so bitterly,
      for no one loves in security,
      love without worry is false.

25 Mes cuers m'a guari et destruit,
   maiz de ce va bien qu'a li pens,
   et ce que je perdre la quit
   me fait doubler mes pensemens.   IV
   Ensi me vient soulaz et fuit,
30 et nonpourquant, selonc mon sens,
   penser a ma dame touz tens
   tieg je, ce sachiez, a deduit.

   Chançon, a ma dame t'envoi
   ançoiz que nus en ait chanté,
35 et si li dites de par moi,
   guardez que ne li soit celé: V
   "Se trecherie n'a en foi
   et trahison en loiauté,
   donc avrai bien ce qu'avoir doi,
40 quar de loial cuer ai amé."

19

   Ire d'amors qui en mon cuer repere
   ne mi let tant que de chanter me tiengne.
   Grant merveille est se chançon en puis trere,
   ne je ne sai don l'acheson me viengne,   I
5 car li desirs et la grant volentez,
   dont je sui si pensis et esgarez,
   m'ont si mené, ce vos puis je bien dire,
   qu'a paine sai quenoistre joie d'ire.

   Et neporquant, touz li cuers m'en esclere
10 d'un bon espoir; Dex dont que il aviengne!
   Mout par devroit a ma dame deplere
   se ceste amor m'ocit; bien l'en couviengne!   II
   Mort m'a ses cors, li genz, li acesmez,

25 My heart has gone on restoring and destroying me,
　　but, doing so, it makes me think of her, and that is good;
　　and so the fear of losing her
　　makes me double my thoughts of her.　　　　　　　IV
　　Thus some pleasure comes my way and flees,
30 and yet, I am so minded
　　that thinking of my lady with pleasure and pain [1]
　　always—now I tell you this—comes sweet to me.

　　Song, I send you to my lady
　　before anyone has sung a word of you.
35 Tell her this for me—
　　be sure not to keep this from her:　　　　　　　　V
　　"If there is no treachery in keeping faith,
　　or treason in loyalty,
　　then I shall have what I ought to have,
40 for I have loved with a loyal heart."

19

　　Grief of love that sojourns in my heart
　　has such a hold on me, I keep from singing.
　　It would be a great miracle if I could draw out a song,
　　and I do not know where the cause could come from,　　I
5 for desire and constant readiness
　　trouble me and fill me with many thoughts,
　　and so have brought me to the point—I can tell you
　　　　　　　this—
　　where I can hardly tell joy from grief.

　　And yet my whole heart brightens
10 with one good hope—God let it come true.
　　For I think my lady would be much displeased
　　if this love kills me—what good could it do her!　　II
　　I have been slain by the grace and ornament of her figure,

[1] Literally, "thinking of her all the time," which in this context means, "with
whatever result."

et ses douz vis freschement colorez,
15 et sa biautez dont il n'est riens a dire.
Dex, por qu'en ot tant a moi desconfire?

Irié me font cele gent de male aire
plus que nus mals que por Amors soustiengne;
més ne lor vaut: ja ne porront deffaire
20 qu'Amors ne m'ait et q'au cuer ne me tiengne.   III
Si fetement me sui a li donez
que ja sanz mort n'en cuit estre tornez.
Puis q'ons se puet vers Amors escondire,
nel doit l'on pas a fins amis eslire?

25 Loial desir, dont j'ai plus de .c. pere,
m'ocirront voir, ainz qu'en la joie viengne
qui toz jorz m'est pramise por atrere;
més je ne cuit qu'a ma dame en souviengne,   IV
cui Dex dona valeur et trop biautez.
30 Més contre moi si est orguels mellez,
si n'ai pouoir de tel tort contredire
puis que mes cuers me veut por li ocirre.

Tres grant amor me fet folie fere,
si ai peür que longues la maintiengne;
35 més je n'en puis mon corage retrere.
Issi me plest, conment q'il m'en aviengne.   V
Par tel reson sui povres asazez
quant je plus vueil ce dont plus sui grevez,
et en l'esmai m'estuet joer et rire:
40 onc més ne vi si decevant martire.

Ha! quens de Blois, vos qui fustes amez,
tiengne vos en si vos en remenbrez,   VI
car qui d'amors oste son cuer et tire,
adventure ert se grant heneur desire.

and her sweet face the color of youth,
15 and her beauty, which cannot be described.
Why did God give her the beauty to destroy me?

I am angered by that bad crowd
more than by any suffering I endure for Love;
But it won't help them, they won't be able to undo
20 the truth that Love possesses me and takes hold in my
heart.
This is how I have given myself to her: III
I do not believe I will ever part from her except by dying.
A man who acquits himself well before Love—
should he not be the one chosen lover?

25 Faithful desires, of which I have more than a hundred
pair,
will surely kill me before that joy comes
long promised me—as bait.
I do not think my lady, whom God gave goodness   IV
and much beauty, will remember.
30 Pride is up in arms against me,
and I don't have the strength to denounce this wrong,
since my heart wants to kill me over her.

This great love makes me act foolishly
and will do so, I'm afraid, for a long time;
35 but I cannot take my heart back.
I like things as they are, whatever happens to me.   V
And so I am poorly contented,
for I want what harms me most,
and dismay makes me laugh and play:
40 I have never seen martyrdom so deceitful.

Ah, Count of Blois, you who would be loved,
keep this in your memory;   VI
for if a man withdraws his heart from love,
it is doubtful he longs for great honor.

20

L'autrier estoie en un vergier,
s'oï deus dames consoillier,
tant qu'eles pristrent a tancier
et lor paroles a haucier;
5 acotez fui lez un rosier
desoz une ente florie.   I
Dist l'une a l'autre: "Consoil quier
d'un mauvais qui m'ainme et prie
pour loier;
10 Amerai je tel chevalier
coart por sa menantie?

"Uns autres me refait proier
frans et cortois et beau parlier,
et quant il reva tornoier
15 en son païs, moillor ne quier;
sages est et tient son cors chier
sanz orguil et sanz folie;   II
mais il n'avroit d'amors mestier
qui tort a mercheandie.
20 Au premier
li fui cruelx a l'acointier,
por le mauvais qui me prie."

Dit la bone: "Je di par droit
que tres bele dame amer doit
25 bon chevalier s'ele aperçoit
que fins et lëaus vers li soit;
et cele cui avoirs deçoit
dame ne l'apel je mie: III
garce est, puis que l'on seit et voit
30 que por loier s'est honie.
Qui la croit

20

The other day in an orchard
I heard two ladies talking quietly,
till they began to quarrel
and raise their voices.
5 I was resting near a rosebush
underneath a grafted tree in flower.   I
One said to the other: "I want advice
about a bad man who loves me and begs
for requital;
10 should I love this knight, the way he is,
a coward, for his money?

"Now there's somebody else who keeps begging me,
he is honest and courteous and well spoken,
and when he goes back to tourney
15 in his country, I won't want a better man.
He is prudent, and dignified,
and he is not proud or foolish.   II
But you don't need love
if you want money.
20 From the first
I was mean to him when I received him,
for the other bad one who keeps begging me."

The good lady says, "I think it is right
that a beautiful lady should love
25 a good knight, if she finds one
true and loyal to her.
And any woman seduced by wealth
I will never call a lady;   III
she's a slut, because everyone knows, everyone sees
30 she has dishonored herself for a price.
Whoever trusts her

fox est et sa folie boit,
quant de l'argent l'a saisie."

Dit la fause: "Qui vos creroit
35 de mesaise et de fain morroit;
n'aing pas chevalier qui tornoit
et erre et despent et acroit
et en yver se muert de froit
quant sa creance est faillie;   IV
40 ne quier que mes druz peceoit
grosse lance por s'amie;
orendroit
prenez l'onor et je l'esploit:
si verrons la mieuz garnie."

45 "Tais toi, pute, va bordeler;
Je ne te puis plus escouter.
Puis que tu vuez a mal aler,
nuns ne t'en porroit destorber.
Coment porras tu endurer
50 en ton lit vil conpaignie?"   V
Li voloit l'un des eulz crever,
mais Gaces nou soffri mie
au torner,
ainz li ala des poins oster:
55 de tant fist il vilenie.[1]

21

Cant voi l'aube dou jor venir,[1]
nulle rien ne doi tant haïr,

[1] Holger Petersen Dyggve, the editor of Gace Brulé's lyrics, prints the speech
in v as a continuation of the one in iv; he seems to attribute both speeches
to the same woman.
[1] The attribution of this song to Gace Brulé is doubtful; it is rejected in the
editions of Dyggve and Huet.

is a fool and will taste his foolishness
when she gets a hold of his money."

The dishonest lady says, "Whoever followed your advice
35 would die of misery and hunger.
I will not love a knight who keeps going on tourneys
and wanders around, and spends a lot, and borrows on
            credit,
and in winter dies of cold
when his credit goes;   IV
40 I don't want my lover to shatter
a big lance for his little friend.
You take
honor any day and I'll take income,
and we'll see who has more in the end."

45 "Shut up, whore, go to a whorehouse,
I can't stand listening to you any more.
Since you want to go to the devil,
no one could stop you.
How will you be able to stand
50 having such trash in your bed?"   V
She wanted to scratch out one of her eyes,
but Gace kept it from happening
as he was going away,
he went and stopped her fists:
55 and in this he did a bad thing.[1]

21

When I see daybreak coming on,[1]
there's nothing I could hate so much,

k'elle fait de moi departir   I
mon amin, cui j'ain per amors:
5   *Or ne hais riens tant com le jour,*
Amins, ke me depairt de vos.

Je ne vos puis de jor veoir,
car trop redout l'apercevoir,
et se vos di trestout por voir   II
10   k'en agait sont li enuious:
Or ne hais riens tant com le jour,
Amins, ke me depairt de vos.

Quant je me gix dedens mon lit
et je resgairde en coste mi,
15   je n'i truis poent de mon amin,   III
se m'en plaing a fins amerous.
Or ne hais riens tant com le jour,
Amins, ke me depairt de vos.

Biaus dous amis, vos en ireis,
20   a Deu soit vos cors comandeis.
Por Deu vos pri, ne m'obleis.   IV
Je n'ain nulle rien tant com vos:
Or ne hais riens tant com le jour,
Amins, ke me depairt de vos.

25   Or pri a tous les vrais amans,
ceste chanson voixent chantant
ens en despit des medixans   V
et des mavais maris jalous:
Or ne hais riens tant com lou jor
30   *Amins, ke me depairt de vos.*

for it makes my lover whom I love   I
with true love part from me.
5   Now I hate nothing as much as day,
which parts me, love, from you.

I cannot see you in the daytime,
I'm so afraid someone will notice us,
and I tell you the truth is every one   II
10   of those killjoys is lying in ambush.
Now I hate nothing as much as day,
which parts me, love, from you.

When I lie down in my bed
and look to my side,
15   I find no trace of my love,   III
and so make this lament to other true lovers.
Now I hate nothing as much as day,
which parts me, love, from you.

Dear sweet love, you will go away,
20   God have your body in keeping.
In God's name I beg you, do not forget me,   IV
there is nothing I love as much as you.
Now I hate nothing as much as day,
which parts me, love, from you.

25   Now I beg all true lovers,
go singing this song,
just in spite of those who spread dirt   V
and of husbands who are jealous and mean.
Now I hate nothing as much as day,
30   which parts me, love, from you.

TWO ANONYMOUS SONGS

(late twelfth or early thirteenth century)

The first song is a *reverdie,* a song set in spring and full of fantasy—a spring morning's dream, in Bédier's words.

The second is a *chanson de mal-mariée,* a song sung by a married woman who takes her pleasures, but not her marriage, seriously, and wherever she can find them.

Text: Karl Bartsch, ed. *Romances et pastourelles françaises des XIIe et XIIIe siècles.* Leipzig, 1870.

22

Volez vos que je vos chant
un son d'amors avenant?
Vilain nel fist mie,   I
ainz le fist un chevalier
5   soz l'onbre d'un olivier
entre les braz s'amie.

Chemisete avoit de lin
et blanc peliçon hermin
et bliaut de soie;   II
10   chauces out de jaglolai
et solers de flors de mai,
estroitement chaucade.

Cainturete avoit de fueille
qui verdist quant li tens mueille,
15   d'or ert boutonade.   III
L'aumosniere estoit d'amor,
li pendant furent de flor:
par amors fu donade.

Et chevauchoit une mule;
20   d'argent ert la ferreure,
la sele ert dorade: IV
sus la crope par derriers
avoit planté trois rosiers
por fere li onbrage.

25   Si s'en vet aval la pree:
chevaliers l'ont encontree,
biau l'ont saluade.   V
"Bele, dont estes vos nee?"
"De France sui la loee,
30   du plus haut parage.

Would you like me to sing you
a sweet song of love?
No country bumpkin made it   I
but a knight
5   beneath the shade of an olive tree
in the arms of his love.

She wore a skirt of fine linen,
and a white cloak of ermine,
and a tunic of silk;   II
10   greaves of gladiolus,
and slippers of May flowers
fitting snug.

She wore a girdle of leaves
that grows green when it rains,
15   the buckle was of gold;   III
her purse was of love,
the pendants of flowers.
it was given for love.

She was riding a mule
20   with silver shoes
and a golden saddle;   IV
behind her on the crupper
she had planted three rose trees
to give her shade.

25   She comes along the meadow;
knights have encountered her
and greeted her courteously.   V
"Beautiful, where were you born?"
"I am of France, the celebrated,
30   of very high degree.

"Li rosgnox est mon pere,
qui chante sor la ramee
el plus haut boscage.   VI
La seraine ele est ma mere,
35   qui chante en la mer salée
el plus haut rivage."

"Bele, bon fussiez vos nee:
bien estes enparentée
et de haut parage.   VII
40   Pleust a deu nostre pere
que vos me fussiez donée
a fame esposade!"

23

Por coi me bait mes maris,
laisette!

Je ne li ai rienz mesfait
ne riens ne li ai mesdit
5   fors c'acolleir mon amin   I
soulette.
Por coi me bait mes maris,
laisette!

Et c'il ne mi lait dureir
10   ne bone vie meneir,
je lou ferai cous clameir,   II
a certes.
Por coi me bait mes maris,
laisette!

15   Or sai bien que je ferai
et coment m'an vangerai:

"My father is the nightingale
who sings on the branch
in the highest trees.   VI
My mother is the siren
35   who sings in the salt sea
on the highest bank."

"Beautiful, may you be born for happiness:
you are of noble kin
and of very high degree.   VII
40   I wish to God our Father
you were given as my
wedded wife to me."

23

Why does my husband beat me,
worn-out wretch?

I've done nothing against him,
or said bad things about him ever,
5   I only put my arms around my lover   I
and that was in private.
Why does my husband beat me,
worn-out wretch?

And if he does not let me live
10   and lead the good life, I warn
I shall make him famous for his horn,   II
for sure.
Why does my husband beat me,
worn-out wretch?

15   Now I know what I shall do
to get my revenge: I intend

avec mon amin geirai   III
nuette.
Por coi me bait mes maris,
20   laisettel

to lie down by my friend
without a stitch.
Why does my husband beat me,
worn-out wretch?

III

COLIN MUSET

(fl. 1230)

Nothing is known of Colin Muset apart from what he tells us in his songs. He was a jongleur and therefore of no social significance, and so no moment of his life is attested. It is inferred that he came from the region touching Lorraine and Champagne.

Joseph Bédier, in his edition of the songs of Colin Muset, lists four poetic themes that recur in this poetry but are otherwise very rare in the courtly lyric: the joys and miseries of the jongleur's profession; moralistic denunciations of stingy lords and praise of generous ones who give big gifts and love fun; the games in the meadow; gourmandise. Bédier also points out that Colin Muset's versification is very carefree, if not careless: he rhymes with the same words, he often uses assonance instead of rhyme, many lines do not scan right, a sentence begun in one strophe runs over into another.

These four themes, as well as his endearing nonchalance regarding technique, are all aspects of the one overriding theme of "the good life," a venerable subject of courtly poetry (particularly in northern France), which Colin Muset authenticates with the hungers and good fortunes of his life as a wandering performer. He is often praised as one of the most "original" of the trouvères—a term rigorously excluded from the commentary in this book as conveying very little, since nearly all of the excellent poets included here are, each in his own way, "original." What we can feel in the lyrics of Colin Muset is the threat that powers his wonderful gaiety, the jongleur's, wanderer's fear of hunger and exposure striking with an inevitably ironic effect against the artificial, indoor conventions of the courtly lyric.

Text: No. 24: Karl Bartsch, ed. *Romances et pastourelles françaises des XIIe et XIIe siècles.* Leipzig, 1870.

Nos. 25, 26, 27, 29, 30: Albert Pauphilet, ed. *Poètes et romanciers du moyen âge*. Paris: Gallimard, 1952. With some emendations.

No. 28: Karl Bartsch and Leo Wiese, edd. *Chrestomathie de l'ancien français*. 12th ed. Leipzig, 1927.

Volez oïr la muse Muset?[1]
En mai fu fete, un matinet,
en un vergier flori, verdet,
au point du jour
5   ou chantoient cil oiselet
par grant baudor,
et j'alai fere un chapelet
en la verdor.
Je le fis bel et cointe et net
10   et plain de flor.   I
Une dancele
avenant et mult bele,
gente pucele,
bouchete riant,
15   qui me rapele:
"Vien ça, si me viele

. . . .

ta muse en chantant
tant mignotement!"

20   J'alai a li el praelet
o tout la viele et l'archet,
si li ai chanté le muset   II
par grant amour:
"J'ai mis mon cuer en si bon cor
25   espris d'amor.

Et quant je vi son chief blondet
et sa color
et son gent cors amoreuset
et si d'ator,   II
30   mon cuer sautele

[1] *Muse*, "song."

24

Would you like to hear the *muse* of Muset? [1]
It was made in May one little morning,
in a flowering orchard, all spring-green,
at the time of day
5   when the little birds sing
from great joy,
and I went to make a chaplet
in the green.
I made it handsome, fine, and elegant,
10   all full of flowers.   I
A young lady,
very beautiful and pleasant,
a pretty girl,
with a little smiling mouth,
15   called me back:
"Come here, fiddle

   . . . . . .

your *muse* while you so
sweetly sing."

20   I went to her in the little field
with fiddle and bow
and sang her my *muset*   II
with great love:
"I have put my heart in a heart so good,
25   aflame with love . . ."

And when I saw her blond head
and her color
and her sweet body with all that love in it,
and so decked out,   II
30   my heart leaps up

pour la damoisele;
mult renouvele
ma joie souvent.
Ele ot gonnele
35   de drap de Castele,
qui restencele.
Douz Dex, je l'aim tant
de cuer loiaument!

Quant j'oi devant li vielé
40   pour avoir s'amour et son gré,
elle m'a bien guerredonné,
soe merci,
d'un besier a ma volenté,
Dex! que j'aim si!
45   Et autre chose m'a donné
com son ami,
que j'avoie tant desirré:
or m'est meri!   III
Plus sui en joie
50   que je ne soloie,
quant cele est moie
que je tant desir;

je n'en prendroie
avoir ne monoie;
55   pour riens que voie
ne m'en quier partir:
ançois vueil morir!

Or a Colin Muset musé
et s'a a devise chanté
60   pour la bele au vis coloré,
de cuer joli.
Maint bon morsel li a doné
et departi.
Et de bon vin fort, a son gré,

for that girl;
my joy keeps on
starting up again.
She had on a tunic
35   of cloth from Castile
that shimmers.
Sweet God, I love her so
with a heart that keep faith.

When I had fiddled to her
40   for her love and pleasure,
she rewarded me well,
she was kind,
with a kiss that I wanted.
God, how I love her!
45   And another thing she gave me,
gave me as her friend,
that I had much desired:
now my wages are paid.   III
I have more joy
50   than I was ever used to,
for the one I desire
is mine.

There's no money or goods
I would take for her,
55   nothing I see could make me
want to part from her,
I'd sooner die.

Now Colin Muset has amused with his *muse*
and sung on demand
60   for that beautiful bright-faced girl,
with a happy heart.
Many a tasty morsel he gave her
and parted.
And good strong wine, the way it should be,

65   gel vous affi.
        Ensi a son siecle mené
        jusques ici: IV
        oncor donoie,
        en chantant maine joie,
70   mult se cointoie,
        qu'Amors veut servir,
        si a grant joie
        el vergier ou donoie,
        bien se conroie,
75   bon vin fet venir
        trestout a loisir.

                        25

        En mai, quant li rossignolet
        chantent cler ou vert boissonet,
        lors m'estuet faire un flajolet,
        si le ferai d'un saucelet,   I
5   qu'il m'estuet d'amors flajoler
        et chapelet de fleur porter
        por moi deduire et deporter,
        qu'adès ne doit on pas muser.

        L'autrier en mai, un matinet,
10   m'esveillerent li oiselet,
        s'alai cuillir un saucelet,
        si en ai fait un flajolet;   II
        mais nuls hons n'en puet flajoler,
        s'il ne fait par tout a loer
15   en bel despendre et en amer
        sanz faintise et sanz guiler.

        Garnier, cui je vi joliet,
        celui donrai mon chapelet.
        De bel despendre s'entremet,

65   I offer *you*.
        This is how he has led his life
        till now: IV
        I go on courting girls
        and singing of great happiness.
70   He decks himself out,
        as he wants to serve love,
        and he has much joy
        in the orchard, courting,
        he feeds well,
75   he makes the good wine come,
        and takes his time.

25

        In May when the nightingale
        sings brightly in the green bushes,
        then I must make a flageolet—
        I shall make it of a willow shoot,   I
5   for I must play on the flageolet about love
        and wear a chaplet of flowers
        to have myself some fun,
        for one can't stand around all day, bemused.

        The other day, it was in May, one morning,
10   the little birds awakened me,
        I picked a little willow shoot
        and made a flageolet;
        but no man can play on this flageolet   II
        unless he is praised by everyone
15   for spending big and making honest love,
        without lies and without tricks.

        Garnier, whom I see gay—
        I shall give him my chaplet,
        he devotes himself to spending big,

20   en lui n'en a point de regret,   III
      et por ce li veuil je doner
      qu'il aimme bruit et hutiner
      et aimme de cuer sanz fausser;
      ensi le covient il ovrer.

25   La damoisele au chief blondet
      me tient tot gai et cointelet;
      en tel joie le cuer me met
      qu'il ne me sovient de mon det.   IV
      Honiz soit qui por endeter
30   laira bone vie a mener!
      Adès les voit on eschaper,
      a quel chief qu'il doie torner.[1]

      L'en m'apele Colin Muset,
      s'ai mangié maint bon chaponet,
35   mainte haste, maint gastelet
      en vergier et en praelet,   V
      et quant je puis hoste trover
      qui vuet acroire et bien prester,
      adonc me prens a sejorner
40   selon la blondete au vis cler.

      N'ai cure de roncin lasser
      après mauvais seignor troter: VI
      s'il heent bien mon demander,
      et je, cent tanz, lor refuser.

                        26

      "Colin Muset, je me plains d'une amor   2
      ke longuement ai servie

[1] Line 31, as it appears here and in the mss., makes no sense. Joseph Bédier, in his edition of Colin Muset, makes this great suggestion: *a dés l'as voit on eschaper,* in dice one can see the snake-eye coming out (of the dicebox). The translation follows Bédier's emendation.

20 and never has any regrets,   III
  and so I want to give it to him,
  because he likes noise and fun,
  and loves with a good heart, never faking it,
  and so he's the one who should wear it.

25 The young lady with the blond head
  keeps me gay and keeps me close;
  she puts such joy into my heart,
  I never think about my debts at all.   IV
  Honi soit who, for fear of debt,
30 gives up the good life.
  You may think you see the snake-eyes coming,
  but you never know how the dice will fall.[1]

  I am called Colin Muset,
  I have eaten many a good little capon,
35 many a barbecue, many a little cake
  in orchard and meadow,   V
  and every time I find somebody with an open hand,
  willing to give a little credit and lend,
  I go and stay
40 with my little bright-faced blonde.

  I do not care to tire out some dray
  trotting after some nasty lord all day: VI
  they all hate my asking,
  and I, a hundred times more, their refusing.

26

"Dear Colin Muset, I have a complaint about a love
that I have long served

de loial cuer, n'ains pitié
n'i poi troveir ne aïe,   I
5   s'i truis je mult semblant de grant dousor,
mais se m'est vis que il sont traïtor,
que bouche et cuers ne s'i acordent mie."

Jaikes d'Amiens,[1] laissiés ceste folor!
fuyés fauce druerie,
10 n'en beau semblant ne vos fiés nul jor:
cil est musairs qui s'i fie!   II
Puisque trovés son cuer a menteor,
se plus l'amés, sovant duel et irour
en averés et pis que je ne die.

15 "Colin Muset, ne m'iert pais deshonor,
se de li fais departie:
pues qu'ai trové son samblant tricheor,
porcherai moy d'amie,   III
car je li ai veü faire tel tour
20 et tel samblant et tel ensaigne aillors,
per coy je haz li et sa compaignie."

Jaikes d'Amiens, il n'est duels ne irour
fors que vient de jalousie.
Povres amans souffre mainte dolor
25 qui bee a grant signorie,   IV
et un usage ont borjoises tous jors:
ja n'amera tant soit de grant richour,
home, c'il n'a la borce bien garnie.

"Colins Muset, gentils dame ait honor
30 qui a ce ne bee mie,
mais la ou voit sen, prouesce et valour,
joliveté, cortoisie!   V
La fauce lais por ceu, se m'en retour
a la belle, la blonde et la mellor
35 qui onkes fust d'amors nul jor proïe."

[1] A trouvère who composed in the second half of the thirteenth century.

with a faithful heart, without ever finding
pity or comfort there— I

5   oh, I find many looks of great tenderness,
but I think these looks are traitors,
for mouth and heart are not at one there."

Jacques d'Amiens,[1] stop this craziness.
Flee false love,

10 and never trust in looks that promise:
whoever trusts in them is a fool. II
Since you find her heart a liar,
if you go on loving her you will know grief
and bitterness often, and worse than I can say.

15 "Colin Muset, it will be no dishonor
for me to leave her:
since I have found that her look is a hypocrite,
I will get myself a friend, III
for I have seen this one do such things

20 and give such looks and make such signs elsewhere,
that I hate her and her company."

Jacques d'Amiens, there is no grief or bitterness
but what comes from jealousy.
A lover without money suffers many griefs

25 if it's a lady of the great nobility he gapes for, IV
and these bourgeois girls have just one way:
not one of them, however rich herself, would love
a man who hasn't the wallet to pay.

"Colin Muset, let there be honor to the noble lady

30 who doesn't gape at money
but looks where she sees judgment, prowess, worth,
merriness, courtesy. V
I'm leaving the false one, just for that, I'm going back
to the beautiful, the blonde, the best

35 ever begged for love."

Jaikes d'Amiens, et j'arant m'en retour
as chaippons en sauce aillie
et as gastiauls qui sont blanc come flor
et a trés bon vin sor lie.   VI
40 As bons morsels ai donee m'amor
et as grans feus per mi ceste froidour:
faites ensi, si menrés bone vie!

"Colin Muset, quier t'aise et ton sejor
et je querrai d'amors joie et baudor,   VII
45 car consireir d'amors ne me puis mie."

27

Sire Cuens, j'ai vielé
devant vous en vostre ostel,
si ne m'avez riens doné
ne mes gages aquité:
5   c'est vilanie!   I
Foi que doi sante Marie,
ensi ne vous sieurré mie.
M'aumosniere est mal garnie
et ma boursse mal farsie.

10   Sire cuens, car conmandez
de moi vostre volenté.
Sire, s'il vous vient a gré,
un beau don car me donez
par courtoisie!   II
15   Car talent ai, n'en doutez mie,
de raler a ma mesnie:
quant g'i vais boursse desgarnie,
ma fame ne me rit mie,

Jacques d'Amiens, I, too, am going back, right now,
to fat capons in garlic sauce,
and cakes as white as flowers,
and to the good wine above the dregs.   VI
40   I have given my love to good eating,
and to big fires in the cold.
You do the same and live the good life.

"Colin Muset, go, seek your comfort and a place to stay,
and I shall seek the joy and happiness of love,   VII
45   for to go without love—I cannot do it."

27

My Lord Count, I have fiddled
for you in your court,
and yet you have given me no gift
nor delivered me my wages:
5   that is ignoble!   I
Faith I owe holy Mary,
I won't follow you like this.
There's poor provisions in my bag,
there's nothing stuffs my wallet.

10   My Lord Count, command me
to do what you want,
only, Lord, if it please you,
make me a nice gift,
out of courtesy.   II
15   For I have a great desire, do not doubt it,
to go home:
when I get there, my wallet bare,
my wife will not smile—

Ainz me dit: "Sire Engelé,
20   en quel terre avez esté,
qui n'avez riens conquesté?
[Trop vos estes deporté] [1]
aval la ville.   III
Vez com vostre male plie!
25   Ele est bien de vent farsie!
Honiz soit qui a envie
d'estre en vostre compaignie!"

Quant je vieng a mon ostel
et ma fame a regardé
30   derrier moi le sac enflé
et je, qui sui bien paré
de robe grise,   IV
sachiez qu'ele a tost jus mise
la quenoille, sanz faintise:
35   ele me rit par franchise,
ses deus braz au col me plie.

Ma fame va destrousser
ma male sanz demorer;
mon garçon va abuvrer
40   mon cheval et conreer;
ma pucele va tuer
deus chapons pour deporter   V
a la jansse alie;
ma fille m'aporte un pigne
45   en sa main par cortoisie.
Lors sui de mon ostel sire
a mult grant joie sanz ire
plus que nuls ne porroit dire.

[1] This line is missing in the mss. The words printed are a conjecture of Gaston Paris.

no, she'll tell me: "Well, well, Lord Numbskull,
20   what far land have you been to,
since you haven't brought back a thing?
[You've had a great time in the tavern] [1]   III
down in the village.
Look how that bag of yours sags,
25   it must be stuffed with wind.
Honi soit whoever the hell
wants you around."

When I come to my house
and my wife has seen
30   behind me the sack swelled out,
and me well provided for
with a gray robe,   IV
let me tell you, she's already put down
her distaff, and puts on no airs:
35   she gives me a great good-natured smile,
her two arms enfold me round my neck.

My wife empties out
my bag without delay.
My boy waters
40   my horse and gives it what it needs,
my girl kills
two capons to make a feast   V
with garlic sauce;
my daughter brings me a comb
45   in her hand, with courtesy.
I am the lord of my house that day,
in great joy, without aggravation.
It is better than anyone could say.

28

Quant voi lo douz tens repairier,
que li rosignols chante en mai,
et je cuiz que doie alegier
li mals et la dolors que j'ai,　　　　　　　　　I
5　adonc m'ocient li delai
d'Amors, qui les font engregnier.
Las! mar vi onques son cors gai,
s'a ma vie ne lo conquier!

Amors de moi ne cuide avoir pechiez,
10　por ceu que sui ses hom liges sosgiez.　　　II
Douce dame, pregne vos en pitiez!
Qui plus s'abaisse, plus est essauciez.

Et qant si grant chose empris ai
con de vostre amor chalengier,
15　toz tens en pardons servirai,
se tout n'en ai altre loieir.　　　　　　　　　III
Ma tresdouce dame honoree,
Je ne vos os nes proier:
cil est mout fols qui si haut bee
20　ou il nen ose aprochier.

Mais tote voie
tresbien revoudroie
vostre amors fust moie
por moi ensengnier,　　　　　　　　　　　IV

25　car a grant joie
vit et s'esbanoie
cui Amors maistroie:
meuz s'en doit proisier.

28

When I see the sweet season returning
when the nightingale sings in May,
and I expect relief
of pain and unease,   I
5   then I am slain by the long delays
of Love, who makes my pain increase.
Alas, what a disaster I ever saw that carefree body,
unless I win it in my life.

Love does not believe it can have wronged me,
10 since I am her liege man and subject.   II
Sweet lady, let pity take hold in you,
who most descends is most exalted.

And since I have undertaken so great a thing
as to lay claim to your love,
15 I will serve for nothing, forever,
though I get no other wages.   III
My most gentle and honored lady,
I don't even dare ask you for love.
He is a great fool who longs for something so exalted
20 he does not dare approach.

And yet
I still wish
your love were mine
to enlighten me,   IV

25 for a man lives in great
joy and has much pleasure
ruled by Love:
then he thinks much better of himself.

Qui bien vuet d'amors joïr,
30   si doit soffrir
et endurer
quan k'ele li vuet merir;
au repentir
ne doit panser,   V
35   c'om puet bien tot a loisir
son boen desir
a point mener.
Endroit de moi, criem morir
meuz que garir
40   par bien amer.

Se je n'ai la joie grant
que mes fins cuers va chacent,
deffenir m'estuet briement.
Douce riens por cui je chant,   VI
45   en mon descort [1] vos demant
un ris debonairemant,
s'en vivrai plus longemant:
moins en avrai de torment.

Bele, j'ai si grant envie
50   d'embracier vostre cors gent,
s'Amors ne m'en fait aïe,
j'en morrai coiteusement.
Amors ne m'en faudrat mie,
car je l'ai trop bien servie   VII
55   et ferai tote ma vie
senz nule fause pansee.
Preuz de tote gent loee
plus que nule qui soit nee,
se vostre amors m'est donee,
60   bien iert ma joie doublee.

---

[1] *Descort,* "a type of lyric in which the strophes, of indeterminate number, are all, or almost all, different from each other" (Bédier). It means "discord" and expresses the discordant, inharmonious experience of the poet's love.

Whoever wants the joy of love
30 should suffer
and accept
whatever she accords him;
should never think
of giving up,   V
35 for in time a man may well
fulfill
his dear desire.
As for me, I am afraid of dying
before I am healed
40 with love.

If I do not get that great joy
my loyal heart pursues,
I must soon die.
Sweet being I sing to,   VI
45 in my descort [1] I ask
courteously for your smile,
then I will live a long while,
my torment will be less.

Beautiful, I have such longing
50 to embrace your gentle body,
if Love does not come to my aid
I will die in a hurry.
I'll never be without Love,
for I have served her very long   VII
55 and will serve all my life
without one straying thought.
O Valiant, praised by all
more than any lady ever born,
if your love is given me
60 my joy will double.

Mon descort ma dame aport,
la bone duchesse, por chanter: VIII
de toz biens a li m'acort,
k'ele aime deport, rire et juer.

65   Dame, or vos voil bien mostrer
que je ne sai vostre per
de bone vie mener
et de leialment amer.   IX
Adès vos voi enmender
70   en vaillance et en doner:
nel lassiez ja por jangler,
que ceu ne vos puet grever!

29

Sospris sui d'une amorette
d'une jone pucelette:
bele est et blonde et blanchette   I
plus que n'est une erminette,
5   s'a la color vermeillette
ensi com une rosette.

Itels estoit la pucele,
la fille au roi de Tudele; [1]
d'un drap d'or qui reflambele   II
10   ot robe fresche et novele:
mantel, sorcot et gonele
mout sist bien a la donzele.

En son chief ot chapel d'or
qui reluist et estancele;
15   saphirs, rubiz i ot encor   III

[1] "Tudela in Navarre. This city is quite often mentioned in the *chansons de geste:* there it is said that such and such a person would not do a certain thing 'for all the gold in Tudela . . .'" (Bédier)

Bring my lady my descort,
the good duchess, to be sung: VIII
for every joy, I follow her,
for she loves disport, laughter, play.

65   Lady, now I want to prove to you
      I do not know your peer
      for living the good life
      and loving loyally.   IX
      Always I see you increase
70   in virtue and generosity:
      do not let slander make you stop,
      for that cannot hurt you.

29

      I am surprised by this sweet love
      for a young girl:
      she is beautiful, blond, and fair,   I
      whiter than a little ermine,
5   she has red in her cheeks
      like a rose.

      That's how this girl was,
      the daughter of the King of Tudela; [1]
      she wore a bright new dress   II
10   of cloth of gold like fire:
      mantel, surcoat, and tunic
      became her very well.

      On her golden head she had a garland of gold
      that shines and glitters
15   with sapphires and rubies   III

et mainte esmeraude bele.
Biaus Deus, et c'or fusse j'or
amis a tel damoisele!

20

Sa ceinture fu de soie,
d'or et de pieres ovree;
toz li cors li reflamboie,   IV
ensi fut enluminee.
Or me doinst Dieus de li joie,
qu'aillors nen ai ma pensee!

25

G'esgardai son cors gai,
qui tant me plaist et agree.
Je morrai, bien lo sai,   V
tant l'ai de cuer enamee!
Se Dieu plaist, non ferai,

30

ainçois m'iert s'amors donee!

En un trop bel vergier
la vi cele matinee
jouer et solacier;   VI
ja par moi n'iert obliee,

35

car bien sai, senz cuidier,
ja si bele n'iert trovee.

Lez un rosier s'est assise,
la trés bele et la sennee;
ele resplant a devise,   VII

40

com estoile a l'anjornee;
s'amors m'esprent et atise,
qui enz el cuer m'est entree.

El regarder m'obliai,
tant qu'ele s'en fu alee.

45

Deus! tant mar la resgardai,   VIII
quant si tost m'est eschapee,
que ja mais joie n'avrai,
se par li ne m'est donee!

and many a beautiful emerald.
Dear God, I wish I were right now
the friend of that young girl.

IV

Her girdle was of silk
20   worked with gold and stones;
her body was all radiant,
she was so full of light.
Now God let me have the joy of her,
I think of nothing else.

V

25   I looked at that alert body
that I liked so much.
I shall die, I know I shall die,
I loved her so with all my heart.
God willing, maybe I won't,
30   before her love is mine.

VI

In a beautiful orchard
I saw her that morning
playing and taking her ease.
She'll never be out of my mind,
35   because I know and do not doubt
one so beautiful will not be found.

VII

She was seated beside a rosebush,
my beautiful and wise;
she shone like a dream,
40   like the morning star;
love of her kindled me with a fire
that caught in my heart.

VIII

Looking at her I forgot myself
till she was gone.
45   God, that was my undoing, looking at her,
she escaped me so fast,
I will never know joy again
if it doesn't come from her.

        Tantost com l'oi regardee,
50   bien cuidai qu'ele fust fee.
        Ne lairoie por riens nee   IX
        qu'encor n'aille en sa contree,
        tant que j'aie demandee
        s'amor, ou mes fins cuers bee,

55   et s'ele devient m'amie,
        ma granz joie iert acomplie,
        ne je n'en prendroie mie   X
        lo roialme de Surie,
        car trop meine bone vie
60   qui aime en tel seignorie.

        Deu pri qu'il me face aïe,
        que d'autre nen ai envie.²   XI

                    30

        Quant je vois yver retorner,
        lors me voudroie sejorner.
        Se je pooie oste trover
        large, qui ne vousist conter,   I
5   qu'eüst porc et buef et mouton,
        maslarz, faisanz et venoison,
        grasses gelines et chapons
        et bons fromages en glaon,

        et la dame fust autresi
10   cortoise come li mariz
        et touz jors feïst mon plesir

² "It is Tobler's honor to be the first to have described the structure of this
piece accurately . . . The first and last [strophes] are constructed on the
same model (the lines are of the same length and the rhymes placed in the
same pattern) and . . . strophe ii . . . is built like strophe ix, strophe iii
like strophe viii, strophe iv like strophe vii, strophe v like strophe vi: so that
the work is divided into two equal parts, of which the second (strophes vi–x)

The moment I saw her
50   I thought she was a fairy.
I shall not for anything born   IX
fail to go back into her country
and ask
for her love, which my heart gapes for,

55   and if she becomes my love,
my great joy will be fulfilled,
and I would not take   X
the kingdom of Syria then,
for the man who loves in such lordship
60   lives the good life.

I pray God for his help,
for I desire no one else.[2]   XI

30

When I see winter coming again,
then I'd like to settle down.
If I could find a host
who was generous and not anxious to count,   I
5   and had pork and beef and mutton,
mallards, pheasants, and venison,
fat chickens and capons
and good cheeses in straw,

and the lady were as full
10   as the husband of solicitude,
and always tried to please me

reproduces the pattern of the first (strophes i–v), but in reverse order . . .
The fine regularity of this architecture, however, is compromised in strophes
iii and viii, which ought to be parallel and are not: in strophe iii, lines of
eight syllables alternate with lines of seven, while in strophe viii the lines
all have seven syllables." (Bédier)

nuit et jor jusqu'au mien partir,   II
et li hostes n'en fust jalous,
ainz nos laissast sovent touz sous,
15   ne seroie pas envious
de chevauchier toz boous
après mauvais prince angoissoux.

night and day till I departed,
and the host would not be jealous over that 11
but would often leave us together in solitude,
15 then I would have no desire
to ride out, covered with mud,
after some bad prince in a penny-pinching mood.

THIBAUT DE CHAMPAGNE

(*1201–1253*)

Thibaut IV, Count of Champagne and of Brie, was the grandson of Marie de Champagne, thus the great-grandson of Eleanor of Aquitaine and Louis VII. In 1234 he became the King of Navarre, inheriting the throne through his mother, Blanche de Navarre. He fought with Louis VIII against the English. He was one of the leaders of the Crusade of 1239 but quit and returned home within a year in disgust over the quarrels of the other leaders. He was deeply resented in Navarre and was castigated in Sordello's famous lament for Blacatz (see Section I, no. 58). He was accused of being the lover of Blanche of Castile and the murderer of her husband, Louis VIII, but these accusations were baseless. By the third quarter of the thirteenth century the story of his love for Blanche took a literary turn: according to this tale, he took up music to help him overcome the melancholy engendered by his love and so created songs equaled only by those of Gace Brulé in beauty and melodiousness. Though the story is false, it testifies to the high esteem accorded these two poets at the time it arose. Dante praises the King of Navarre (DVE I, ix; II, v and vi) and treats him as the equal of Giraut de Bornelh and Guido Guinizelli.

In Thibaut we can get a clear idea of how the trouvères reacted to the songs of the troubadours: we can see what they adopted and what they rejected. To begin with, the influence of the troubadours hardly needs comment. Its presence is obvious both in the techniques and the themes of the trouvères: in the strophic forms, the vocabulary, the opening gambits; and in the celebration of refined love as the exclusive experience of the courtly class, in the familiar cast of characters, in the lover's essential state of exile, remembrance, and renunciation. One can gauge the influence of the troubadours by comparing the songs of the trouvères included here with the precourtly songs that flourished in northern France before this influence and that the courtly poets often adopted: owing to the nature of this anthology these precourtly songs are sparsely represented, but a glance at the *chanson de mal-mariée* (no. 23) will suffice.

One can also detect this influence of the troubadours in the singer's repertory of postures and forms. No one plays so many rôles, in so many different genres, more skillfully than Thibaut. In the selection included here we see Thibaut the aspiring lover of the *chanson;* the "précieux ridicule" of the *jeu-parti;* the lustful dope of the *pastourelle;* the Christian knight of the crusading song. From the earliest moments of the vernacular courtly lyric, with Guillaume IX, this virtuosity with voices was a proud achievement of the courtly poet. It is a testimony to the pervasiveness of troubadour influence that the northern French poets most highly esteemed in their own and in subsequent generations —for example, Gace Brulé—were the ones who most closely adhered to the troubadour model.

Nevertheless, it is also clear that the trouvères created a body of poetry all their own. They took what they could use from the troubadours and then went their own way. They gladly accepted the principal forms and themes of the southern lyric, but they rejected other elements, including its most characteristic technique.

One of the key elements of the troubadour love lyric was a cast of characters whom the singer explicitly identified as his attending audience: they were there before him as he performed his song. The troubadours used the image of the audience as the key to the meaning and the structure of their lyrics.

The troubadour differentiated the people in this audience according to their attitudes toward "the courtly lover," a character he impersonated. From the point of view of those whom he regarded as his friends, the performer's song was an expression of the refinement and the ethical aspiration of the courtly class. The love of a distant and virtuous lady, the renunciation of every demand for requital, the lover's steadfastness despite his suffering—

these well-known themes of the troubadour love song were, to the friends, representations of the moral qualities that define court-liness. Mindful of their attitude, the performer sang of a rare and lonely joy that made all his suffering worth while; for through his devotion to this distant beloved his own courtly quality was enhanced and revealed, and the ethical commitment of his friends was confirmed: he was recognized by the friends as a courtly man, as one of them.

But the singer gave equal expression to the attitude of those whom he called his "enemies" and who also listened to his song. Though they were further differentiated by the singer, these enemies are all united in their cynicism regarding moral values. They believe in no higher reality than their own smug carnality. They regard "courtly love" simply as disguised lust, or lack of manliness, or madness, or an outrageous lie foisted upon the audience for reasons they cannot fathom, and they respond to the singer's words, as he himself informs us, with accusations of insincerity or with coarse mockery.

This audience was set out before the singer like an array of perspectives. Each sector of the audience considered the courtly love relation from its own point of view, each revealing in its re-sponse its own moral quality. In the course of his performance, the singer scanned the entire audience and responded to each segment in a certain order. When he responded to the friends, he spoke like a "courtly lover,"and conformed to their image of him. When he turned his eyes to the eyes of the enemies, he spoke like one of them and proceeded to ridicule that same exalted love he had celebrated a strophe, or perhaps only a line, earlier; and he would boast of his own carnality and mock the devotion that he had, in his rôle as "courtly lover," earlier af-firmed. The troubadour love song, as a result, is full of sur-prising contrasts in tone and diction.

Thus Bernart de Ventadorn, for example, in *Be m'an perdut lai enves Ventadorn,* vows, for three and a half strophes, that he would never part from his lady and swears that he cannot think of one bad thing to say of her. In the fourth strophe, his gaze moves from the sector of the friends to that of the enemies. In one of the most cunning and illogical strophes ever com-

posed, he declares that since no one can constrain a heart without killing it, he is free to love any lady he wants to, whether
she likes it or not. In the fifth strophe, completely under the
influence of the *vilana gens,* "the vulgar people," he announces
that he is now available to all other women; anyone who wants
him can have him, provided she does not make him pay too
high a price for the good she has it in her heart to do him, for
there is nothing worse than vain entreaty—he knows this from
his own experience, for he has been betrayed by a beautiful
lady with a vicious nature. In other songs he boasts of his new-
found joy with his new lady. Bernart was in fact criticized for
his inconsistency in this song some time after 1240 by Ramon
Vidal, in the *Razos de Trobar.* And yet this inconsistency, re-
flecting a clash of perspectives in the audience, this continual
and cadenced alternation between different kinds of love and
desire, was part of the troubadours' definitive technique.

Thus the troubadour lyric was an arrangement of several con-
flicting points of view, each perspective representing some sector
of the attending audience. Through the performance, and in the
figure of the singer, the song expressed every attitude toward
love, from unredeemed carnality to the most spiritual and
aspiring devotion. This dialectical arrangement of audience
perspectives was finally the meaning of the lyric: the song comes
into being through the audience's effect on the performer. An
implicit performance situation is therefore essential to the meaning of nearly every troubadour love song; in fact, the song was
created in order to reveal the meaning of the situation in which
it was performed. That situation, in which the singer incor-
porated in his own person every mode of love and lust, was a
metaphor, a re-enactment of courtly life itself, of its harmony
and dignity, where destructive impulses were controlled by
moral and aesthetic ideals. Through his performance the singer
sets all of the perspectives in the situation into a hierarchical
order: the ideal view is supreme, the vision of "the vulgar ones"
confirms its supremacy. This was the basic conviction, the essential experience, of courtliness.

This technique of involving the audience as a witness and co-
creator of the song was an aesthetic strategy, a way of putting the

lines and strophes of a song into a significant order, and a way of representing courtly life at once in its totality. Of all the courtly poets of western Europe, only the Minnesänger adopted this technique and made further brilliant innovations in it. The stilnovisti, lacking the court situation in which alone it can make any sense, abandoned it altogether, substituting for the old courtly society their fellowship of poets, and thus a monolithic audience.

Now the northern French poets, even though they wrote for a courtly audience, did not try to involve it in their songs in the manner of the troubadours. One of the most striking features of the northern lyric, in comparison with the lyrics of the troubadours and minnesingers, is that the "I" does not show any signs of being aware of, or responsive to, a present audience. Though the French poets differentiate courtly society into the same types and characters as the other poets of the Continent and often call them by the same names—*li losengier, gent de male aire, faus dru, faus ameour,* and *cil autre chanteor,* the insincere singers from whom the performer desperately wants to be distinguished, —they rarely, if ever, depict that society as exerting an effect on the singer during his performance. In making the structure of their songs independent of the effect of the audience, the French poets clearly, and deliberately, reject one of the basic techniques of their models.

One of the simplest ways to see this difference is to compare the three bodies of poetry with respect to the use of words that imply a demonstrative gesture on the part of the singer and thus a direct reference to a live audience. In the songs of the troubadours and the minnesingers, as we might expect, such words occur continually. We need only recall the two little words that reverberate constantly throughout the songs of Bernart de Ventadorn, *sai* and *lai,* "here" and "there"—"here," where I am now, alone with the sympathy of these friends, surrounded by these enemies who defame my devotion; "there," where she is, in that direction, in the glory of distance. Among the Minnesänger we need take but one example, Hartmann von Aue, whose famous song of leave-taking, *Ich var mit iuwern hulden, herren unde mâge,* requires a singer in the dress of a crusader: *seht!* he calls out, look here and see how Love loves me—and points to the Cross sewn on his tunic (Hugo Kuhn, "Minnesang and the Form of Performance," in *Formal Aspects of Medieval German Poetry,* ed. Stanley N. Werbow, 1969). And perhaps no other courtly poet wove these gestures into his lyrics with greater effect than Heinrich von Morungen.

When we turn to the love songs of Thibaut de Champagne, we find no suggestion of any performing gesture penetrating space, nothing that calls upon the audience to look where the singer is pointing, no expression that requires a performance situation, and therefore the presence of an audience, to achieve its fullest meaning. In this respect he is typical of the French poets, who completely rejected the dialectical technique of the troubadours. Thibaut and the others deliberately strove to create a lyric that would not require the perspectives of an audience; and though these songs were meant to be performed, the performance was intended primarily to realize the sounds and harmonies of the words and music, not to involve the audience. And we can say this with certainty because we rarely, if ever, find in the *chansons* of any French poet a continuous and ever-modulated reference to a class of observers. Compare, for example, the songs of Gace Brulé, who is as close to the troubadours as any trouvère ever cares to be: neither the live audience nor the performance situation has any important part in his songs.

Once the dialectical audience is removed, the words of the song must be formed into an independent structure: the lyric becomes a self-sufficient verbal organism, entirely self-referring. It is true that friends and patrons are often named; but their names appear in the *envoi,* or at any rate in a context explicitly detachable from the rest of the song, so that this mention of some member of the courtly audience is intended as a graceful and flattering ornament. And it is true that this poetry, with all its talk of polite devotions and spies and homages, makes no sense except in a courtly society. But that amounts to saying what is true of every lyric, indeed of every human utterance: that it requires some kind of ethical and social context. Every speaker must define this context; but, in doing so, he does not necessarily involve the audience in a game he wants to play with them.

It is true, too, that there is a wonderful effect created by the figure of the poet in this case—Thibaut IV, Count of Champagne and of Brie, King of Navarre. It is pleasant to speculate on the audience's response to the sight of this powerful man masquerading as a passive and sentimental "courtly lover." In the contrast between the regality of his person and the mask of submissiveness he puts on, there is, indeed, an implicit necessity for an audience of intimate acquaintances.

But Thibaut, though he creates this situation, hardly exploits it. This is easy to see if we compare him to Guillaume IX, who, in a precisely similar situation, played upon it endlessly. Guillaume may begin his song in the posture of a man rendering homage, but it is never long before he changes his attitude with an imprecation and a demand—"By the head of Saint Gregory, I'll die if she doesn't kiss me in some chamber or underneath a tree; I think you want to become a nun; what good could I do you in a cloister?" (see Section I, no. 7)—thus playing off, before an audience well acquainted with his boasts and his merry stories, the facts of his political and sexual mightiness against the ridiculous fiction of his timidity.

What does Thibaut do in this same situation? The "I" of his songs regularly denounces hypocrites, false lovers, and slanderers, heaps his scorn on their vulgarity and lust. But where a southern poet would have played a merry game with them, would have become the imbecile they think they see when they see a "courtly lover," and would have gladly agreed with the common sense of their carnality, Thibaut dissociates himself from them in all respects except as their victim. He denounces them with wonderful wit; but, though he has to share his world with these liars, he never hints that he shares their attitude. He never departs from his initial posture as an adoring suppliant, even though in other genres (for example, the *pastourelle* and the *jeu-parti*) he shows himself a master at speaking in their voices. Thibaut and the trouvères followed the principle of "one genre, one ethic, one style, one voice."

We can get an idea of the aspirations and the virtues of the northern French lyric if we look at the elaborate metaphorical system of *Ausi conme unicorne sui* (no. 35), a song which, though not typical of Thibaut's manner, reveals the possibilities of his technique. This song begins with an image drawn from the bestiaries (see note to no. 35). Now there was a troubadour named Rigaut de Berbezilh (c. 1170–1210) who was famous for such imagery, and his influence on this song of Thibaut's has been noted, among others by Rigaut de Berbezilh's' editor, Alberto Varvaro. Here is the first strophe of one of Rigaut's songs:

> Atressi con l'orifanz,
> que quant chai no·s pot levar
> tro li autre, ab lor cridar,
> de lor voz lo levon sus,
> et eu voill segre aquel us,
> que mos mesfaitz es tan greus e pesanz
> que si la cortz del Puoi e lo bobanz
> e l'adreitz pretz dels lials amadors
> no·m relevon, iamais non serai sors,
> que deingnesson per mi clamar merce
> lai on preiars ni merces no·m val re.
>
> (*Liriche,* ed. Alberto Varvaro. Bari: Adriatica, 1960)

> Like the elephant,
> who, when he falls, cannot raise himself
> till the others, crying out,
> raise him with their voices,
> I, too, want to do the same,
> for my misdeed is so grave and burdensome
> that unless the magnificent court of Puy
> and the true merit of loyal lovers
> raise me up again, I shall never get on my feet,
> not unless they deign to call for pity for my sake
> there where prayer and pity do not help me.

It will be noted that Rigaut, immediately after that farfetched image, calls on his friends in the court of Puy-en-Velay for help. Thus he orients his song to the live audience before him.

However, this explicit mention of the audience is still not the clearest indication of the distance that separates the trouvères from Rigaut, who, it should be noted, is one of those troubadours most nearly like the poets of northern France. As a matter of fact, as Varvaro points out, Rigaut himself differs from most of the other troubadours in that the usual cast of characters is missing from his songs, the relation between lady and lover being "always direct, free of intermediaries and obstacles, bound only to the personal will of the two." As a consequence, Rigaut does not usually employ the troubadour technique of audience perspectives, and he found many sympathetic imitators among the French.

And yet, there is nothing in Rigaut's songs that can compare with the extended metaphor—extended over twenty-three lines —in *Ausi conme unicorne.* An extended figure of this sort would be hard, if not impossible, to find in any of the troubadours, and Rigaut, though he does not follow the usual technique, does not break away from it either: he simply stops short. The troubadours avoided the extended metaphor because, by imposing its own frame of reference on the words of the singer, it separates the singer from the audience. As long as a metaphor lasts, it obliterates the world that the singer and the audience share: it forms a complete and exclusive world of its own, inhabited only by the terms of a comparison; and the longer it is extended, the less effective is the singer's figure, the less his personal reality affects the meaning of his song. There is no opportunity, unless the metaphor is intended as part of a rôle, for the singer to celebrate the gathering of his peers, or to take note of their various attitudes toward his song. The metaphor—especially one drawn from an alien realm such as the bestiaries—is purely figurative and its effect is therefore completely independent of the conditions in which it is uttered or preceived. That is why, when metaphors appear in the songs of the troubadours, they are kept short, rarely if ever extending more than a few lines, three or four. In the case of Rigaut de Berbezilh, the longest of his innumerable metaphors and similes amounts to six lines, corresponding to one metrical division of one strophe. That such extended figures are common among the trouvères is made clear by Roger Dragonetti, in his chapter entitled, "Des moyens de développement." Thus, in Thibaut's song, when we hear at such length about "the prison of love," we know that we are listening to a poet whose technique and whose poetic ambitions

are altogether different from those of the troubadours, even the
troubadours whose style comes closest to his own.

The "prison" in which the "prisoner of love" is arrested has
replaced the court as the location in which love is experienced.
The detailed secularity of the troubadour lyric, the setting of a
fictional love in the actual world, is in marked contrast to the
artificial setting in a great part of Thibaut's lyric. The social
world is replaced by the metaphorical world, geographical space
by allegorical space. Not until strophe v, when the lover says that
even if he goes away his heart will always be in "prison," does
the perspective change (Roland and Olivier, in strophe iv, belong to the same imaginative realm as the metaphor) : then the
secular world is suddenly envisioned, with a wonderful effect.
The "prison" is revealed in its true nature as a metaphor, a way
of expressing the inner experience of a love that has to make its
way in a vast and ordinary world, in a realm of geographical
and temporal extent, in which one may "go away," and may "remember"—put distance between himself and the place where he
has some significance, and time between his moment and his
joy. The deepest effect of this lyric lies in this sudden replace-
ment of one world by another, of one persepctive (confined
within the metaphor) by another (coinciding with poor, dull,
normal reality). "My heart would . . . always be/in prison
though with me": so intense was the love in his heart, that for
a while all beloved reality was contained within that heart, till
suddenly the singer finds himself in the world of every day, with
its welter, its formless distances, its meaninglessness without love.

Here we have, indeed, a playing with perspectives—and a way
of comparing trouvère with troubadour. The troubadour played
with audience perspectives; the trouvère, with verbal perspectives, with the points of view created by forms of speech, by
metaphor, by grammar. The form of the French lyric is determined purely from within, never by some extra-verbal pattern
such as the traceable effects of an attending audience.

This abandonment of the dialogue with the audience is typical also of the courtly lyric of the later Middle Ages, though not
all of these later poets had the skill and restraint of a Thibaut
de Champagne. They, too, set their lyrics within "the heart,"

for the court no longer served as the realm of experience; they, too, allegorized the faculties of the inner life. Or else they sought to create an effect principally from patterns of sounds. In either case, it was a poetry that relied for its effect on the elaboration of rhetorical patterns. In Germany, this new kind of poetry was far below the level of the Minnesänger; in Italy, enriched with a new vocabulary and new sources of imagery, it had a great flowering.

The momentous change in medieval courtly poetry—and the end of the early courtly lyric—occurred when poetry moved out of the court. That was when poets renounced the dialectic of the troubadours, the patterning of audience perspectives, and set their lyrics entirely within the inner life of the singer, which they treated as the ground of a metaphor. This removal of the song from the context of the court to that of the inner life prepared the way for one of the most characteristic poetic figures of the later Middle Ages and the Renaissance, the conceit, the extended self-referring metaphor.

The dialectical technique of the troubadour lyric was bound to play itself out, for its moves were limited. Its range of expression could never be as great as that of a lyric which does not depend on external perspectives but rather on the possibilities of language itself. Whatever historical or social circumstances may also account for the difference between the northern and the southern lyric, there was an inherent technical reason for the rejection of audience perspectives among the trouvères: once the song's significance no longer lay in the performance situation and the singer was freed from the necessity of responding to an attending audience, then lyric poetry was permitted to explore and develop the possibilities of figurative language.[1]

Text: A. Wallensköld, ed. *Les Chansons de Thibaut de Champagne*. Société des anciens textes français. Paris: Edouard Champion, 1925.

[1] A portion of this introduction was read before the French 1 section at the eighty-seventh annual meeting of the Modern Language Association of America, December 29, 1972.

31

De bone amor vient seance et bonté,
et amors vient de ces deus autresi.
Tuit troi sunt un, qui bien i a pensé;
ja a nul jor ne seront departi.   I
5 Par un conseil ont ensenble establi
li coreor, qui sont avant alé:
de mon cuer ont fet leur chemin ferré;
tant l'ont usé, ja n'en seront parti.

Li coreor sunt la nuit en clarté
10 et le jor sont por la gent oscurci:
li douz regart plesant et savoré,
la granz biautez et li bien que g'i vi;   II
n'est merveille se je m'en esbahi.
De li a Deus le siecle enluminé,
15 car qui avroit le plus biau jor d'esté,
lez li seroit oscurs a plain midi.

En amor a paor et hardement:
li dui sont troi et du tierz sont li dui,
et grant valeur est a eus apendant,
20 ou tout li bien ont retret et refui.   III
Por c'est Amors li hospitaus d'autrui
que nus n'i faut selonc son avenant.
G'i ai failli, dame, qui valez tant,
a vostre ostel, si ne sai ou je sui.

25 Or n'i a plus fors qu'a li me conmant,
car touz biens fez ai lessié pour cestui:
ma bele joie ou ma mort i atent,
ne sai le quel, dès que devant li fui.   IV
Ne me firent lors si oeil point d'ennui,
30 ainz me vindrent ferir si doucement

454

From true love come wisdom and goodness,
and love comes from these two in its turn.
All three are one, to whoever gives it some thought.
They shall never once separate from one another.   I
5 With one mind they have together chosen
the harbingers that announce their coming:
they have made their beaten path out of my heart,
they have worn it so well they shall never abandon it.

At night these harbingers are in splendor
10 and in the daylight dark to everyone:
the sweet and pleasant and rejoicing looks,
the great beauty and the virtues I have beheld in her;   II
it is no wonder I am astonished by these things,
God has lit up the world with her;
15 for take the most beautiful day of summer—
beside her it would be dark at high noon.

In love there is fear and bravery,
these two are three and from the third come the two,
and true worth belongs to their essence
20 where every virtue finds shelter and retreat.   III
For love is the refuge of all,
and not one is absent that belongs there.
But I have been absent in your residence,
my lady whose worth is so great, and do not know
                    where I am.

25 Nothing is stronger than she when she commands me,
for I have relinquished every blessing for that one:
my greatest joy awaits me, or my death,
I do not know which, and have not known since I stood   IV
                    before her.
Then her eyes gave me no distress,
30 no—they turned to strike so gently

par mi le cuer d'un amoreus talent;
oncore i est li cous que j'en reçui.

Li cous fu granz, il ne fet qu'enpoirier,
ne nus mires ne m'en porroit saner,
35 se cele non qui le dart fist lancier.
Se de sa main i daignoit adeser,   V
bien en porroit le coup mortel oster
a tout le fust, dont j'ai grant desirrier;
mès la pointe du fer n'en puet sachier,
40 qu'ele bruisa dedenz au cop doner.

Dame, vers vous n'ai autre messagier
par cui vous os mon corage envoier   VI
fors ma chançon, se la volez chanter.[1]

32

Tuit mi desir et tuit mi grief torment
viennent de la ou sont tuit mi pensé.
Grant poor ai, pour ce que toute gent
qui ont veü son gent cors acesmé   I
5 son si vers li de bone volenté.
Nès Deus l'aime, gel sai a escïent;
grant merveille est, quant il s'en suesfre tant.

Touz esbahiz m'obli en merveillant
ou Deus trouva si estrange biauté;
10 quant il la mist ça jus entre la gent,
mult nous en fist grant debounereté.   II
Trestout le mont en a enluminé,
qu'en sa valor sont tuit li bien si grant;
nus ne la voit ne vous en die autant.

[1] Dante cites this song for praise in DVE I, ix.

a longing for love into my heart;
the wound I received there is still fresh.

The wound was great and can only get worse,
nor can any doctor cure me
35 except her who shot the arrow.
   If she deigns to touch it with her hand,   v
she would take away that mortal wound—
at least the shaft, which I greatly want.
   But she cannot draw out the iron point,
40 for that broke off inside my heart when the arrow struck.

Lady, I have no other messenger to you
   with whom I dare send you my heart   VI
except my song, if you consent to sing it.[1]

32

All my desires and all my heavy torments
come from the one place where all my thoughts reside.
   I am much afraid, because everyone
who has seen her noble figure adorned   I
5 is much inclined toward her.
   God himself loves her, I know.
It is a great wonder how He does without her.

In great unrest I forget myself wondering
   where God found such strange beauty;
10 when he set her down here among mankind
it was a great act of kindness for us.   II
   He lit the whole world with her light,
for every virtue is present in her worth.
No one who sees her would tell you less.

15 Bone aventure aviengne fol espoir,
   qui mainz amanz fet vivre et resjoïr!
   Desperance fet languir et doloir,
   et mes fous cuers me fet cuidier guerir;   III
   si'il fust sages, il me feïst morir.
20 Pour ce fet bon de la folie avoir,
   qu'en trop grant sens puet il bien mescheoir.

   Qui la voldroit souvent ramentevoir,
   ja n'avroit mal ne l'esteüst guerir,
   car ele fet trestoz ceus melz valoir
25 cui ele veut belement acoillir.   IV
   Deus! tant me fu grief de li departir!
   Amors, merci! Fetes li a savoir:
   Cuers qui n'ainme ne puet grant joie avoir.

   Souviengne vous, dame, du douz acueil
30 qui ja fu fez par si grant desirrier,
   que n'orent pas tant de pouoir mi oeil
   que je vers vous les osasse lancier;   V
   de ma bouche ne vos osai prïer,
   ne poi dire, dame, ce que je vueil;
35 tant fui coarz, las, chetis! q'or m'en dueil.

   Dame, se je vos puis mès aresnier,
   je parlerai mult melz que je ne sueil,   VI
   s'Amors me let, qui trop me maine orgueil.

   Chançon, va t'en droit a Raoul[1] noncier
40 qu'il serve Amors et face bel acueil   VII
   et chant souvent com oiselez en brueil.

[1] Raoul de Soissons, nobleman and poet, born some time after 1210.

15 Good luck to foolish hope!
for hope lets a lover live and rejoice.
Despair makes me suffer and pine away,
but my heart, in its foolishness, makes me believe in my   III
        recovery;
now if the heart were wise, it would make me die.
20 Therefore it is good to be a little foolish,
for with too much good sense, things can go badly.

Anyone who would call her to mind again and again
would suffer no disease and need no remedy,
for she makes everyone stronger and worth more
25 whom she is willing to welcome.   IV
God, how bitter it was to part from her!
Love, have pity, let her know:
a heart that does not love cannot know great joy.

Lady, remember when you received me gently:
30 my desire was so great,
my eyes did not have such strength
that I could dare turn them toward you;   V
I did not dare open my mouth to pray for love,
I cannot tell you, my lady, what I want,
35 I am such a coward, weary, so wretched! and now I suffer
        for it.

Lady, if I can speak with you again,
I will speak much better than I do,   VI
if Love allows it, who treats me now with such disdain.

Song, go straight to Raoul [1] and tell him
40 to serve Love and receive her well   VII
and sing and sing like the birds in the woods.

33

Chançon ferai, que talenz m'en est pris,
de la meilleur qui soit en tout le mont.
De la meilleur? Je cuit que j'ai mespris.
S'ele fust teus, se Deus joie me dont,
5 de moi li fust aucune pitié prise,   I
qui sui touz siens et sui a sa devise.
Pitiez de cuer, Deus! que ne s'est assise
en sa biauté? Dame, qui merci proi,
Je sent les maus d'amer por vos.
10 *Sentez les vos por moi!*

Douce dame, sanz amor fui jadis,
quant je choisi vostre gente façon;
et quant je vi vostre tres biau cler vis,
si me raprist mes cuers autre reson:
15 De vos amer me semont et justise,
a vos en est a vostre conmandise.   II
Li cors remaint, qui sent felon juïse,
se n'en avez merci de vostre gré.
Li douz mal dont j'atent joie
20 *m'ont si grevé*
morz sui, s'ele m'i delaie.

Mult a Amors grant force et grant pouoir,
qui sanz reson fet choisir a son gré.
Sanz reson? Deus! je ne di pas savoir,
25 car a mes euz en set mes cuers bon gré,
qui choisirent si tres bele senblance,   III
dont jamès jor ne ferai desevrance,
ainz sousfrirai por li grief penitance,
tant que pitiez et merciz l'en prendra.
30 *Diré vos qui mon cuer enblé m'a?*
Li douz ris et li bel oeil qu'ele a.

33

I shall make a song, for the desire has come on me,
about the best one in the world.
The best? I guess I'm wrong.
If she were the best, so God give me joy,
5 some bit of pity would have taken hold in her   I
for me, who am all hers and at her will.
The heart's pity—God! why has it not settled
in her beauty? Lady of whom I crave mercy,
I feel the pains of love for you,
10 *now feel such things for me!*

Sweet lady, once I was free of love,
and then I picked out your gentle ways;
and when I saw your beautiful bright face,
my heart had still another cause;
15 now it summons me and directs me to love you,
it has gone into your power.   II
My body will perish suffering cruel punishment,
unless you are pleased to take pity on its state.
The sweet pains in which I look for joy
20 *have so weighed down on me,*
I am dead if my lady makes me wait.

Love has great power, great force
which makes you search things out without reason, at her
            pleasure.
Without reason? God, I'm not making any sense:
25 my heart gives thanks to my eyes
for seeking out a form so beautiful,   III
which I shall never part from,
no, I shall suffer heavy penance for her sake,
till pity and mercy take hold in her.
30 *Shall I tell you who stole away my heart?*
The beautiful eyes and sweet smile of her.

Douce dame, s'il vos plesoit un soir,
m'avrïez vos plus de joie doné
c'onques Tristans, qui en fist son pouoir,
35 n'en pout avoir nul jor de son aé;
la moie joie est tornee a pesance.   IV
Hé, cors sanz cuer! de vos fet grant venjance
cele qui m'a navré sanz defiance,
et ne por quant je ne la lerai ja.
40 *L'en doit bien bele dame amer*
et s'amor garder, qui l'a.

Dame, por vos vueil aler foloiant,
que je en aim mes maus et ma dolor,
qu'après les maus la grant joie en atent
45 que je avrai, se Deu plest, a brief jor.
Amors, merci! ne soiez oublïee!   V
S'or me failliez, c'iert traïson doublee,
que mes granz maus por vos si fort m'agree.
Ne me metez longuement en oubli!
50 *Se la bele n'a de moi merci,*
je ne vivrai mie longuement ensi.

La grant biautez qui m'esprent et agree,
qui seur toutes est la plus desirree,
m'a si lacié mon cuer en sa prison.   VI
55 *Deus! je ne pens s'a li non.*
A moi que ne pense ele donc? [1]

34

Coustume est bien, quant on tient un prison,
qu'on ne le veut oïr ne escouter,

---

[1] This song is built on six varying refrains, none of which was composed by Thibaut. The scheme of each strophe is 10ababcccx plus refrain. Each refrain provides the rhyme demanded by x (Wallensköld).

Sweet lady, you could if you wanted to,
one night, give me greater joy
than ever Tristan, who struggled hard for it,
35 could win even once in his life.
Now my joy is turned to grief.   IV
Alas, body without its heart, how she has punished you,
she wounded me without ever calling out a challenge.
And yet I shall not leave.
40 *A man must love a beautiful lady,*
   and guard, if he gets it, her love.

Lady, for you I willingly do crazy things,
for I love my pains and suffering for your sake,
for after my pains I await that great joy of you
45 that I shall have, God willing, very soon.
O Love, mercy! do not forget!   V
If you fail me now, it will be a double treason,
for my great suffering for you is my great pleasure.
Do not send me into long oblivion.
50 *If my beautiful does not pity me,*
   I shall not, as I am, long live on.

Her great beauty, which burns and pleases me
and above all others is most desired,
has bound up, in her prison, the heart of me.   VI
55 *God! I have no thought except for her.*
   Why, then, has she no thought for me? [1]

34

It is common for a man who holds a prisoner
to be unwilling even to listen to him speak,

car nule riens ne fet tant cuer felon
con grant pouoir, qui mal en veut user.   I
5 Pour ce, dame, de moi m'estuet douter,
car je n'i os parler de raençon
n'estre ostagiez s'en bele guise non.
Après tout ce ne puis je eschaper.

D'une chose ai au cuer grant soupeçon,
10 et c'est la riens qui plus me fet douter:
que tant de genz li vont tout environ.
Je sai de voir que c'est por moi grever;   II
adès dïent: "Dame, on vos veut guiler;
ja par amors n'amera riches hom".
15 Mès il mentent, li losengier felon,
car qui plus a, melz doit amors garder.

Se ma dame ne veut amer nului,
moi ne autrui, cinq cenz merciz l'en rent,
qu'assez i a d'autres que je ne sui
20 qui la prïent de faus cuer baudement.   III
Esbaudise fet gaaingnier souvent,
mès ne sé riens, quant je devant li sui;
tant ai de mal et de paine et d'ennui,
quant me couvient dire: "A Dieu vous conmant!"

25 Vous savez bien qu'en ne conoist en lui
ce qu'en conoist en autrui plainement.
Ma grant folie onques jor ne conui,
tant ai amé de fin cuer loiaument;   IV
mès une riens m'i fet alegement:
30 qu'en esperance ai un pou de refui.
Li oiselez se va ferir el glui,
quant il ne puet trouver autre garant.

Souvent m'avient, quant je pens bien a li,
qu'a mes dolors une douçors me vient

for nothing makes a heart so cruel
as great power which it wants to make bad use of.   I
5 Therefore, Lady, I must fear for myself,
for I do not dare speak to you about ransom
or be freed for hostages, except with great eloquence.
I cannot, after all, escape this prison.

One thing puts a great worry in my heart,
10 it's the thing that makes me most afraid:
so many people go to her from all around.
I know well enough it is all to do me harm.   II
They keep on telling her, "Madame, he's trying to trick
        you;
a man that rich and noble never makes love with true
        love."
15 But they are lying, those cruel slanderers,
for if a man has more, he must be better at attending to
        love.

If my lady does not want to love anyone,
neither me nor anyone else, I will give her five hundred
        thanks for it,
for there are plenty of others unlike myself
20 who ask boldly for her love with an empty heart.   III
Boldness is often the only way to victory,
but I can't do a thing when I am in her presence;
I suffer such great unease and pain and irritation
when I'm supposed to say hello.[1]

25 You know, of course, one never sees in himself
what he can see quite clearly in another.
My own great foolishness I never see,
I have loved so deeply with a true and loyal heart.   IV
But there is one thing that gives me some relief:
30 I have found, in hope, a bit of refuge.
Thus the bird hurtles right into the trap [2]
when it cannot find another shelter.

Often when I think of her it happens,
with my pains a sweetness comes

[1] Literally, "I commend you to God."
[2] Literally, "into the birdlime."

35 si granz au cuer que trestouz m'entroubli,
   et m'est a vis qu'entre ses braz me tient;   v
   et après ce, quant li sens me revient
   et je voi bien qu'a tout ce ai failli,
   lors me courrouz et ledange et maudi,
40 car je sai bien que il ne l'en souvient.

   Bele du tout et dure de merci,
   se mi travail ne sont par vous meri,   vi
   mult vivrai mal, s'a vivre me couvient.

35

   Ausi conme unicorne sui   3
   qui s'esbahist en regardant,
   quant la pucele va mirant.
   Tant est liee de son ennui,
5   pasmee chiet en son giron;   i
   lors l'ocit on en traïson.[1]
   Et moi ont mort d'autel senblant
   Amors et ma dame, por voir:
   mon cuer ont, n'en puis point ravoir.

10   Dame, quant je devant vous fui
   et je vous vi premierement,
   mes cuers aloit si tressaillant
   qu'il vous remest, quant je m'en mui.
   Lors fu menez sanz raençon   ii
15   en la douce chartre en prison
   dont li piler sont de talent

---

[1] "The Unicorn . . . is a very small animal like a kid, excessively swift, with one horn in the middle of his forehead, and no hunter can catch him. But he can be trapped by the following stratagem.

"A virgin girl is led to where he lurks, and there she is sent off by herself into the wood. He soon leaps into her lap when he sees her, and embraces her, and hence he gets caught." (*The Bestiary*, translated by T. H. White)

35 into my heart, so great that I completely forget myself,
and then it seems to me she holds me in her arms; V
and afterwards, when my sense returns
and I see clearly I have missed all that,
then I rage and speak insults against myself,
40 for I realize she has no thought for me.

Beautiful in all things, hard in mercy,
if you do not reward my pains, VI
I shall live very badly, if I am meant to live.

35

I am like the unicorn
astonished as he gazes,
beholding the virgin.
He is so rejoiced by his chagrin,
5 he falls in a faint in her lap; I
then they kill him, in treachery.[1]
Now Love and my lady
have killed me just that way:
they have my heart, I cannot get it back.

10 Lady, when I was around you
and saw you for the first time,
my heart leaped over so,
it stayed with you when I went away.
Then I was led without ransom II
15 into sweet captivity in prison,
where the pillars are made of Desire,

et li huis sont de biau veoir
et li anel de bon espoir.

De la chartre a la clef Amors
20   et si a mis trois portiers:
Biau Senblant a non li premiers,
et Biautez cele en fet seignors;
Dangier a mis a l'uis devant,   III
un ort, felon, vilain, puant,

25   qui mult est maus et pautoniers.
Cil troi sont et viste et hardi:
mult ont tost un honme saisi.

Qui porroit sousfrir les tristors
et les assauz de ces huissiers?
30   Onques Rollanz ne Oliviers
ne vainquirent si granz estors;
il vainquirent en conbatant,   IV
mès ceus vaint on humiliant.
Sousfrirs en est gonfanoniers;
35   en cest estor dont je vous di
n'a nul secors fors de merci.

Dame, je ne dout mès riens plus
que tant que faille a vous amer.
Tant ai apris a endurer
40   que je sui vostres tout par us;
et se il vous en pesoit bien,   V
ne m'en puis je partir pour rien
que je n'aie le remenbrer
et que mes cuers ne soit adès
45   en la prison et de moi près.

Dame, quant je ne sai guiler,
merciz seroit de seson mès   VI
de soustenir si greveus fès.

the gates of Pleasant Sight,
the chains of Good Hope.

Love holds the key to the prison
20 and has set three watchmen there:
the name of the first is Kindly Look,
and Love makes Beauty their chief;
and has put Rejection at the outer gate,   III
a dirty, cruel, vulgar, stinking,

25 vicious scoundrel.
These three are nimble and strong,
they have fallen many times suddenly on a man.

Who could withstand the strategies
and the assaults of these watchmen?
30 Never did Roland or Olivier
conquer with such great onslaughts: IV
they conquered by striking blows in combat,
but these you conquer by humbling yourself.
Suffering is their standard-bearer;
35 In this assault I'm telling you of
there is no rescue outside of pity.

Lady, I fear nothing more
than failing in my love for you.
I have learned so well to bear up
40 that I am yours by habit.
And if even that annoys you,   V
I do not know how to go away
so that I would not always have the memory
and my heart would not always be
45 in prison, though with me.

Lady, as I do not know how to deceive,
mercy now would be seasonably given,   VI
to help me bear so grave a burden.

36

Une chose, Baudoÿn,[1] vos demant:
s'il avenoit a fin, leal ami,
qui sa dame a amee longuement
et proiee tant qu'ele en a merci
5 et li mande que parler veingne a li   I
tout por sa volenté faire,
que fera il tot avant por li plaire,
quant li dira: "Beaus amis, bien veingniez"?
Baisera il ou sa bouche ou ses piez?

10 "Sire, je lo que il premierement
en la bouche la baist, car je vos di
que de baisier la boche au cuer descent
une douçours dont sunt tuit acompli
li grant desir par qu'il s'entrainment si;   II
15 Et joie qui cuer esclaire
ne puet celer lëaus amis ne taire,
ainz li semble qu'il soit toz alegiez,
quant de la boche a sa dame est baisiez."

Baudoÿn, voir! je n'en mentirai ja:
20 qui sa dame vuet tout avant baisier
en la bouche, de cuer onques n'ama;
qu'ainsi baise on la fille a un bergier.
J'aing mieuz baisier ses piez et mercïer   III
que faire si grant outrage.
25 L'en doit cuidier que sa dame soit sage,
et sens done que granz humilitez
doit vien valoir a estre mieuz amez.

---

[1] "Baudoÿn" has not been identified with certainty.

36

One thing I ask you, Baudoin: [1]
if it should happen to a true, loyal lover
who has long loved his lady
and prayed her have mercy on him till finally
5 she sends for him to come and speak with her,   I
all in order to do his pleasure,
what should he do first of all to please her
when she says, "Sweet Friend, welcome"?
Should he kiss her mouth first, or her feet?

10 "Lord, I advise him first of all
to kiss her on the mouth, for I tell you,
from kissing the mouth there descends to the heart
a sweetness which fulfills
all the great desires with which they love each other;   II
15 and a joy lights up the heart
no loyal lover can conceal or silence;
no, he feels all relieved,
when he kisses the mouth of his lady."

Baudoin, listen, I won't lie about this:
20 whoever wants to kiss his lady before anything else
on the mouth never loved from the heart;
because that is how you kiss a shepherd's daughter.
I'd rather kiss her feet and say thanks   III
and not commit such an outrage.
25 One must believe his lady is wise,
and good sense tells us that deep humility
must do a lot to make one loved.

"Sire, j'ai bien oï dire pieç'a
qu'umilitez fait l'amant avancier,
30 et puis qu'Amors par humilité l'a
tant avancié que rende le loier,
qu'il ait cele que tant ainme et tient chier,   IV
je di qu'il feroit folage
s'en la bouche ne li feïst honmage,
35 car j'oï dire, et vos bien le savez:
qui bouche lait por piez, c'est nicetez."

Baudoÿn, voir! ice ne di je pas
qu'en sa bouche laist por ses piez avoir,
mais baisier vuil ses piez eneslepas
40 et puis après sa bouche a mon voloir
et son beau cors, c'on ne tient mie a noir,   V
et ses beaus eulz et sa face
et son chief blont, qui le fin or efface.
Mais vos estes bauz et desmesurez,
45 si semble bien que pou d'amour savez.

"Sire, bien est et recreanz et las
qui congié a de baisier et d'avoir
le douz solaz dou cors lonc, graille et gras
et met douçour de bouche en nonchaloir
50 por piez baisier; ne fait mie savoir.   VI
Ja Deus ne doint que il face
jamès chose par guoi il ait sa grace,
que mil tanz est li baisiers savorez
de la bouche que cil des piez assez!"

55 Baudoÿn, cil qui tant chace
que il ataint, bien se tient a eschace,   VII
quant a sez piez ne chiet toz enclinez;
je di qu'il est deables forsennez.

"Lord, certainly I have heard for a long time
that humility helps the lover advance;
30 but when Love, because of his humility
has advanced him so far that she gives him his reward
and he has her whom he loves so much and holds dear,   IV
then I say he'd be acting like a fool
if he did not do her homage on the mouth,
35 for I have also heard, and you know it well:
whoever bypasses the mouth for the sake of the feet has
         done something stupid."

Baudoin, listen, I do not say
that one should bypass the mouth to get to her feet,
but I want to kiss her feet right away
40 and then, afterwards, her mouth, as I like,
and her beautiful body, which no one could call un-
         pleasant,
and her beautiful eyes, and her face,   V
and her blond head, which turns fine gold into nothing.
But you are rash and do things out of order,
45 and I don't think you know very much about love.

"Lord, any man must be fainthearted and a loser
who, having leave to kiss and to enjoy
the sweet solace of that body long, slender, plump,
treats the sweetness of the mouth with such indifference
50 in order to kiss feet; that makes no sense.   VI
God never let such a man do
anything that wins his lady's grace.
For a kiss is a thousand times more sweet
on a lady's mouth than on her feet."

55 Baudoin, whoever pursues so long
till he gets what he wants behaves too proudly   VII
if he does not fall flat at her feet—
I say he's a devil in his crazy conceit.

"Sire, cil cui Amors lace
60 ne puet muër, quant il a leu n'espace　　　　VIII
qu'asevir puist toutes ses volentez,
tost n'ait les piez por la boche oblïez."

37

L'autrier par la matinee　　　　3
entre un bois et un vergier
une pastore ai trouvee
chantant por soi envoisier,
5　et disoit un son premier:　　　　I
"Ci me tient li maus d'amor."
Tantost cele part m'en tor
que je l'oï desresnier,
si li dis sanz delaier:
10　"Bele, Deus vos dont bon jor!"

Mon salu sanz demoree
me rendi et sanz targier.
Mult ert fresche et coloree,
si m'i plot a acointier:
15　"Bele, vostre amor vous qier,　　　　II
s'avroiz de moi riche ator."
Ele respont: "Tricheor
sont mès trop li chevalier.
Melz aim Perrin, mon bergier,
20　que riche honme menteor."

"Bele, ce ne dites mie;
chevalier sont trop vaillant.
Qui set donc avoir amie
ne servir a son talent
25　fors chevalier et tel gent?　　　　III
Mès l'amor d'un bergeron
certes ne vaut un bouton.

"Lord, a man bound by love
60 cannot keep, when he has the place and time   VIII
to make all his joys complete,
from quickly forgetting, for the sake of the mouth, all
    about the feet."

37

The other day in the morning
between some woods and an orchard
I found a shepherdess
singing for her pleasure;
5   it was a song about love in the spring: I
"Here I feel the pain of love."
I turned in that direction right away
where I heard her speaking her mind
and said to her, without much ado,
10   "Beautiful, God give you good day."

She gave me my greeting
right back, without hesitating.
She was young, with good color,
and I wanted to know her.
15   "Beautiful, I want your love,   II
afterwards I'll give you something nice to put on."
She says, "Traitors
are what knights are, the lot of them.
I love Perrin, my own shepherd,
20   better than any rich and noble liar."

"Beautiful, don't say that;
knights are men you can count on.
For who knows how to have a little friend
and serve her as she likes
25   but a knight, and one of that class?   III
But the love of an insignificant shepherd,
that's really not worth a button.

  Partez vos en a itant
  et m'amez; je vous creant:
30 de moi avrez riche don."

  "Sire, par sainte Marie,
  vous en parlez por noient.
  Mainte dame avront trichie
  cil chevalier soudoiant.
35 Trop sont faus et mal pensant,   IV
  pis valent de Guenelon.
  Je m'en revois en meson,
  que Perrinez, qui m'atent,
  m'aime de cuer loiaument.
40 Abessiez vostre reson!"

  G'entendi bien la bergiere,
  qu'ele me veut eschaper.
  Mult li fis longue proiere,
  mès n'i poi riens conquester.
45 Lors la pris a acoler,   V
  et ele gete un haut cri:
  "Perrinet, traï, traï!"
  Du bois prenent a huper;
  Je la lais sanz demorer,
50 seur mon cheval m'en parti.

  Quant ele m'en vit aler,
  si me dist par ranposner: VI
  "Chevalier sont trop hardi!"

38

Seigneurs, sachiez: qui or ne s'en ira
en cele terre ou Deus fu morz et vis
et qui la croiz d'Outremer ne prendra,

Come on off to the side there
and make love with me.   I promise you:
30   I'll give you something nice."

"You lord, by holy Mary
you're wasting your breath.
These knights are traitors,
how many ladies have they tricked!
35   They're all hypocrites, with nasty ideas,   IV
they're worse than Ganelon.
I'm going home,
Perrinet is waiting for me,
he loves me with an honest heart.
40   Keep your proposition."

I got the idea this shepherdess
wants to escape me.
I made her a long speech full of prayer
but couldn't get anything there.
45   So then I tried to use a little force,[1]   V
and she starts to rant and rave:
"Perrinet, help! He's raping me!"[2]
The shouts start coming from the woods.
I dropped her one-two-three
50   and took off on my horse.

When she saw me running away,
she called out to embarrass me,   VI
"Noble knights are very brave."

38

Lords, be sure of this: whoever does not now depart
for that land where God died and lived,
and does not take the cross of the Holy Land,

[1] Literally, "I started to embrace her, take her round the neck."
[2] Literally, " (I'm) betrayed!"

a paines mès ira en Paradis.   I
5 Qui a en soi pitié ne remenbrance,
  au haut Seigneur doit querre sa venjance
  et delivrer sa terre et son païs.

  Tuit li mauvès demorront par deça,
  qui n'aiment Dieu, bien ne honor ne pris;
10 et chascus dit: "Ma fame, que fera?
  Je ne leroie a nul fuer mes amis."   II
  Cil sont cheoit en trop fole atendance,
  q'il n'est amis fors que cil, sanz dotance,
  qui pour nos fu en la vraie croiz mis.

15 Or s'en iront cil vaillant bacheler
  qui aiment Dieu et l'eneur de cest mont,
  qui sagement vuelent a Dieu aler,
  et li morveus, li cendreus demorront;   III
  avugle sont, de ce ne dout je mie.
20 Qui un secors ne fet Dieu en sa vie,
  et por si pou pert la gloire du mont.

  Deus se lessa por nos en croiz pener
  et nos dira au jor ou tuit vendront:
  "Vous qui ma croiz m'aidastes a porter,
25 vos en iroiz la ou mi angre sont;   IV
  la me verroiz et ma mere Marie.
  Et vos par qui je n'oi onques aïe
  descendroiz tuit en Enfer le parfont."

  Chascuns cuide demorer touz hetiez
30 et que jamès ne doie mal avoir;
  ensi les tient Anemis et pechiez
  que il n'ont sens, hardement ne pouoir.   V
  Biaus sire Deus, ostez leur tel pensee
  et nos metez en la vostre contree
35 si saintement que vos puissons veoir!

will hardly go to Paradise.   I
5 Whoever has pity and remembrance
must go forth to revenge the Lord on high
and deliver his country and his land.

All the bad ones will stay behind right here,
who love neither God nor virtue nor honor nor renown;
10 and each will say: "My poor wife, what will she do?
I would not leave my friends for any price."   II
They are trapped in a foolish expectation,
for surely we have no friend except the one
who was put on the true cross for us.

15 Now those valiant knights will go away,
who love their God and the honor of their world,
who wisely want to go to God;
and those other snots, dirty with the ashes of their fire-
          place, will stay: III
they are blind, I know that.
20 Whoever does not once give God succor in his life
loses, for so little, the glory of the world.

God let himself be tortured on the Cross for us,
and He will tell us on that day to which all come:
"You who helped me bear my cross,
25 you will go where my angels dwell;   IV
there you will see me, and my mother, Mary.
And you from whom no help ever came,
you will go down to the depths of Hell."

Everyone thinks he lives safe and sound
30 and will never be touched by suffering.
That is how the Enemy, and sin, hold them in such
          embrace,
they have no sense, no courage, no strength.   V
Dear Lord God, free them from such thoughts
and put us in your country
35 in such sanctity that we can see You face to face.

Douce dame, roïne coronee,
prïez pour nos, Virge bone eüree!
et puis après ne nos puet mescheoir.

VI

Sweet Lady, Queen crowned in heaven,
pray for us, Virgin in bliss!   VI
and we shall never fall on evil days.

ADAM de la HALLE

(*c. 1240–c. 1288*)

The poet, better known as Adam le Bossu, the Hunchback, was born in Arras. He was a prominent member of the *puy*, or literary fraternity, of Arras. In 1272 he entered the retinue of the Count of Artois and went with him to Naples, soon after the Sicilian Vespers of 1282, where he was much esteemed in the court of Charles of Anjou, King of Naples and Sicily.

He is best known for his plays, *Le Jeu de la feuillée* and *Le Jeu de Robin et Marion,* which are both monuments of the drama in France. He was as well an accomplished and versatile poet, participating in several *jeux-partis* (no. 39) , and composing many *chansons* and *rondeaux* (dance songs of one strophe, with a refrain at the beginning, the middle, and the end; nos. 40 and 42) . He is regarded as one of the most important musicians of his time.

"Adans, mout fu Aritotes sachans;[1]
et si fu il par Amours tieus menés
k'enselés fu coume chevaus ferans
et chevauchiés ensi que vous savés   I
5 de celi qui il voloit a amie,
qui, en la fin, couvent ne li tint mie.
Vaurïés estre atournés ensement
de vo dame, si vous tenist couvent?"

Sire, ki prent as fais des soufisans
10 essample et cuer n'en doit estre blamés.
Aritotes fu de moi plus vaillans
en renoumee, en sïence, en bontés.   II
Et qant il eut le plaisance acomplie
de sa dame, n'en eut il mie aïe;
15 dont doi jou bien faire tel hardement,
qui mains vail, et s'arai alegement.

"Adan, or estes vous trop esmaians
et poi en vo vaillance vous fiés,
ki vauriés estre a tel honte eskaans
20 que cevauchiés fuissiés pour estre amés!   III
Trop en avés abaissie clergie!
Mais ce fait perece qui vous maistrie.
Pour eskiever la paine que on sent
au deservir, volés goïr vieument."

25 Sire Jehan, cieus ki est desirans
a paines cuide estre a tans saoulés.
Parmi tous prieus doit faire fins amans
a sa dame toutes ses volentés,   IV
n'on ne li doit pas tourner a folie;
30 car bien d'Amours sont de tel signourie

[1] Text: Newly edited for this volume. Base ms.: R.

39

"Adam, Aristotle was very wise,[1]
and he was led by love to such a point
that he was saddled like a horse
and ridden around, as you know,
5 by the girl he wanted for his lover,
who, in the end, didn't even keep her word.
How would you like the same treatment
from your lady if she *did* keep her word?"

   I

Sire, whoever takes heart and example
10 from the deeds of wise men can't be blamed.
Aristotle was a better man than I
in reputation, knowledge, good qualities.
And when he had done the pleasure
of his lady, he got nothing for it;
15 well, then, I, who am worth less and yet will get some
       relief,
surely ought to do this dashing deed.

   II

"Adam, now you're being much too timid
and have little confidence in your own worth,
if you would willingly descend to such shame
20 as to be ridden in order to be loved.
Now you have debased every man of culture.
You lack vigor, and that's what's the matter with you.
To escape the pains one undergoes
to be worthy of love, you want your pleasure like a
       vulgar man."

   III

25 Sire Jean, a man who is full of desire
hardly expects to be quickly satisfied.
Whatever the dangers, a true lover ought to obey
his lady's every wish,
nor should anyone call it foolish;
30 for the virtues of Love are so noble,

   IV

c'on n'i puet emploiier mauvaisement
honte a soufrir, disfame ne torment.

"Adan, jamais ne soiés counisans
que vous soiiés a tel honte livrés
35 c'on vous chevaucl C'est bien kose aparants
que vous autrement desservir n'osés   v
que vous aiiés soulas ne druerie.
Bon en fait en secré soufrir haschie,
mais nus n'en doit soufrir apertement
40 blasme commun, car Amours le desfent."

Sire, voire, mais se jou sui faillans
a ma dame, g'ere desesperés.
Je voi que cuers de feme est si cangans
que li loiaus est souvent refusés,   vi
45 et cieus ki sert Amours par tricerie
a de sa dame hounour et conpaignie.
Par qoi je douc pour cest pril seulement
que jou servi n'eüsse pour noient.

"Evrart, avoirs mal aquis apovrie,
50 mais biens d'Amours a droit pris monteplie.   vii
On doit d'Amours goïr secreement
et ki ensi ne le fait, il mesprent."

Ferris, faus est cil qui sen preu detrie
et qui on osfre a faire courtoisie   viii
55 pour pau de honte avoir, s'il ne le prent;
car ki premiers coisist ne se repent.

[2] Evrart and Ferri are to be the judges of this dispute. Sire Jehan, or Jean
Bretel, who died in 1272, was Adam's partner in all but two of the seventeen
jeux-partis. The story of Aristotle's embarrassing experience was well known
in the Middle Ages and was recounted in the *Lai d'Aristote* in the 1230s.
"Alexander [the Great], in love with a young Indian girl, spends all his time
with her and neglects his military campaign. Aristotle, Alexander's tutor,
tries to get him to leave her. The young lady hears about this and sets a trap

it can't be wrong to undergo a little shame
for its sake, or make use of dishonor and torment.

"Adam, I hope you never have the experience
of letting yourself be brought to such disgrace
35 that someone rides you! For it is easy to see
you don't have the nerve to be worthy   V
of pleasure and friendship in any other way.
It's all right to suffer torture for it in secret,
but no one should suffer public blame
40 for making a spectacle of himself, Love forbids it."

Sire, true; but if I fail
with my lady I will be in despair.
I see that a woman's heart changes so constantly
that the loyal lover is often refused,   VI
45 and someone who serves Love with trickery
gets the honor and the company of his lady.
Therefore, the only danger I'm afraid of
is that I will have served for nothing.

"Evrart, wealth ill-gotten becomes poor,
50 but the riches of Love, justly won, increase.   VII
One should enjoy Love secretly,
and whoever does otherwise is wrong."

Ferri, he is a false lover who rejects his own advantage
and who, when someone offers to do him some courtesty VIII
55 in exchange for a little shame, does not accept;
for whoever chooses first has no regret.[2]

for him to get her revenge. Dressed in veils, barefoot, her hair loosely flow-
ing, she walks beneath the windows of the Philosopher, singing love songs.
Aristotle immediately falls in love with her, but she promises him her love
only if he will satisfy a bizarre caprice of hers first. He must serve as her
mount and, saddled and bridled, carry her on his back. The wretched man
is in this position when Alexander . . . arrives . . ." (L. Nicod).

40

    Je muir, je muir d'amourete,[1]
    las! aimi!
    par defaute d'amiete,
    de merchi.
5   A premiers le vi douchete;
    . . . .
    je muir, je muir d'amourete,
    las! aimi!   I
    d'une atraiant manierete
10   adont le vi,
    et puis le truis si fierete,
    quant li pri.
    Je muir, je muir d'amourete,
    las! aimi!
15   par defaute d'amiete,
    de merchi.

41

    Bergeronnete,[1]
    douche baisselete,
    donnés le moi, vostre chapelet,
    donnés le moi, vostre chapelet.
5   "Robin, veus tu que che le meche
    seur ton chief par amourete?"   I
    "Oïl, et vous serez m'amiete;

---

[1] Text: Friedrich Gennrich, ed. *Rondeaux, Virelais und Balladen aus dem Ende des XII., dem XIII. und dem ersten Drittel des XIV. Jahrhunderts mit den überlieferten Melodien.* Gesellschaft für romanische Literatur. Vol. I: Dresden: Max Niemeyer, 1921; Vol II: Göttingen: Max Niemeyer, 1927.
[1] From Adam's play *Robin et Marion.* Text: Gennrich.

40

I die, I die of love,[1]
oh weary, oh me,
it is my beloved's want
of all mercy.

5   At first I saw her gentle;

. . . .

I die, I die of love,
oh weary, oh me,   I
with that catching little way she has

10   I saw her then,
and find her since so proud
when I beg her for love.
I die, I die of love,
oh weary, oh me,

15   it is my beloved's want
of all mercy.

41

Little shepherdess,[1]
sweet kid,
give me the garland on your head,
give me the garland on your head.

5   "Robin, would you like me to set it
on your head for love?"
Sure, that means you'll be my girl,   I

vous averés ma chainturete,
m'aumosniere et mon fremalet.

10   Bergeronnete,
douche baisselete,
donnés le moi, vostre chapelet."
"Volentiers, mon douc amiet!"

42

Fi, maris, de vostre amour,[1]
car j'ai ami!
Biaus est et de noble atour;
fi, maris, de vostre amour!   1

5   Il me sert et nuit et jour
pour che l'aim si.
Fi, maris, de vostre amour,
car j'ai ami!

43

Merveille est, kel talent j'ai [1]
de canter;
car je ne puis ne ne sai
tant penser

5   ke puisse voie trouver,   1
c'on ëust de moi merchi!
On a par fausser goui!
Mais anchois mouroie,
ke je vausisse avoir goie

10   par avoir menti!

Ja mais jour ne chesserai
d'esperer

[1] Text: Gennrich.
[1] Text: R. Berger, ed. *Canchons et Partures des altfranzösischen Trouvère Adam de la Hale le Bochu d'Aras*. Romanische Bibliothek, 17. Halle: Max Niemeyer, 1900.

you will get my little belt,
my wallet, and my buckle.
10   Little shepherdess,
sweet kid,
give me the garland on your head.
"My sweet little friend, with pleasure."

42

Husband, fooey on your love,[1]
I've got a lover!
He is handsome and nobly turned out;
husband, fooey on your love.   I
5   He serves me day and night,
and I love him so for that.
Husband, fooey on your love,
I've got a lover!

43

It is a miracle what a wish I have [1]
to sing;
for I cannot
think anything up
5   to find a way   I
to get someone to take pity on me.
Others have enjoyed love by faking it,
but I would sooner die
than be willing to have joy
10   because I lied.

I shall never stop
hoping

merchi; ne sai se l'arai,
mais anter
15   n'os me dame n'aparler;   II
car je n'afierch mïe a li
et si me douch trop aussi,
se je l'aparloie,
tost me dëist, "Va te voie!"
20   S'aim mius estre ensi!

Se j'ai merchi? J'i venrai
par amer,
ne ja ne le conkerai
par rouver!
25   Car me dame voit tout cler   III
ke je l'ain trop mius ke mi!
Cant li plaira, tost gari
m'ara, mais, se le veoie
assés, nul mal n'averoie
30   fors douch et joli!

Vremeille, ke rose em mai,
pour mirer,
clere, ke souleus ou rai,
ainc lasser
35   ne me peuch de raconter   IV
le sens de saison cueilli
et le bien c'avés nouri,
ke vos viaires otroie!
Dius vous tenoit bien a soie,
40   cant i vous fourni!

Dame, je vous prïerai
au finer
de chou dont sui en esmai
d'akiever,

for pity; I don't know whether I will get it,
only I don't dare

15 visit my lady or speak to her;   II
for I am not equal to her,
and so I greatly fear,
if I spoke to her
she would tell me straight off, "Go your way!"

20 And so I prefer to stay like this.

Will I find pity? I shall come to it
by loving,
I shall never get it
by insisting.

25 For my lady sees quite clearly   III
I love her much more than myself.
When she wants to, she'll have quickly
made me well again; still, if I could see her
often, every pain I get

30 would be sweet and pleasant.

You who are of the red of the rose of May,
to shine forth,
in splendor, like the sun in its radiance,
I could not

35 ever weary of recounting   IV
the wisdom that has ripened in your youth
and the goodness you have brought forth,
to which your look gives witness.
Surely God meant you for his own

40 when He endowed you with the way you look.

Lady, I shall entreat you,
here at the end,
for that which I am in despair
of attaining:

45   ke vous daignies escouter   v
       et canter che cant seri,
       si m'arés mout enreki
       et mius em feroie
       canchon, s'a faire l'avoie!
50   Pour che le vous di!

44

       Por che, se je n'ai esté [1]
       cantans et jolis,
       n'a je mïe mains amé,
       ains sui plus espris,
5   c'onkes mais, et plus soupris;
       car beours, reube envesïe,   I
       biaus canters, langue polïe
       ne soulers agus
       l'amour pas ne senefïe,
10   mais fins cuers loiaus repus,
       c'on n'em mesdïe!

       De tel cuer ait om pité,
       nient des soursalis,
       om voit tant oume effronté
15   em fais et en dis,
       en resgars et em faus ris,
       et tante feme hounïe,   II
       par coi chele ki n'a mïe
       lour assaus ëus,
20   doit estre bien castoïe!
       On doit dire: "Levés sus!" [2]
       a tel mainïe!

[1] Text: Berger.
[2] *Levés sus:* this phrase translates the biblical passage; see Matthew 4, 10 and 16, 23; Luke 4, 8; III Kings 21, 15 (Rudolf Berger).

45 that you consent to hear   V
  and sing this merry song,
  and then you shall have ennobled me,
  and then I would make a better
  song, if I had one to make—
50 which is why I'm saying this to you.

44

  If I have not been [1]
  lusty to sing and happy in love,
  it does not mean I have loved any less;
  in fact, I am yet more inflamed
5 than ever, more overwhelmed;
  For pageantry and tournaments, lusty dress, I
  fine singing, a polished tongue,
  pointed shoes—
  these things do not signify love,
10 only a true and loyal heart that keeps faith
  lest anyone slander its devotion.

  One could take pity on such a heart,
  but no pity for those strutting types
  one sees so many of, shameless
15 in deeds and words,
  in their looks and their fake smiles;
  and so many women shamed.   II
  And so, any woman who has never
  known their assaults
20 had better be forewarned.
  One must say, "Get thee behind me!" [2]
  to such a crowd.

Li mesdisant ont parlé
seur aucuns amis,
25　ke, s'i se fussent mené
en sinples abis,
ja n'em fust issus mesdis;
mais par lour conte veulïe　　　　　III
font sage autrui de lour vïe,
30　tant c'on lour met sus,
mais cors ki desire amïe,
doit estre con cos enplius,[3]
et li cuers rïe!

[3] "That is, 'shiver,' . . . and then, 'approach something like a coward,' then proceed cautiously and circumspectly.' " (Berger)

The slanderers have talked
about many a lover,
25   but if these lovers had gone around
in simple clothes,
there never would have been such talk.
But with their fancy vanity   III
they put everyone wise about their life,
30   till something is found to accuse them of;
but a man who wants a love
must be like a rained-on cock,[3]
and let his heart laugh.

Selected Bibliography

Battaglia, S. *La lirica medioevale*. Naples: 1954.

Bec, Pierre. *Nouvelle anthologie de la lyrique occitane du moyen âge*. Avignon: Aubanel, 1970.

Bezzola, Reto R. *Les origines et la formation de la littérature courtoise en occident (500–1200)*. 5 vols. Paris: Honoré Champion, 1958–1967.

Camproux, Charles. *Histoire de la littérature occitane*. Paris: Payot, 1953.

Davenson, Henri. *Les Troubadours*. Paris: Éditions du Seuil, 1961.

Der provenzalische Minnesang, ed. Rudolph Baehr. Darmstadt: Wissenschaftliche Buchgesellschaft, 1967.

Dragonetti, Roger. *La technique poétique des trouvères dans la chanson courtoise*. Bruges: De Tempel, 1960.

Dronke, Peter. *The Medieval Lyric*. London: Hutchinson, 1968; New York: Harper & Row, 1969.

Frank, István. *Trouvères et Minnesänger*. Saarbrücken: West-Ost-Verlag, 1952.

Frappier, Jean. *La poésie lyrique en France aux XIIe et XIIIe siècles*. Paris: Centre de Documentation Universitaire, n.d. [around 1958]

———. "Vues sur les conceptions courtoises dans les littératures d'oc et d'oïl au XIIe siècle," *Cahiers de civilisation médiévale*, 2 (1959), 135–56.

Goldin, Frederick. *The Mirror of Narcissus in the Courtly Love Lyric*. Ithaca: Cornell University Press, 1967.

Hamlin, Frank R., Peter T. Ricketts, and John Hathaway. *Introduction à l'étude de l'ancien provençal*. Publications romanes et françaises, 96. Geneva: Droz, 1967.

Hoepffner, Ernest. *Les Troubadours*. Paris: Armand Colin, 1955.

Imbs, P. "De la *fin' amor*," *Cahiers de civilisation médiévale*, 12 (1969).

Jackson, W. H. T. *The Literature of the Middle Ages*. New York: Columbia University Press, 1960.

Jeanroy, Alfred. *La poésie lyrique des troubadours*. Toulouse and Paris: Didier-Privat, 1934.

———. *Les origines de la poésie lyrique en France au Moyen Age*. 4th ed. Paris: Champion, 1965.

Klein, Karen W. *The Partisan Voice. A Study of the Political Lyric in France and Germany, 1180–1230.* The Hague and Paris: Mouton, 1971.

Köhler, Erich. *Trobadorlyrik und höfischer Roman.* Berlin: Rütten and Loening, 1962.

———. "Observations historiques et sociologiques sur la poésie des troubadours," *Cahiers de Civilisation Médiévales,* 7 (1964), 27–51.

Kolb, Herbert. *Der Begriff der Minne und das Entstehen der höfischen Lyrik.* Hermaea: Germanische Forschungen, 4. Tübingen: Max Niemeyer, 1958.

LaFonte, Robert and Christian Anatole, *Nouvelle histoire de la littérature occitane.* Publications de l'institut d'études occitanes, I. Paris: Presses Universitaires de France, 1970.

Lazar, Moshé. *Amour courtois et Fin' amors.* Paris: Klincksieck, 1964.

Spoerri, Theophil. "Wilhelm von Poitiers und die Anfänge der abendländischen Poesie," *Trivium,* 2 (1944), 255–277; reprinted in *Der provenzalische Minnesang.*

Topsfield, L. T. "The Burlesque Poetry of Guilhem IX of Aquitaine," *Neuphilologische Mitteilungen,* 69 (1968), 280–302.

Valency, Maurice. *In Praise of Love.* New York: The Macmillan Company, 1958.

Wilhelm, James J. *The Cruelest Month.* New Haven and London: Yale University Press, 1965.

Zumthor, Paul. *Langue et techniques poétiques à l'époque romane (XIe–XIIIe siècles).* Paris: Klincksieck, 1963.

O3